I Owe Y

I Owe You Nothing

My Story

———

LUKE GOSS

Grafton
An Imprint of HarperCollins*Publishers*

Grafton
An Imprint of HarperCollins*Publishers*
77–85 Fulham Palace Road,
Hammersmith, London W6 8JB

A Grafton Original 1993
1 3 5 7 9 8 6 4 2

A catalogue record for this book is
available from the British Library

ISBN 0 586 21863 7

Set in Ehrhardt

Printed in Great Britain by
HarperCollinsManufacturing Glasgow

Contents

I picked up this book to read with a mixture of emotions. It is Luke's book, Luke's story, but it is also to a large extent my story. Luke and I are brothers, twins, best friends and, until recently, we were also partners in Bros. Many of the things that happened to Luke happened also to me. I could not help wondering how he would tell our story, how he would deal with the triumphs and traumas of our career. I put the book down, having read it from cover to cover, with a feeling of overwhelming pride that he has written about his life – and my life – so sensitively and well. The book has revealed depths in Luke that even I, who have been so close to him all our lives, did not know he had. He has told the story of Bros brilliantly, and he has also told of his personal life with tenderness and compassion. It is, I believe, a great book.

Matt Goss

Foreword

I'm sure most autobiographies are written to set the record straight, to tell the true story and put right the popular misconceptions. Mine is no exception. As you read this book I hope you will begin to know and understand me better and see beyond the two-dimensional image created in the Bros fame days.

I realize that changing people's perception of me will be a very high wall to climb, but if this book helps you to see me and my work, be it music or otherwise, through different eyes, then I shall be happy.

This book is about the real me.

In hope,

Luke Goss

To Shirley

CHAPTER ONE

Break My Silence

The whole of terminal three at London's Heathrow Airport was in chaos. Three thousand young girls blocked the ramps, the escalators, the whole concourse. The police outriders who were escorting our limo piloted us to a side entrance, and we clambered out. Immediately our five burly bodyguards linked arms in a ring around us, and around the seal of their muscular biceps came another ring, of twenty-five policemen.

We paused for a second, a last moment of sanity before the girls spotted where we were. I breathed deeply and psyched myself up, like a runner before a race or an actor before going on stage. Then a scream arose, and the shriek was taken up and sustained by three thousand adolescent voices. The force of several hundred girls running at speed hit the outer wall of our defences, but they held firm, and slowly but surely we were edged through the tide of yelling fans, across the terminal to the customs gate.

It was 23 October 1988, and the madness and mayhem of Brosmania was at its height. A year earlier, nobody had even heard of us. Yet on that day, as Matt, Craig and I left Britain to start a world tour, we could be forgiven for thinking that every teenage girl in the country was there to wave us off. As far as my eyes could see, there were excited, clamouring faces and arms outstretched towards us.

Then, just as suddenly as we had been besieged by them,

the fans were cut off from us as we made the quantum leap into the comparative calm of the airport departure area. A thick belt of uniformed police prevented the madness pursuing us. We were on our way.

As we dozed, played video games and watched films on the twenty-seven-hour flight, I remember wondering what kind of reception we would get in Australia. We were on our way to the other side of the world, a place we had never been to before, where we knew nobody. Perhaps, in contrast to the crazy struggle we'd had to get to the plane, we would be disembarking like ordinary passengers, queuing to get through immigration and waiting to pick up our bags off the carousel. Perhaps life would be back to normal.

But when the plane touched down, before anyone could get off, a posse of airport security men got on. They told us to stay where we were while the rest of the passengers were cleared. Then steps were wheeled up to the plane and as we reached the top of them I was hit by two waves: a wave of heat, even though it was only seven thirty in the morning, and a wave of noise, as a huge cheer went up from the five thousand fans who were waiting for us. It took a moment or two for my eyes to focus in the clear, bright light. Below us, at the bottom of the steps on the tarmac, was a line-up of about a hundred and fifty airport staff waiting to meet us. Held at bay by security men were fifty journalists and photographers. And in the background was a blurred sea of screaming faces.

We had travelled 12,000 miles and nothing had changed except the weather. My main emotion was one of excitement and pleasure. We were a pop band, I'd been working hard and planning a pop career since the age of twelve, and there was no way I wasn't going to be pleased and excited by success. But there was also a now familiar sense of unreality about it all. When we got to our plush Sydney hotel and switched on the television, one of the main items on the news was a film of our arrival. I watched myself coming down the steps of the plane and thought: *Wow, this is incredible, I'm world-famous.* But at the back of my mind there was the niggling question: *Surely there must be more important things happening in the world to put on the news bulletins?*

Although we'd had nearly a year to get used to it, it was a weird feeling, getting your head round the kind of adulation and fan-worship we encountered everywhere we went. I really had thought that once we got out of Britain, out of our own backyard, we would find ourselves back to 'normal' again. But watching that television news, I knew there was no more 'normal' for me. And there hasn't been. For the last five years I have been on a crazy roller coaster, with tremendous highs and terrible lows. I have had no experience of ordinary life. I am not complaining: I would not change my experiences for anything. But I would like people to understand just how surreal it has all been.

I have been screamed at hysterically by girls of all ages, some as young as eleven and twelve. I have been spat at, punched and jeered at, for no reason that I can come close to understanding. Bros has generated adulation – and hatred. There has been very little indifference and even less genuine respect. Yet what have we done? We made some successful records, brought a lot of pleasure to a lot of kids. We hurt nobody, certainly never intention-ally. Yet our fall from success has been greeted with the kind of gloating glee that is normally reserved for the arrest of a mass murderer – and that has been even harder to get my head round than the scale and suddenness of our success.

I hope that by writing this book I am going to help myself – and others – come to terms with the strange

Bros phenomenon and the whole phenomenon of the pop business that created it. It was just an episode in my life, not my whole life. There was a time pre-Bros, and there is going to be a long, productive and successful time post-Bros, for both me and my brother Matt. But before we can get on with this next stage, I want to lay to rest some of the myths about Bros.

The popular ideas about us are that we are a pair of arrogant spendthrifts who ran through millions of pounds on extravagant living, that we ditched our mate Craig from the group, that neither of us had a thought in our heads save how to be hyped into yet more success, that we were an artificially created band who didn't even perform on our own records, that we quarrelled and split up acrimoniously.

Every single one of those ideas is wrong.

First of all, let's go back to the beginning and get the gynaecological bit over. I obviously don't remember a great deal about being born – but my mum and dad both have vivid memories of it all.

They had friends round to dinner the night Mum went into labour with me and Matt, two months before we were due. She had no idea she was expecting twins. When her waters broke at the dinner table she didn't know what it was and didn't want to embarrass anyone, so went into the bedroom and mopped up with a few towels. At three o'clock in the morning of 29 September 1968 the pain was so bad that my dad sent for an ambulance to take her to Lewisham Hospital, and fifteen hours later I emerged first into the world. I was bald, had no fingernails and weighed four pounds two ounces.

Even at that stage, nobody knew there was another baby to be born. It was my dad who first sussed it. When the nurse was telling Mum to bear down because the afterbirth was very high, he said, 'You'd better be quick, there might be another one in there.' It was a jokey remark, not a deep premonition. But when the midwife put her ear-trumpet to Mum's stomach, she looked up in alarm: there *was* another heartbeat in there.

Mum was delirious and in great pain, but she remembers the sudden panic. 'I took one look at the instruments coming towards me and closed my eyes tight,' she says.

Dad is the one who really remembers what happened. 'The nurse looked startled when I joked about another baby, but as soon as she detected the heartbeat all hell broke loose. Suddenly there were doctors and nurses everywhere. I stood in the corner, trying to look inconspicuous, pretending I was a drip-feed. But when the doctor spotted me he said, "You – out!" and ordered me through the door.

'I tried to peep in and see what was happening, and nearly got my nose caught in the door as it was shut firmly. It seemed to take an eternity, but in reality it was very quick. Officially, Matthew is eleven minutes younger that Luke, but I think it was actually less than that. It was quite hairy: the staff appeared to be panicking and all rushing about. Both the babies needed special care, and incubators were rushed to the delivery room. I had seen Luke immediately after he was born, but I didn't see Matthew until later.'

Mum remembers that Matt was very blue when he was born, because his lungs had not inflated. Although he was two and a half ounces heavier than me, he was even more delicate because he had had a more difficult birth.

The doctors explained to Mum that we had been lying back to back in her womb and that our heartbeats had been synchronized, which was why they had failed to detect that there were two of us. It was the next day before she was taken in a wheelchair to see us in our incubators. She could not feed us herself, we had to be tube-fed straight into our stomachs.

'I loved them desperately from the moment I saw them,' she says. 'I know the experts say that mothers need to touch their babies to bond with them – well, it's not true. I was longing to hold them, but even though I wasn't allowed to it certainly didn't stop me loving them. It was such an intense emotion it hurt.

'They were in incubators next to one another, alike as two peas in a pod. But even then I could see a difference between them. Matthew had a rounder face than Luke, he was tubbier even though they were so tiny.'

When Dad saw us in the incubators his main feeling was pride. 'I felt so incredibly proud of them – and yet at the same time I felt a fraud, because I didn't seem to have done much. I felt so sorry for my wife Carol: she'd had a difficult pregnancy and a difficult birth, and I seemed to have got off very lightly. Just looking at them lying there, so small and yet perfect, I was amazed that it was anything to do with me.

'I remember someone asking me if I had insured against having twins, and I felt insulted – as though having twins was a disaster, like a flood, to be insured against. But I must admit the money would have come in handy!

'I don't really think I did have a premonition about twins, but I can remember waiting inside the hospital once while Carol was attending an antenatal class and fantasizing about the possibility. For some reason I thought if one was a boy and one a girl I would phone Carol's parents and tell her mum that she had a grandson and her dad that he had a granddaughter, and leave them to work it out for themselves. I never thought about two boys.'

If they had thought about two boys, they might have had another name ready. They had chosen my name before the birth: Luke Damon. If I'd been a girl I would have been Rebecca! They weren't ready with another boy's name, and it was Mum who chose Matthew Weston when the registrar called at the hospital to register the new babies.

Dad remembers her telling him about it when he visited her in hospital. 'Carol told me she had named the second baby after her father, who everyone called Harry. I said, "Harry? You called him Harry?" She shook her head and I remembered that her father was also known as Sam. Harry and Sam are fashionable names now, but they weren't then and I wasn't keen on either of them. But she shook her head again – her father's name is actually Samuel Matthew, and it was Matthew she had chosen, to my relief.

'Then she said she'd given him a second name after *my* father. "Denis?" I asked, because that's my stepfather's name, and I didn't like that much. No, Weston, she said – that's his surname. I liked that, and unbeknown to us both at the time my real father also has Weston as his second Christian name, so it worked out fine.

'It was only afterwards that I realized Luke and Matthew together made us sound a very Biblical family, which we weren't. But I liked both the names very much.'

So that's how my brother and I were launched on the world.

It was the week that Mary Hopkin hit the top of the charts with 'Those Were the Days' – and they certainly were for my parents. Coping with one baby is difficult, but twins are a nightmare.

But to understand anything about anybody, you have to go back a long way before their birth. How any of us ends up is influenced by a great many factors, but our parents have the most crucial role to play . . .

My mother, Carol, was born in Peckham, south-east London, in 1946. Her father Harry, my granddad, was in the building trade: the war had interfered with his studies to become a surveyor, but he ended up as a building-site foreman. My grandmother, Win, worked in a variety of different jobs, usually as a shop assistant.

Harry and Win's home had been blown up during the war, and afterwards Harry made such a stink that the housing department of the local council found them a prefab – he threatened to pitch a tent for his family outside the council offices if they didn't get a home.

'Prefabs' were prefabricated buildings that were put up hastily all over the country after the war, to help with the massive housing problem caused by the popu-lation bulge. Lots of men, like my granddad, came back from fighting and didn't waste any time before having families. They'd given seven years of their lives to their country, and they weren't prepared to wait any longer, certainly not until the government got around to building enough houses for them all.

Prefabs were far from being shanty-style houses, even though they were put up very quickly and didn't have traditional brick walls. They were warm – they had central heating before it became standard in British houses – and they came fully equipped with fridges and cookers, back in the days when fridges were luxury items. So my nan and granddad were very happy there with their two daughters – my auntie Ann was born within a couple of years of my mum.

When my nan was thirty-nine she had another baby, as much to her astonishment as everyone else's. My aunt Sally was born on my mother's twelfth birthday, and because of that my mum has always regarded her as a bit special.

'I thought she was my own personal present, an extra-special birthday gift,' says Mum.

About the same time Sally was born, the family were moved by the council to a maisonette in Camberwell Green, because the prefabs were being pulled down. Tower blocks were put up in their place – soulless, miserable places compared to the prefab community, where everyone had taken a pride in their home and where there were annual competitions for the best gardens.

Because my grandmother worked, my mum and her sisters were largely brought up by their grandmother – my great grandmother – a smashing old lady I remember from my own childhood.

Mum stayed at school until she was fifteen and a half, when she left to take up an apprenticeship at a hairdresser's. She had learned shorthand and typing at school, and her teachers had wanted her to stay on and take exams, but she was set on leaving and starting work.

My dad, Alan Goss, was born in a stately home. But there was no silver spoon in his mouth – his mother had been evacuated there for the birth to get away from the bombing raids on London. Dad is two years older than my mum, and he, too, comes from south-east London. His mother was sent to Luton Hoo, a stately home belonging to the Wernher family (relatives of the Royal family) in the Bedfordshire countryside near to Luton, a week or so before he was born. It was used as a maternity home for mothers from areas where there was a high risk of bombing. The London hospitals were overstretched dealing with casualties from the raids, and, besides, it was safer for the mothers and newborn babies to be out in the country.

After he was born, my dad and his mother went to live

in Norfolk, where his father was stationed with the RAF. My grandfather was a technician who became an expert in the development and use of X-rays (after the war he stayed on in the RAF, and many years later worked for British Aerospace until his retirement). My grandparents and my dad lived in the village of Horsford for the last year of the war. Dad was a sickly baby and everyone was very worried about him for a few months because he did not feed well. But he survived, which is more than his parents' marriage did: after the war his mother brought him back to Walworth and he never saw his real father until many years later, not until after his mother had died.

Life in a single-parent family was not easy, even though my grandmother received a maintenance payment from my grandfather every week. It was twelve shillings (60p), which was not a bad amount immediately after the war but one which never increased, despite inflation. So my grandmother worked as a typist to support herself and my dad. They lived in a one-bedroom flat in a house without electricity, only gas lights. There was no bath, so my father was taken to Manor Street baths for a weekly wallow, and the rest of the week his mother stood him on the kitchen table and scrubbed him down.

He was introduced to music at an early age. His mother took him with her to her favourite ballets and to a concert by Edmundo Ross at the Albert Hall. She didn't trust babysitters, so she always took him along. He remembers buying his first pop record – a Little Richard EP, when he was twelve – and having to go round to his cousin's house to play it, because without electricity he couldn't plug in a record player. He had a good singing voice, singing in the South London Schools Choir, until his voice broke.

When Dad was thirteen his mother remarried. His new

stepfather was Denis Weston, who worked with his mother at the local electricity board. They all moved into a council flat in East Dulwich, where my father could play his records! Dad left school at sixteen with only one O level, GCE Art: he admits that, like his sons, he wasted his time at school and didn't enjoy studying. He was good at art, but nobody encouraged him to take that any further. His only other interest was cars, so he became a trainee motor mechanic at a local garage. After a year he was transferred to the reception desk because he was good at handling customers. Three years later, dissatisfied because he wasn't progressing fast enough, he left and joined the London Electricity Board for a short spell. Ten years after leaving school he had been through ten different jobs, including two jobs as a sales rep, one selling tyres and the other selling hosiery.

'I wanted to go into car sales but there were no openings. I was young and naïve – I expected everything to happen quickly, I wasn't prepared to wait. I was seriously planning to emigrate to Australia, but I met a girlfriend who changed my mind about that.'

Whilst he was in his teens Dad taught himself to play the harmonica and the guitar. By the time he was twenty the Beatles and the Rolling Stones were dominating the charts, and Dad was singing with a band, or a group as they were called in those days. It was a group which never had a name, and they only played one gig – disastrously. They used to practise at the Heal's furniture store canteen, because the lead guitarist worked there. They were booked to fill in when the main group took a break during a dance at the Heal's social club, in Kent. After watching the main group fail to get anybody up on their feet to dance, Dad knew they were on to a loser.

By then he was going out with Mum, and she and the

girlfriend of one of the other members of the group gamely danced the whole time they were playing, although they were the only ones on the dance floor. Dad now admits this might have had something to do with the fact that they were dreadful.

It was in 1967 that my mum and my dad met; she was just twenty-one and he was twenty-three. Regardless of all that was to happen later between them, they were very much in love at the beginning – in fact, it was almost love at first sight. My mum was visiting her gran in hospital. As she walked down the corridor with her sister she saw Dad coming the other way, and they fancied each other instantly.

'He was very attractive, and we gave each other the eye,' says Mum. 'When I came out after visiting-time he was waiting, and we started chatting. I'd just finished with another boyfriend who I knew was watching, so I played up to Alan like mad.'

They went out together for quite a few months, and by Christmas 1967 Dad proposed. They decided to get married the following September, but Matt and I changed their minds about that. When Mum found out she was pregnant they brought the wedding forward to April.

'We didn't get married because Carol was pregnant: we simply brought it forward. We'd already agreed we wanted to be married and I suppose after that we threw caution to the wind a bit,' says Dad. 'It was a surprise when Carol became pregnant, but not a nasty shock. We were both pleased: it was just sooner than we'd planned.'

Their main problem was finding somewhere to live. Then, only a week or two before their wedding day, they found a one-bedroom flat at the top of a house in Brockley. They didn't let the landlady know that Mum was pregnant and managed to get away with it as Mum stayed slim for quite a few months – remarkable when you consider that she was carrying twins. Eventually the landlady found out there was a baby on the way and though she wasn't heartless enough to throw them out, she certainly didn't make life easy for a young mother. Although there was a big wide hall in the house, she would not let Mum leave a pram downstairs.

For the first three months of their married life Mum was able to carry on working, first as a hairdresser and later as a telephonist. But it hadn't been an easy pregnancy: Mum had anaemia, low blood pressure, renal colic and, when she was three months pregnant, a threatened miscarriage that meant she had to spend two weeks in hospital.

She admits now that she knew nothing about babies and how they were born. 'We went to a film about childbirth at the hospital,' she says. 'I assumed that by the wonders of nature the stomach opened up, the doctor lifted the baby out, and the stomach closed up again, an everyday miracle. When I saw what really happens I passed out. Alan had to get me outside. He drove to the nearest pub, dashed in and brought a double brandy out to the car for me. It seems incredible now that I could ever have been so naïve.

'It was supposed to be the swinging sixties with everyone being permissive. But nobody had ever bothered to explain the fundamental facts of life to me.'

Soon after learning about it, Mum had to go through it. After we were born she spent ten days in hospital, and then went home to the flat in Brockley without her babies. We stayed in hospital for another month. She says:

'It was a very strange experience, walking out of the hospital without them. I felt dreadful. I spent hours travelling back there to see them, and I was always pestering the life out of the staff on the phone. I remember one day being told that Luke was out of his incubator and holding his own. Matthew had also been taken out but then had to go back in.

'I spent the weeks when they were in hospital getting ready for them at home. The pram had to be changed for a twin one, and I had to get lots of extra clothes, nappies and everything else.

'Then, when they came home, it was a matter of survival. They were being fed every three hours, day and night. I was so, so tired, and there was no help. Alan was scarcely there – he was working very long hours. It was very hard work and I was very lonely. I had a boiler for the nappies, and the kitchen seemed to be permanently full of steam.

'If I took them out I had to first carry the base of the pram down three floors to the hallway, go back for the body of the pram, go back again for the first baby and then make a fourth trip up and down for the second one. Coming back in I had to repeat the same procedure. I was dying of tiredness.

'But despite that, I adored having them. I sat for hours by their cot – they shared one at first – just watching them.'

At this time Dad had a job working for a firm that supplied and stocked kiosks selling souvenirs all over the tourist areas of London. It paid well and gave him a car, but the hours were appalling. He worked for thirteen weeks with only one day off, and that was the day we were born.

He remembers coming in one night, late, and disturbing us. 'The noise of me coming in woke Luke and Matthew. Carol automatically started to climb out of bed to see to them. Her eyes were closed and she was operating on automatic pilot – she was so tired. I did the feeding and changing for her that night: it took me three hours, and by that time they were ready to start again. I don't know how she coped, but I have nothing but admiration for the way she did. I know I wasn't around enough to take any pressure off her.'

Things were already starting to go wrong between my parents. Mum remembers when she came home from hospital after having us and found that Dad had not even washed the dishes from the dinner party on the night she went into labour, or changed the bed. She remembers feeling very alone during the eight months they lived at the Brockley flat after our birth.

But there were some good times as well. Mum has a really great singing voice, and they shared the same taste in music: Stevie Wonder, Gladys Knight and the Pips, the Beatles, James Taylor. Wherever they lived, and however little money they had, my parents always surrounded themselves with music. Dad would get his guitar and his harmonica out, and Mum would sing. Because she was shy, she preferred to sing in the dark: they would lie in bed together singing. Even before we were old enough to remember it, Matt and I were surrounded by music.

Soon we moved from the flat in Brockley to a ground-floor maisonette at Hither Green. It was bigger and better than Brockley, although the tiny boxroom bedroom that Matt and I shared was damp and Mum constantly had to redecorate it.

For the first year of our lives, me and my brother were both bald, and then we sprouted a mop of blond, downy hair. We had big blue eyes and dimples. Mum says that wherever she took us, people stopped her and commented on how lovely we were. I'm sure that all parents of twins will know what it is like: one baby gets a lot of attention and fuss made over it; two are guaranteed twice the attention and twice the fuss.

Mum was completely wrapped up in us: 'They were my

saviours, they made my life worth living,' she says. 'We used to giggle together all the time, and I'd be so busy talking to them as we walked along the street that more than once I pushed the pram into a lamp-post. I loved them to pieces. My mum adored them, too. They were her first grandchildren, after all, and she was forever buying them clothes and toys. I'd go to see her once a week and she'd make sure I had a huge meal – she knew that money was tight and that I'd be making sure that the boys and Alan had everything, without worrying about myself. I never had to tell her, she just knew, and there would be a package of things for me to take back home with me.'

Dad was now working as a hosiery salesman, and he was also doing evening jobs to raise more money. It was while he was knocking on doors doing market research for Gillette that he met a man who is still a friend of his to this day, and who sparked in him an interest in joining the police.

'This chap admitted bluntly that he had joined to get a police house and to have job security. He suggested that if I was interested I should try the City of London police, not the Metropolitan Police. I was worried about it, I thought we might alienate family and friends by joining the police. But Carol was philosophical: she said that if we lost friends because we needed good housing and a steady wage, they weren't worth having,' he says.

It took a long time for Dad to be accepted. The police force weren't too happy about his employment record, but eventually they accepted him for training, when we were two and a half years old. Mum was very pleased and proud, and thought that life was going to get better for us all. She didn't realize that her problems were just beginning.

CHAPTER TWO

Just Another Tear

It was the most violent thunderstorm I have ever seen. I was four years old, and terrified. I huddled on my bed with my brother Matt, both of us crying. Suddenly a flash of lightning crackled across the window, lighting up the room. In the brightness I saw my mum and dad, standing by the French windows, side by side. Just the sight of them made me feel warm and safe and secure. It was one of those lovely childhood feelings when you know, deep down know, that because they are there, everything will be all right. You cannot be harmed while your mum and dad stand guard, and they were standing by the window guarding Matt and me from the storm. I stopped crying and snuggled down to sleep, a happy little boy.

Three weeks later my childhood happiness would be shattered: my dad left us, for good.

The storm broke in Majorca, on the only foreign holiday we ever went on. It was the summer before my fifth birthday, so I was old enough to have clear memories of it. It was a week of perfect fun: swimming, playing, Mum rubbing suntan oil on our backs. It felt like a family should feel.

Unknown to me at the time, the holiday was a farewell gesture from my father. When my parents had booked it, they did not know they were going to split up; but by the time we all went away, Mum already knew that when we got back Dad would be leaving. I think going on the holiday was probably a mistake. On the one hand, it gave us some happy memories to treasure of our parents together, but on the other hand it lulled us into a false sense of security. However young we were, my brother and I had some inkling that things were not quite right, we were aware of the friction: but seeing them playing happy families on holiday in Majorca soothed any doubts we had, and left us unprepared for the shattering blow of Dad leaving. Looking back on the memory of them both standing at the French window while the storm raged is particularly poignant because to me it summed up all the happiness and security that a child has the right to be given, and it left an indelible image of their togetherness, which made my sense of loss so much more acute.

Things had not been going well for Mum and Dad from the time that Dad joined the police, more than two years earlier. He was sent away to Oxford for three months training, and that was a lonely time for Mum, as Dad only got home at weekends. But when the course finished, she was determined to see his passing out parade: she was very proud of him. She had saved some money for the train fare, she borrowed her sister Ann's boots so that she looked her smartest despite the tight budget we lived on, she dressed my brother and me in our best clothes and set off for Oxford. We were nearly three years old, so we were a handful to control during the journey and the ceremony, but Mum was determined that we should see Dad's big moment.

  She arrived to an uncomfortable reception. Dad asked her if she had received his letter: apparently he had sent her a six-page letter telling her that he thought their marriage was over and that he would not be returning to live with us after the course. Mum had not received it before

setting out. Not surprisingly, there was a huge row and a
terrible journey home for us all. Mum at least had the
satisfaction of forcing Dad to tell her to her face, but none
the less she was devastated. She had honestly not realized
that there was anything seriously wrong with the marriage,
and she loved Dad very deeply.

'I had a boyfriend before Alan, but Alan was the first
real love of my life,' she says. 'I was young and inexperienced, but I believed that marriage was for ever and that
children need a father. I wanted him back and I was so
miserably unhappy.'

We went back without Dad to the maisonette in Hither
Green, and he was still away at the start of 1972, the year
of the miners' strike when the whole country went on to
a three-day working week, and when electricity supplies
were cut off for long periods each day. The flat at Hither
Green was all-electric, and it was cold and damp at the
best of times, so my great grandmother said we could go
and stay at her flat. She moved in with her daughter, my
gran, and we took over her home at Nunhead, which is
between Lewisham and Brixton. Mum walked there with
the two of us, a suitcase full of clothes, and our cat in a
bag. We must have looked a sorry sight.

Our new home was in a big old block of flats in a
tough area, a place where kids put lighted matches
through the letter box for sport. Mum was ill while we
were there, and she remembers it as the worst period
of her whole life. I don't remember it at all, although
I have clear memories of my great grandmother, who
died when I was seven.

After we'd been there a few weeks my dad decided to
come back home again. He and Mum talked, and in the
end determined to give their marriage another go.

'I hated being away from my kids, I really missed them

very badly, missed knowing what they were up to every day,' he says.

Dad by this time qualified for a police house, so we moved to a three-bedroom 1930s mid-terrace house in Lee, south-east London. It was the best home we had ever had, with hot and cold running water and an upstairs bathroom, and they both thought this would give them the break they needed to get their marriage together again. The clearest memory I have of this house is of the 'ghost' who shared a bedroom with Matt and me. Both of us saw the figure of an old man in our room. We weren't terribly frightened; he seemed to be a kindly presence who stood between our beds, looking at us. When we called for Mum he would disappear.

Mum also thought the house was haunted. She always went upstairs with her back against the wall because she was sure there was 'something' on the stairs, where it was always very cold, no matter how hard she tried to heat it. On one occasion, after a row with Dad, Mum went to sleep in the small back bedroom. She heard footsteps on the landing that couldn't possibly be Dad's, and she felt the bedroom turn icy cold. When her sister Ann came round she, too, sensed some presence. Our granddad Harry was also aware of it; he says he never liked that house. Granddad has discovered since then that he is psychic, and I believe that Matt and I have inherited some of his abilities. We certainly have a very highly developed ability to communicate with each other without talking, something many twins have.

At this stage of our lives we even had our own language, which Mum says started when we lay side by side in our shared cot. We would babble away together, understanding each other but excluding everyone else. Gradually it lapsed, as we became able to speak properly, but the bond between us did not lessen; to this day we have a sixth sense which tells us if the other is in pain or is upset.

'They were so close that I could not come between them even when they were fighting,' says Mum. 'If I told one of them off the other would turn to me with big round eyes and defend his brother – even though that brother had been thumping him only a moment before. They made me feel wicked for even suggesting one of them was in the wrong! It was always the two of them against everyone else. I sometimes felt excluded, even as their mother.'

It was at this house, though, that I thought I had eliminated Matt from my life for ever: I really did think I had killed him. He was perched on a kitchen stool which had wheels, and I gave it a hard push. He careered down the kitchen and hit his head on the corner of a cupboard. There was so much blood I was sure he was dead, and he's still got the scar to prove it. I think I cried more than he did, I was so worried.

While we were living at Lee my grandmother, Win, died of cancer. I wish she had lived longer as I would have loved to have got to know her better, although I even now sometimes have a very strong feeling that she is close to me. From everything I have heard about her from my mum and granddad, I know she was a terrific person, and I have a dim memory of her crawling around on the floor on her hands and knees, with me on her back. Mum was devastated when she died and still misses her after all these years.

We got a transfer to another police house, in Mitcham. It was more modern, but still not modern enough to have central heating, and Mum seemed to spend a lot of her time carrying in coal for the fire and cleaning out grates. She was also very busy trying to earn some extra money for the family: she did typing at home, made jewellery, addressed envelopes. At one stage she got a job as a secretary, which earned enough money for her to pay for our extras. We were looked after at a nursery in Blackheath. I can remember that we had to go to bed for a sleep every afternoon on little camp beds, with itchy blankets over us, and Matt and I never wanted to sleep. I can also remember having jam sandwiches for lunch.

But that arrangement did not last long because we both caught measles, and Matt had complications that meant that he had to be kept in the dark for several days, to protect his eyes. Mum had only had the job for three weeks, and had to give it up to look after us. Dad was away on a four-week course.

Things were breaking down again between my parents, but I do have some very happy memories of my early childhood: of them singing together, Dad playing the harmonica and trying to teach Mum the guitar; of Mum sitting on the floor between our two beds, holding hands with each of us and singing us to sleep, songs like 'Toora Loora Loora' and 'Fly, Fly Superbird'; of her putting on funny little shows for us on the landing while we were in bed, singing 'Hey, Big Spender' with all the actions. I remember going to a music shop on Lewisham High Street with Dad, and staring at a drum kit in the window. I was so small that only half of my face came above the windowsill, but I could see these huge, gleaming drums and I knew then that I wanted them. The kit might as well have been made from solid gold, it was so far out of my reach, but I dreamed about it for the rest of my childhood, and even now when I think about it I can feel again that same mixture of excitement and longing.

It was while we were living at Mitcham that we went on the holiday to Majorca. The only holiday I have a memory of before that was camping in the New Forest in a tent. Just Dad and Matt and me, which was fun. Strangely enough, for several years after the holiday in Majorca I pretended I could not remember it. It was as though I were blocking it out. Dad would ask about holidays we remembered, and I would always talk about the New Forest, and when he asked me about Majorca I'd say I couldn't remember. But in fact it is the holiday of which I have the clearest memories: I think, in my very young way, I felt that I was somehow betraying my own unhappiness by talking about it. To me, my father leaving home for good was always linked with that holiday.

He left soon after we got back from Majorca. Apparently, when he told Mum he was leaving us as soon as he found somewhere to stay, he offered to let the three of us go on holiday without him. But she insisted that he came, hoping it would be a last chance to get everything right. She remembers 'that awful, pathetic feeling of just hoping that someone will love you again, when their love for you has died'. But when we returned she knew it was finally over.

I've never believed in using the breakdown of my parents' marriage as an excuse for anything I've done in my own life. Lots of kids play on it, and make out it causes them all sorts of problems. I cannot pretend it made us happy, but I don't believe it lets me off the hook for my own actions, and in some ways it may even have helped me. It made me more independent and stronger than I perhaps otherwise would have been. We weren't shielded from it: Mum levelled with us that Dad wasn't coming back, and I can remember sobbing my heart out.

The worst thing was the unnaturalness of our relationship with Dad when he came to see us at weekends. Every time we saw him felt something like the first day at a new school – that strange feeling of having to get to know your way round, having to re-establish yourself, even the way we had to put on our best clothes and have our hair neatly brushed to go out with him. We had to build some sort of relationship afresh every time we saw him, and I always had huge butterflies in my stomach when I knew he was coming.

I developed a sort of tunnel vision, shutting out a great deal of the thoughts and memories around me and concentrating on getting on with life from one day to the next; I'm sure that's how lots of kids cope with it. It's such a common experience, but I do think you have to live through it to fully understand what it's like. You feel as excited at seeing your missing parent each time as you do, much later in life, when you are meeting a lover. It's a different emotion, but just as strong, and you are just as desperate to make a good impression, be the person they want you to be. Somehow, in a childish way, you think that if you can be perfect maybe your dad will come back home.

We went from seeing our dad every day of our lives to seeing him every couple of weeks – and that feels like a lifetime to a child. He became almost a stranger to us; we had things in common to talk about, but the closeness was gone, the comfortableness of a well-worn and familiar relationship where you don't even need to talk. He would take us for a meal, and that was always a nightmare because I don't think Dad was really cut out to sit in a restaurant with two small boys whose table manners weren't always immaculate. He was probably not ready for young kids, he didn't want to be embarrassed or shown up. Then we'd go to the pictures or the zoo or something. The worst bit was the gap between the meal and the start of the film, because he would sit with us in his car or on a park bench and lecture us on how we ought to be getting on at school, how we ought to behave, all sorts of things. He was trying to make judgements about us based on one-day visits; we were rapidly becoming strangers to each other.

He says now that he didn't see us more often because he encountered a lot of hostility from Mum. I'm sure that's true: her life had been devastated by him walking out, and she wasn't about to put down a welcome mat for him. But I believe he should have persevered for at least the first two or three years, seeing us more regularly, for our sakes. As it was, he copped out and let his visits slide, so that when we did see each other it was such hard work for all of us. At the end of the day we used to say goodbye with a little peck on the cheek, when all along I was desperate for him to fling his arms round me and hug me. I used to walk into our house with tears in my eyes, trying hard not to let him see them.

I don't believe that the break-up of any marriage or long-term relationship is entirely black and white: there are faults on both parts and I have tried not to take sides between Mum and Dad. But I do know that in terms of bringing us up on her own my mum was brilliant, and my dad was just not there, however much we wanted and needed him.

When you have a child you immediately become a fully-fledged parent. You don't have any training courses, you don't have to produce a CV or any other certificates, you are what that child has got. You are taken for granted by that small person you have created; that's part of the deal of being a parent. It's a responsibility you have to take very seriously, no matter how difficult it is at times. You can't cop out, like my dad did. Even though I now understand everything better, I know what he was going through and I get on with him brilliantly today, in spite of this there are still huge, unresolved miseries inside me when I think back to those years.

If we were suffering, so was Mum. 'I don't fall in love easily and I don't fall out of love easily,' she says. 'It takes me a long time to turn. But part of me wanted the marriage to end because at least I would know where I stood, we had been messing around for so long trying to keep the thing going. I was terrified of being on my own with just the boys, petrified. It sounds cowardly, but it's the truth. I didn't want the loneliness, the poverty. I didn't even feel secure in our home, which was a police house.

'But it was a question of dusting myself down, and doing my crying when the boys were in bed. But they did know how upset I was, and they did their share of crying, too. I didn't hide from them the fact that their dad wasn't coming back: I thought that if I lied to them they would have nobody left in the world they could trust.

'They became very insular, very dependent on me. I once went down the road to the phone box, which you could see from our house, to ring my father. I'd only been gone a couple of minutes and I could hear them crying. They were at the end of our path looking for me, clinging together with tears pouring down their faces. "You won't leave us, Mummy, will you?" they kept asking. It was heart-breaking. It cracks me up even now to think about it. I just had to give them hugs and hugs to reassure them.

'Alan and I were probably both too young when we married, but he was able to pick himself up and walk away from it, doing his growing up somewhere else in a way that suited him. I was forced to grow up and get on with life because of the children. But I would never, ever change places with him: he missed out on so much joy by not being with Luke and Matthew.

'If we had stayed together, the boys would have had a

tougher upbringing and may not have turned out the way
they did. I don't regret my marriage to Alan: I loved him,
my children were conceived in love and born in love – how
can anyone regret that?'

We had started school by the time they split up, at first
going to St Mark's Junior School in Mitcham, but transfer-
ring after a while to Beechholme, also in Mitcham. One
of my happiest memories is of being met by Mum at the
gate and going home to sit on her lap with tea and biccies.
It was a ritual that I loved. It sounds like something out
of *Little House on the Prairie*, but it's true. I fell in love with
my first teacher, who had glasses and long hair, and I
sobbed when I had to leave her class.

We were typically naughty little boys in those days. I can
remember dunking my head in a puddle to try to catch a
cold, so that I could stay home from school. Unfortunately
a woman saw me and followed me home to tell my mum,
and I was in trouble. Another time Mum nearly caught me
and a girl called Jenny showing each other our naughty
bits in the garage – we hid in a wardrobe that was stored
in there, terrified of being caught with our pants down.
The garage, which was at the back of the house, was a
favourite place. We spent all our pocket money on bubble
gum and practised for hours trying to blow bigger and
bigger bubbles.

Money was very tight. We were offered free school
dinners, but Mum was too proud to accept them. She put
cardboard in her shoes and borrowed a friend's sewing
machine to make our clothes, to save money. One day, in
desperation, we went in the pouring rain with Mum to the
phone box so that she could ring granddad and ask him
for some money. She called me into the phone box because
I was getting wet outside, and as I went in I noticed

something that looked like a pound note on the floor. When I picked it up I saw that it had the Queen's head on both sides – I was very disappointed, because I thought it must be toy money. But when I gave it to Mum she realized that it was two pound notes stuck together, probably worth about ten pounds today, and enough to buy us all some food for the rest of the week. We all hugged each other in delight.

Mum got a part-time job working in an employment agency in Streatham. Her boss would not let her leave the office five minutes early to catch the bus back to Mitcham, so when she finished work she literally had to run all the way to be sure of being at the school gates when we came out: we were so insecure we would be distraught if we could not see her face among those of the other mums.

When Dad first moved out he went into rented accommodation in Finchley, sharing a house with some people much younger than him, but he was already seeing Margaret, the woman who was to become his second wife and our stepmother. They met on the train when he was travelling to work from Mitcham. She was also married, but was separated from her husband, and before too long she had bought a flat in Sutton where they lived together. It was a while before we met her, and it was never really an easy relationship.

'Both the women in my life were unhelpful with my relationship with my sons,' says Dad. 'It was understandable from Carol, she felt a great deal of animosity towards me and she made it hard work for me to visit them. I could see how they were affected by the bad feeling. I was also given a hard time at home afterwards from Margaret, who I felt resented the time I spent with them. In the end it was too taxing, too sad, too hard to go back each week, and I cut my visits down to once a month, and then every six weeks, even every eight weeks. I can see now that Luke is right, I should have worked harder at being with them more. But I never actually stopped seeing them, even at the risk of my relationship with Margaret, and even after being told by their teachers and doctor that my visits were too upsetting for them. It was not a good situation, but it was probably typical of many, many broken marriages where children are involved.'

Dad married Margaret in 1976, and we weren't told about it or invited to the wedding. Luckily for us, Margaret did not have any children from her first marriage, and she and Dad did not give us any little half-brothers or sisters: I don't know how I would have coped with sharing him with other children, especially knowing that he was living with them and therefore much closer to them than he was to us. I know lots of kids have to live with that situation, but I'm just grateful it didn't happen to us.

Mum had also met a man six months previously who was to become our new stepfather, and play a very large role in our lives: Tony Phillips. She went out one evening with a crowd of her girlfriends and found herself chatting to a man with 'twinkling eyes', as she describes it.

'I didn't fall in love instantly, but I thought he was very cute and I was attracted to him straightaway,' she says. 'I'd tried going out with one or two other fellas after Alan left, but I'd never met anyone that I wanted to see again, until Tony came along. For a few weeks he came round to see me every Tuesday, but I wouldn't let him over the threshold until the children were asleep. He was the only man I allowed into the house: I'd no intention of the boys having to cope with a succession of strange men.

'Then one Tuesday Tony came round and Luke and Matthew were still awake, in bed. He asked if he could go up and see them. I was very possessive about them, and very reluctant, but eventually I agreed.'

I can remember clearly the night Tony first walked into our bedroom. He's not very tall and he has a very slight limp caused by the arthritis he has suffered with all his life. He didn't talk down to us or try to buy our affection. He simply said 'hello', and then told us a story about a little bird, which he made up as he went along. The bird lost all its feathers, but found some new ones to stick on. Unfortunately, it was only a little bird and the new feathers were from an eagle. Tony said that if we ever saw a bird flying around faster than Concorde we'd know it was our bird from the story. We took to him straight away.

But we were only seven years old at the time and very used to being on our own with our mother: I don't think we made life easy for Tony when he moved in, despite such a good start.

Looking back, I can see that Mum didn't help the situation either. She didn't give him enough authority over us, she never allowed him to make decisions about us or to exercise discipline. Tony can be philosophical about it now, but I think he's looking back through rose-tinted spectacles: at the time I'm sure he thought we were a couple of spoiled little brats, and I don't think he liked us at all.

Tony now says: 'I learned quickly that Carol's relationship with the boys was the number one relationship, I couldn't compete. They had created a very close bond, which overruled everything else, an even closer mother–son bond than normal. So I learned to keep quiet and just get on with things. After all, I was courting their mother, so I didn't want to fall out with them. There was certainly friction and I know Luke took it personally. But I only got involved in confrontation with them when I felt they

needed it, in the same way that all children do from time
to time: it wasn't personal for me at all.'

Tony, who is a year older than Mum, has led an interesting
life. He was involved in the 1970s' property boom, but the
boom collapsed into a slump and cost him a lot of money.
At the time Mum met him he had a garage in Holborn,
but when the council put double yellow lines in front of it
business was wiped out. Since then, he's done a great
variety of different jobs, almost always being self-
employed. He's not a nine-to-five person, and he's not a
person who ever lets life get on top of him for long: he
always finds another scheme to keep himself going.
    He is very different from Dad. At times I have felt
Tony to be very cold, because he is not a demonstrative
person who shows his feelings. Mum says this does not
mean that he does not feel anything: he is just more
restrained than the rest of the family – we are all the
sort of people who hug and kiss and say 'I love you'
all the time. Tony knows that our nickname for him in
the family is 'the robot'.
    We've had our problems, but I have a lot of love and
respect for him. I've seen him go through tremendous
business problems, and I've seen him cope bravely with
the pain from his arthritis. I've learned a lot from Tony,
and I like him as well as love him.
    Shortly after Tony moved in we were threatened with
eviction from the police house. From the moment Dad left
us we were not really entitled to go on living there, but we
had nowhere else to go, and it took quite a while for the
police force to catch up with the fact that Dad had gone.
Mum tried to get the council to re-house us, but they
had a very long waiting list, so she and Tony scraped
together a deposit, arranged a mortgage and bought a small

end-of-terrace modern house on an estate in Cheshunt, Hertfordshire. They married a year after we had first met Tony.

We transferred to another school, St Clement's, in Cheshunt, and while living there we joined swimming and karate clubs. We settled down quite well, singing in the school choir and playing football for the school. I was the more active of the two of us: Mum says I have always been hyperactive. Even when I'm supposed to be sitting still I tend to fidget and from a very early age I was forever drumming with my fingers on the arm of a chair or a table. It drove the grown-ups wild at times.

It was at Cheshunt that I had my first taste of rejection in love, when I was ten years old. The object of my affections was a girl called Tina, who was two years older than me and not remotely interested. I used to race out of school so that I could be sitting on the wall when she walked past. Up to that point, you could guarantee that Matt and I would be the last out of school, always larking about in the cloakrooms, but Tina changed all that for me. It must have been infectious, because Matt then decided he was in love with her, too, and we had our first rivalry over a woman. It didn't really matter, because to Tina we were both too young to even be considered as boyfriends.

While we were living at Mitcham, my parents had a very angry showdown. Dad wrote to say that he had now decided not to see us any more: he said he had been advised by our teachers and a doctor and social worker who he had consulted that it would be better for us to have a clean break from him, at least until we were older. When Mum told us, we were desperately upset: I can remember crying my eyes out. We never got used to the idea of not seeing Dad and eventually Tony got very angry, the angr-

iest I have ever seen him. He picked up the phone and
rang Dad, and held the receiver out so that Dad could
hear us crying. 'That's your sons,' he said. Tony handed
the phone to me and Dad just said, 'Hello, son.' The word
'son' was enough to choke me with tears, I couldn't talk
to him for crying.

Dad accepted that we needed him and started to come
and see us again. But it was a very bad time for our relationship with him and both Matt and I got through by camou-
flaging our feelings, putting him out of our minds as much
as we could. That year he actually left our Christmas presents on the doorstep on Christmas Day. I could not
believe it: I thought it was a joke, and that he was hiding
round the corner and would jump out to wish us a Merry
Christmas. It was devastating to think that he had been so
near to us and had not seen us. On another occasion, when
I was about nine or ten, I called him 'Daddy' and he told
me I was a bit old for that, and should call him 'Dad' in
the future. Perhaps if I'd been seeing him frequently the
change to 'Dad' would have occurred naturally by then,
but I still clung to the name I had called him by when we
were little and he lived with us. I was hurt that he had to
say that to me.

Our new life in Cheshunt did not just entail a new house,
a new school and a new stepfather. We also acquired a
new stepsister and stepbrother, Tony's children Carolyn
and Adam. Carolyn was a year younger than us, Adam
three years younger. They lived with Tony's ex-wife, but
visited us at weekends. We were determined to hate them
from the word go, but the first time we actually saw them
they were in the bath – how can you be standoffish with
two kids who are in the bath?

Every weekend when they came to our house we would

start out dreading it, not wanting them to come. And every weekend when it was time for them to go home all four of us would be pleading to stay together. Matt and I enjoyed horse riding, and they would come with us to the stables. Sometimes we would all pile into the car – Mum and Tony had an E-type Jag, a leftover from his prosperous days – and drive out to Billing Aquadrome with the caravan in tow. We'd spend the whole weekend fooling around in inflatable dinghies, fishing, making dens in the woods. There was a permanent fairground nearby and we spent all our pocket money there.

I can see now how hard it was for everyone. Broken families are an equation and different people solve it differently: Tony and his ex-wife Pauline got on better than Mum and Dad, for instance; Mum had plenty of troublesome times with Carolyn and Adam; we were not exactly pleasant to Dad's wife Margaret and we gave Tony a few problems. On the other hand, the adults were not always as sensitive as they might have been in handling us, and at times their behaviour was downright unforgivable.

All in all, we had far more problems with the adults than we ever did with Carolyn and Adam, although we were envious of the way Tony could show affection for them more easily than he could for us. There were jealousies and suspicions all around, but children always find their own level and come to terms with each other better than they do with grown-ups. Tony himself says he measured the success of our relationship with Adam and Carolyn by the fact that before too long we had all dropped the word 'step' and referred to each other simply as brothers and sisters.

CHAPTER THREE

Leave Me Alone

I always feel weird when I see other identical twins. If they are very alike, they look to me like something from the twilight zone. Freaks. Clones. Then I wonder if people feel that about Matt and me. I hope they don't, because I don't think we go out of our way, like some twins do, to look and be spookily alike.

There was no single moment when I realized that I was different from other kids because I was a twin – I always knew it. There are pluses and minuses in being a twin, but on balance I think the minuses outweigh the pluses. It's not that I don't love having Matt as a brother: I wouldn't have missed that for anything. There's an indestructible bond between us. But we have both had to fight all our lives to be treated as individuals, and I expect all other identical twins will understand and recognize that problem.

As a twin and a young child, individuality is virtually impossible. You are regarded as being half of a whole: anyone who knows your brother assumes that you have an identical personality, simply because you look the same. At school you are both tarred with the same brush: if I was bad, Matt was assumed to be bad also, and vice versa. Children, in particular, ask you stupid questions – but you also get a fair amount from adults. When Matt broke his arm, all the other kids wanted to know why I didn't have a plaster cast on mine, too. When he wore a brace on his teeth I was asked – even by adults – why I didn't have one. And I got heartily fed up with well-meaning shop assistants and old ladies in the street asking us if our mother could tell us apart.

Mum did not deliberately dress us alike, but it is difficult to be creative with shopping when you are struggling around with two lively little boys in tow: it was easier to buy two of everything. When we got dressed in the mornings the clothes were all kept together, there was no clear sense of his and mine. When Tony moved in with us, he admits it took him a while to recognize us as individuals, and he asked Mum to make sure we were dressed differently.

Later on, when we were buying our own clothes, we guarded them jealously. When they were no longer new we would lend them to each other, but we both had certain things which were out of bounds to the other one. We respected the unwritten rules because the battle for even that much individuality had been hard won.

When we started at school we had to wear badges with our names on. Later on, at secondary school, when all the other kids were being called by their first names, we had to put up with being addressed as 'Goss' because teachers did not know who was who. I was constantly in trouble for saying 'I have a name, sir' to teachers. Like most twins, we hated being referred to as 'the twins' or 'the Goss twins', we were desperate from an early age to be treated as individuals.

The confusion between us probably cost me a GCE in maths. I was always much better at maths than Matt, but for some reason he was put into a higher set than me in our last year at school. When I protested to the teachers I was told that they would move me in a few weeks, but a few weeks later they claimed it was too late to switch me.

I'm afraid I lost all interest in the subject under my new teacher. I continued doing Matt's maths homework for him, which was more difficult than mine, but didn't bother with my own. I'm not claiming that this put paid to a brilliant academic career – I couldn't wait to leave school and I had no intention of doing any further studies – but it is an example of how little we were regarded as individuals.

We actually asked to be put into separate classes at school when we were thirteen; that was a very big step for us, because until then we had never been apart for such long hours on a regular basis. We both felt we needed more time away from each other, and we developed separate groups of friends for a while.

There is also a physical disadvantage in being twins: we knocked hell out of each other as kids. Because we were the same size and weight we were evenly matched in fights, and because we are equally pig-headed neither of us would ever give in, so we slugged each other as hard as we could for as long as we could. We both have scars on our bodies to prove it. Had one of us been a year or two older, we would perhaps still have fought, but never for so long or so hard. As we got older we agreed not to be so rough: our fights in recent years may have involved a bit of pushing, but we don't hit each other any more.

The advantages in being a twin are obvious. From birth onwards I had a constant, close companion. There was always a friend of my own age to play with, someone to get into trouble with, an ally against the adult world. When we were unhappy, it was shared, and we could give each other support. I know that Matt and me have a means of communication that does not rely on speech. We feel things for each other even when we are thousands of miles apart, and when we are together we often only have to glance at the other to know what he's thinking. My Mum will probably hate to read this, but I know that if I was in an aeroplane that was about to crash, the two people I would think about would be my girlfriend Shirley and my brother Matt.

It may sound a contradiction of everything I have said about the quest for individuality, but being a twin certainly gets you noticed. It gives you, from birth, a title. The new teacher will go home after her first day in front of the class with only a few pupils firmly fixed in her mind: the twins will always be among those she gets to know first. In other words, the struggle for individuality was between me and my twin, not between us and the rest of the kids. We were designated as special and different from birth, and we liked that.

We had the usual fun and games that twins enjoy. We used to deliberately confuse teachers, usually when they were trying to punish one of us. We would go out of the class to the toilet and when we came back in we would sit in each other's chairs, that kind of silliness. It was always easier to get into trouble: when Matt suggested something wicked it was like suggesting it to myself, he was so much part of me, and because there were two of us we could always egg the other one on to mischief. But in a way we could get away with more – twins are expected to be 'double trouble'. That expression and 'as like as two peas in a pod' are so familiar, you simply learn to put up with hearing them. I wouldn't mind a tenner for each time they've been said about us.

Occasionally we could even confuse our mum, especially at night when we would change beds. But she always sussed us pretty quickly. Both Mum and Dad knew us apart automatically, not just by looks but by personality. We are very different people, however alike we look. I am much more practical, down-to-earth, self-sufficient than

Matt. He is a dreamer, more relaxed than me. My family and friends tell me I'm deeper than he is: I think about things more. He takes what comes. We're both impulsive and mad, but I've always been more sensible than he is. He's likely to want to do really crazy things that could end in total disaster, and I have to restrain him. You can see the differences in our personalities when you look at the words we write for songs: his are more lyrical, more descriptive; mine are simpler, more direct.

I have always assumed the role of older brother. Studies of twins have shown that it is very common for one of them to take on a surrogate mother role with the other. It isn't necessarily the one who was born first who does this, but in our case that's the way it has worked. As a child I saw it as my job to look after Matt, to protect him. I was always, physically, ahead of him. Dad remembers us cycling down the road on our little bikes when we were four, the first two-wheelers we ever had, and I suddenly put my feet up on the handlebars. Three days later Matt did it. That was a pattern that would be repeated many times. I was also a bit ahead of him physically in another way: girls. We both had girlfriends from an early age, but I was the first to get into sexual relationships.

There is a deep underlying rivalry between us but it is softened and reduced by the great love we have for one another, which means that we genuinely both want only good things to happen for the other. In other words, neither of us wants to do well at the other's expense, but we still want to do as well as each other. It was characterized in my early relationships with girls: whenever I went out with a girl I always had to ask her if she fancied my brother. I needed to know. We were, after all, alike to look at, so I felt that if she wanted me she probably also wanted him. I needed reassurance that it was something individual about me that she found attractive. Of course, in those early schoolboy–schoolgirl relationships that are over after a couple of days, looks are probably the most vital ingredient, and so it often happened that girlfriends were passed between us: I stole his girlfriends and he stole mine.

Having a twin who looks like you is not as hard to cope with as many people might think: and that's because to us, and to those who are close to us, we don't look alike at all. We are the same height now, six feet two inches, but Matt is more heavily built than me; he weighs a stone more than I do; he has a rounder face than mine: he looks more like our father and I look more like our mother.

Occasionally, looking at photographs, I realize how alike we are, but the rest of the time I see the differences rather than the similarities. I have always believed he is better looking than I am. At school I was the one with the skinny legs, and I was convinced girls would fancy him more than me.

Until we were twelve there was an easy way to tell us apart: I was the one with the sticking-out ears. I had serious jugs; I made Prince Charles look streamlined. I always had my hair long to cover my ears until eventually I had an operation to pin them back. At one school sports day I remember an older girl shouting out to me 'Cheers, big ears', which upset me so much that I ran off the track and all the way home. It was then that Mum agreed to fix up the operation privately, because I was so self-conscious about them, but in the nick of time we received an NHS appointment from the local hospital. They had to take cartilage out of my left ear to put in my right, which was the more prominent. Afterwards my ears were badly bruised and a lovely colour combination of yellow, mauve, brown and black for a few weeks.

Our singing voices are very different, but that owes more

to the influences in our music than to nature. Matt has
cultivated a higher voice because he admired Michael Jackson. I have always preferred a soul sound, deeper than his.
But if our singing voices are different, our speaking voices
are identical. Even our nearest and dearest have trouble
recognizing which one of us is on the other end of the
telephone. We used this to great advantage as teenagers,
chatting up each other's girlfriends shamelessly.

In the final analysis, I would not swap having Matt as a
brother for anything. But I do not like being pigeonholed
as 'a twin', and in my experience being a twin is jam-packed
with insecurities.

I have Richard Briers and Felicity Kendal to thank for the
year I spent living in Cheddar, in Somerset. *The Good Life*,
a television series in which they played a married couple
who gave up their nine-to-five existence to run a smallhold-
ing, was a great hit in our household, particularly with
Mum. When Tony's property maintenance business collapsed, she persuaded us all that we should opt out and
move to the country. The attraction was to be self-
sufficient, and it certainly looked fun on telly. I had always
lived in or near to London, but I was only eleven at the
time and the prospect of moving did not bother me: we'd
already lived in quite a few different houses.

Mum and Tony took off for a week of house-hunting
and, with a loan from Tony's father, who was a chartered
surveyor and insurance claims consultant, they bought a
'cottage' in Cheddar, the beautiful little village famous for
the nearby Cheddar Gorge. I'm using the word cottage
because 'tumbledown wreck' sounds a bit harsh, though it
is probably a fairer description. Matt and I didn't see it
until the day we moved in.

I travelled from Cheshunt to Cheddar with Mum, in

the Jag. Tony and Matt followed behind in a transit van containing some of our furniture, and with our caravan hitched on the back, stuffed full with a set of kitchen units for the new house.

Mum and I nearly didn't make it. As we were travelling down the M4 in the middle lane, a woman in a white Mini suddenly pulled out of the inside lane in front of us. Mum swerved, slammed on the brakes, and our car went into a spin in a cloud of white smoke. We performed three complete circles, the last one on two wheels, and ended up broadside on across the motorway, with the engine cut out. Mum sat behind the wheel, transfixed. I broke the spell by saying 'At least, Mum, we would have died together.' She snapped into life and tried the engine. At the first turn of the key it would not start, but luckily at her second attempt it did. We were very close to a motorway service area and we pulled off for a cup of coffee to calm us down. After we parked and started to walk towards the café, a car passed quite close to me and I jumped in fright, my nerves shattered. Mum put her arm round me and we had a big hug.

If we had died on the motorway that day, it would not have been Mum's fault. She is a good driver, and she was doing everything right. Even to this day I have a very firm idea of what I would like to do to the driver of that Mini, who pulled out without looking in her mirror and drove on, safe and sound, almost leaving death in her wake. We were lucky that no other cars were close enough to ram into us: if the motorway had been busier the consequences could have been appalling.

Despite the near-accident, we still arrived first at the house in Cheddar. I couldn't believe it. There were no windows, the doors were hanging off, it was a dilapidated mess. 'That's not where we're going to live, is it, Mummy?

We can't live there, it's worse than a shed,' I said, praying that she would say there was a mistake and we had pulled up outside the wrong house. But there was no mistake: this was our new home, Jasmine Cottage.

We were too frightened even to go inside. A woman was coming down the hill and Mum asked her if she would mind going in with us. She must have thought we were mad, but she was very kind and accompanied us. It was far worse than Mum had remembered it: local kids had been using it for all sorts of things, and it was full of used condoms, cigarette ends, matches and every other kind of litter. We pitched the caravan in a nearby farm field and lived there until the place was habitable. It was a good choice of field: the farmer had a son, Robert, who was the same age as us, and became one of our best friends down there.

Living in Cheddar did not work out for our family, but in many ways it was a great year, and I would not have missed it. Mum was able to get work easily: she worked as a secretary at the local electricity board, which was just up the lane from us. She made friends and loved the life there, as did our dog, a Yorkshire terrier called James, who came with us. To our dismay he was run over in our quiet little backwater – ironic after surviving life in London and Cheshunt. We buried him in the garden and replaced him with two mongrels called Bill and Ben. We also had a cat called Jessica, who had the quickest sex change in history when we discovered that she was a he and renamed her Jesse. The cat was the Madonna of the feline world, because he seemed to like nothing better than letting the dogs inflict pain on him.

We also bought a goat called Mary who attached herself romantically to Tony. I learned to milk the goat, and came to prefer chilled goat's milk on my cornflakes to cow's milk from a bottle. Unfortunately, Mary died giving birth and we had to bury her in the garden, too.

Matt and I used to go fishing in a private pond nearby, with a big *No Fishing* sign – it was poaching, to give it its correct name. We did not have expensive fishing tackle, just worms on the end of a line, but when my granddad came down to stay with us for a few days we caught the biggest trout he has ever eaten. It must have weighed three pounds and was probably the prize specimen in the pond.

We had a lot of fun and a very strong feeling of being up against the odds together: we all worked hard at getting the cottage straight and, although it was never completely finished, when we moved out it was a very attractive and picturesque home. We never really got to grips with the garden though: it was waist deep in nettles when we moved in, and then one day when I returned from school it had all been ploughed up. It looked like a muddy field, with deep furrows across it. It stayed like that until we left.

We went to Fairlands School, our first secondary school. We made friends and we were not unhappy, but we always felt we were outsiders. Our strong London accents made for a communication problem with the local kids, who had country accents as broad as ours. Some of them asked us if we were Australian! We had to learn a new language: 'daps' meant trainers, 'scrap' was a fight. Because we were already very interested in clothes and always believed in personal hygiene (Matt and I were using deodorants and anti-perspirants before most boys had heard of them), we tended to be more popular with the girls than the boys. That made us even less popular with the boys, but we were already tall and strong (five feet ten inches by the time we were eleven) and we defended ourselves pretty well in any punch-ups.

For a time I went out with a girl called Karen, who was

a year older than me and the most popular girl in the school. One day her sister phoned up and said she didn't want to go out with me any more, and I found out later that behind my back Matt had been round to her house and chatted her up. It didn't always work that way, though: I took great delight one day in introducing him to my new girlfriend, a girl called Nicky: she'd been going out with him the previous week!

When we were told by Mum and Tony, a year after moving to Cheddar, that we were going back to London I had mixed emotions: I didn't want to leave my girlfriend, a small, pretty blonde girl who I thought I was devoted to at the time, and, much worse, I did not want to be parted from our puppies, Bill and Ben, who had to be given away. But I did want to get back to the city.

It was Tony who had the worst time down there. He could not find work. The good life is great if you have lots of money: when you are trying to pay back a loan and support yourselves, it can be a nightmare. Tony travelled as far as South Wales to work, but could find only casual jobs. Village people don't exactly open their arms to outsiders and he found it difficult to fit in. At times he had to hunt around the garden for firewood to keep us all warm.

He tried lots of schemes to make money, and we all trudged miles sticking leaflets through doors for him. We had great fun helping him to train as a double glazing salesman. He did a course, and then he practised knocking on our door and trying to sell to Mum or Matt or me. We loved it because it was an excuse to open the door and be rude to him, which most kids would enjoy. I know that whatever else becomes of me, I could always work as a trainer for door-to-door salesmen: I perfected all sorts of excuses for not buying from him. When he had to do it for real, the whole family went out in the car with him and literally pushed him up the first drive.

Mum and Tony protected us from the worst of it, but they were at a very low ebb during that year in Cheddar. They used up all their savings, they could not afford to pay Tony's father the money they owed him, and Tony was so unhappy he was close to a breakdown. He's definitely a city person; country life was not for him. Unknown to Tony at the time, and because she was desperate, Mum went to see his father and asked him to give Tony a job, which he did.

We sold the house in Cheddar and made sufficient profit to pay off the debt and put down the deposit on a house in Camberley. Mum chose the house by herself: Tony told her to get on with it. But there was a hiccup, and the purchase of the original house they were buying fell through at the last minute. Mum rushed around and found another, but we were unable to move in for a few weeks, so when we first moved back to London we were once again living in a caravan, this time on a site at Henley. I hate caravans and I cannot for the life of me imagine why people go on holiday in them.

Because we were enrolled at Collingwood School in Camberley, and because Mum did not want our education to be messed around any more by changing schools, she drove us to Camberley from Henley every morning in the rush hour, a round trip of one and a half hours, which she repeated every afternoon.

It was while we were in Cheddar that the relationship between Mum and Dad had gone through its most critical and unpleasant phase. There had been disputes between them before, over maintenance payments, and they both felt they had grievances. As I have already said, I love Dad and have a great relationship with him now, and I have also tried to understand why he behaved the way he did. But he admits himself he was way out of order in some of his actions, both to us and to Mum. Even today, with so much water under the bridge, I can feel a physical pain when I think about it.

Dad received a bad school report about us and was very angry. He assumed that we weren't trying: we were, but we had moved about so much that our schooling had been disrupted. He wrote to us: it was a typed letter and it was a 'harsh, dogmatic attack'; those are his own words to describe it and he accepts that he should never have sent it.

We each received identical letters and we were desperately upset. It was as formal as a letter to a bank manager, but much nastier. He even signed it 'Alan Goss'. To me, it seemed like yet more proof that my father did not love me. A child does not understand about marriage breakdown: when one parent leaves, the child always imagines that in some way they are at fault, that the parent does not love them. Not enough was done to compensate for that; Dad never went out of his way to explain it to us, nor did he demonstrate his affection physically. So when we read the letter we were convinced that he did not love us. We were so upset that we did not go to school that day.

Mum went berserk and there was a loud slanging match down the phone. She said that she would not let us go to stay with Dad: he and his wife Margaret had recently moved to a house that was big enough for us to visit, and he wanted us to spend a week with him for the first time since he had left home. Dad retaliated by taking Mum to court, claiming that she was refusing him access to see us: this after he had been dissuaded from dropping out of our lives altogether a couple of years earlier. Mum explained to the court that she was not denying him the right to have his children stay with him, she simply wanted him and Margaret to build a closer relationship with us before we were taken off to stay with a woman we did not know in an unfamiliar house. The court agreed, and ordered Dad and Margaret to travel to Cheddar and see us at least three times before we could stay with them. They did it within ten days, and we went to stay with them for a week.

Margaret made a great effort to welcome us. She cooked our favourite foods, made me my favourite tuna and mayonnaise sandwiches, and we in turn behaved ourselves and the week passed very well. I remember being so nervous before we went there that I felt sick, but at the end of the week I had developed an affection for her. It was the only time that things worked out between her and us though, and I cannot really explain why. I suspect we were all trying too hard that week and in real life nobody can keep up that level of effort. Dad says we were cold, sullen and withdrawn on our next visit: we probably were. We were eleven years old and wracked with guilt about enjoying being with Dad; we felt it was a betrayal of Mum, even though she did not consciously impose that view on us, and I think we just put the shutters up on our relationship with Margaret.

Mum says, 'Watching them going off to stay with another woman tore me apart. I tried hard not to let them know how I felt. I genuinely wanted them to get on well with their Dad because blood is thicker than water. But I'm sure they sensed how unhappy I was seeing them go.'

When we moved back to London, just before we went to the caravan, we stayed with my granddad; I have some lovely memories of that time. Granddad has been the most constant father figure in my life, always there for me whenever I needed him. While we were there, Dad did not know where we were living: he found out that we had left Cheddar by contacting the school, because in all the rush to get back to London nobody had given him our new address. He was livid, and applied to the court for care and control of us (he and Mum had been awarded joint custody at the time of the divorce).

He wanted us to go and live with him and Margaret, and he was claiming that Mum was an unfit mother. Mum received the letter from the court making these allegations when we were living in the caravan at Henley. That morning, driving us to school in Camberley, she hit a bus and wrecked the Jag. It was an old car by then, but she really loved it. The accident was totally her fault; she couldn't concentrate on the driving because the words 'unfit mother' were pounding through her brain.

I detested my father at this point. It was bad enough as a family having to live in a caravan, but to have the added grief and pain of his court action was dreadful, and there were times when Mum and Matt and I all clung together, crying.

The court arranged for a welfare worker to visit us and assess whether or not we were being properly cared for. By the time she came, we had moved into the house in Camberley. Matt and I had chosen the colours for our bedrooms: his was red and white stripes and mine was green and white. The day the social worker came we dashed in from school as usual, and Mum didn't tell us who the lady there was, although we soon guessed when we were asked to show her round the house. We were so obviously well-cared for, the social worker decided very quickly that the whole thing was a waste of court time.

My father's point of view was that we were leading very unsettled lives and that our schooling was suffering. He thought the caravan was an unsuitable place for us to live and did not realize that it was only a temporary home. There were some very angry scenes between him and Mum at this time, and we were not sheltered from them. Our loyalty was with Mum, who had been there for us all our lives, and that partly accounts for why we became as difficult as we did with Margaret.

Living in the kind of jigsaw puzzle family in which we grew up is now very common: almost half of all school children in Britain today come from a broken family, and there are literally millions of kids struggling to come to terms with step-parents, half-brothers and -sisters, step-brothers and stepsisters, several sets of grandparents and all the other baggage of multi marriages. Our situation was probably no better and no worse than the average, and I know that the other people involved – Mum, Tony, Dad, Margaret – were also in a lot of pain, but that didn't make things any easier.

Looking back now, Dad accepts that he handled this stage of our lives badly.

'My marriage to Margaret was good for me in many ways, so I shut my eyes to the fact that she had problems with my kids. She did talk to me about it once, and I understood it wasn't easy for her to have a sort of part-time relationship with two boys who clearly resented her existence.

'When Carol and I were together, we never argued about the way the children were being brought up: even now, after many years of being divorced from her, I think Carol did a remarkable job with them, and must take credit for the fact that they have turned into two caring, decent, honest young men. There were problems between Carol and me over the years, as is inevitable perhaps when there has been a rather bitter divorce, and there was a time when I was very worried about the conditions they were living in. But looking back, I think she did the best possible job in view of all the upheaval and moving.'

It was soon after we left Cheddar that Matt achieved a milestone in his life: he stopped wetting the bed. I wet the bed until I was about five and a half, then I stopped until I was seven when I became disturbed at Tony's arrival in our lives, and I wet every night for another year. By the time I was eight I was dry at night, but it took Matt longer. The problem could be equated with the traumas in our lives: I expect that's what the amateur psychologists would say. But I'm not so sure. I was old enough to be aware of it, and so was Matt. I came to the conclusion that Matt simply went into a very deep sleep every night, much deeper than most people. He is a very dreamy person even during the day: if you want to attract his attention you often have to say his name four or five times. I think he stopped wetting the bed when he reached an age where he may have started sleeping less deeply, because we were at secondary school by then, and had busy lives and more pressures than a small child has.

I'm not claiming to have any solution to the problem but I believe it should be talked about, because I'm sure there are lots of kids who are deeply embarrassed by it. It's treated like a taboo although in reality it is probably very common. There are lots of parents, too, going through hell because of it, blaming themselves and getting angry with their children. I'd like to tell everyone to relax about it. It will eventually go away, and the less everyone gets on to the kid about it, the sooner it will happen.

Some parents think their kid is too lazy to go to the toilet in the middle of the night. Let me tell you, no kid is so lazy that he wouldn't walk the twenty yards to the toilet when he knows what will happen the next morning if he wets the bed. Nobody does it through choice, nobody. You wake up in the morning and you lie still, and for a moment or two you can convince yourself that you haven't done it, and then you roll over and hit that horrible cold wet patch. It's disgusting. You hate yourself.

I've seen Matt work himself up into a terrible state, chanting to himself before bed to try to make himself wake up, and yet he still wet. He went through hell. Mum bought a device with a buzzer that sounded the minute even a drop of water touched the sheet: many a night I've woken up, in the next room, to hear Matt's buzzer going off and he was still sound asleep. I'd have to go in to him to wake him. Then he might climb into bed with me – and sometimes, before morning, he'd wet again, in my bed. It made him so utterly miserable. I've seen that panicky, frightened look on his face so many mornings and I've hated it.

You can try all the tricks that people suggest, nothing works. You can go to the toilet ten times before you go to bed, you can stop drinking five hours before bed, your mother can get you up and take you to the toilet when she goes to bed. Nothing works. You could be in a desert, seriously dehydrated, and you'd still wet the bed. It is not something you can control.

Tony had the idea of putting a chart up on the wall in our kitchen, with ticks and crosses for when we were dry or wet. Gradually my crosses changed into ticks, but Matt's stayed as crosses: I don't think that helped him.

I understand what a terrific burden it is on a mother, having to wash sheets every day. But as soon as the kid is old enough, I think the parents should get him involved in washing his own sheets. They should try not to see it as such a big chore that they end up taking their anger out on the child, giving him an even bigger hang-up about it.

It caused problems for Matt right through his childhood. He could never go away on school trips or stay over at a friend's house – and I never did, either. We always made a joint excuse. I would never have gone without him, I always felt his problem was mine, too.

CHAPTER FOUR

Try

My Mum, Tony and I walked up to the counter of the music shop in Fleet, near our Camberley home. The assistant said, 'Hello, Mr Phillips, do you want it now?' He pulled up from behind the counter an electronic drum kit. I couldn't believe my eyes, and I was so excited my legs were shaking. It was the best, the greatest, most wonderful present I have ever been given. My mum says I carried it to the car with such reverence, as if it were a crate of delicate china.

I was twelve years old, and they had scraped together the money to buy me a £400 kit, with eight pads. I had dreamed about owning a drum kit all my life, from when I was a toddler and drove Mum mad banging spoons against saucepan lids. I had been in trouble at school and at home for endlessly drumming rhythms with my fingers. I had fantasized about having my own kit, and now I did. It was a terrific gesture by Mum and Tony because they could ill-afford the money at that stage of our lives, after we had just returned from Cheddar. They had even been considering paying for it in instalments, but in the end had managed to put all the money down at once.

Matt had been given a saxophone, and lessons. He never progressed much beyond painstakingly picking his way through 'Baa Baa Black Sheep', although if you hear Mum talk you'd think he was orchestral standard. I'm glad he never persevered with the sax because he might have ended up concentrating on that and not singing, which would have been a great loss. He used the sax to great effect to impress girls, but when they asked him to play something he usually had an excuse ready.

One of the nicest things about the present was that it was not for Christmas or a birthday, it was simply an extra loving gesture, and I know that Tony was the main force behind it, so I owe him an enormous debt. Looking back, they must have been mad buying a drum kit for a twelve-year-old, especially if they wanted to stay on friendly terms with the neighbours. But because I was so desperate to play, and because I worked so hard at it, it was no time at all before I could do it properly. Our first neighbours, though, did take the soft option – they moved. After that we had a crowd of young people living next door and they did not seem to mind. Mum and Tony insisted that I never played late at night, so I don't remember too much friction. Mum knew how desperate I had been to have drums, and she appreciated that I had to learn, so she was my defender. When she said 'Not now, Luke', I stopped, however itchy my fingers were.

'If Luke is interested in something, it doesn't take him long to master it,' she says. 'I don't blame the neighbours for moving, I think I would have too if I'd had a choice! But within a couple of months he was making professional-sounding noises on his drums, and it just got better and better. The most irritating thing was not the noise, it was trying to get him to do anything else.'

It is hard to describe the pleasure I had from owning that kit. Every time I went into my bedroom, I forgot whatever else I was supposed to be doing and sat down at the drums. When I woke in the morning it was the first thing I looked at, because it was a huge kit that filled half the bedroom, and for a few weeks I had to keep reminding myself that it was really mine.

There were times in those first few months when I felt so frustrated by the limits of my ability; when I felt like stabbing the drum kit with a knife; when my aching ankles would not do what they were supposed to do and when I could hear in my head what I wanted it to sound like, but I simply did not have the muscle development to produce that sound. But I worked at it every day, until my arms ached, my fingers bled and my head span.

I had one drum lesson at school in a lunch break, but it was simply a matter of banging sticks on a desk, and I was able to teach myself much better at home. Learning any instrument comes down to practice, practice and more practice, and because I enjoyed it I never found that a struggle.

What is the first thing a boy who plays the drums does? He forms a band. There were a group of other kids at school who were keen on the idea, but I was the main force behind it. Matt and I met Craig Logan, who was a year younger than us, when we started at Collingwood School. He came round to our house and we gave him a lift home on the back of one of our bikes; he decided we were completely crazy because we cycled across people's gardens. Craig's family were resolutely middle class – big house, two cars on the drive, so clean that you felt you couldn't stand on the carpet – and Craig had been brought up to be more conventional, less rebellious than we were.

Craig had a bass guitar. Another mate, Peter Kirtley, played the keyboards. He was always known as 'Little Pete', which is ironic because he is now over six feet tall. He still plays, and his band has just been signed by a record company. His father was a jazz musician, so there was no problem about rehearsing at his house.

We called the first band Caviar. We didn't know what

caviar was, but it sounded posh. We dressed like the early Duran Duran: long hair, frilly shirts, earrings. With hindsight, we probably looked and sounded dreadful, but at the time we thought we were fantastic.

My hair and my slavish interest in music did not do me any favours with the teaching staff at school, and neither did my refusal to conform. We'd had a fairly gypsy-like upbringing, travelling about and meeting lots of different people through Tony's and Mum's work. We had never been treated like children, and we found it hard to fit into a vast school of 2,000 pupils where there was no scope for any individuality. I didn't like school, I felt too old to be there and I desperately wanted to get on with my life. It did little to prepare us for the harsh realities of life ahead: one simple lesson about the difference between gross and net might have saved Matt and me a small fortune.

No doubt there were some kids who got what they wanted from that school, who enjoyed it and did well there. But I felt let down and betrayed by the whole system.

I could not understand – then or now – why there had to be such a formal gulf between teachers and pupils. Teachers were not allowed to act like human beings any more than pupils were. There were a couple of teachers I liked, and once when one of them looked really upset I wanted to go up to her and put my arm around her, but of course that was out of the question. Apart from a formal 'good morning' and 'good afternoon', you were not supposed to have any social chat with the staff.

We joined the school a year after everyone else, because of our move from Cheddar, but it did not take us long to make friends. We soon became part of the school 'in-crowd', mainly because of our style and music. Craig was a 'boff' – one of the boffins who took school seriously.

Our school uniform was black trousers, jumper and shoes, a white shirt and a red, yellow and green striped tie. Small collars were fashionable at the time, and I would tie my tie with the thin side on top and the thick side tucked into my shirt. I was always very neat and clean, but I was in trouble because my hair was long. Mum and Tony went to see the headmaster about it, and Tony argued forcibly that because we were otherwise so tidy and clean, and our hair was freshly washed every day, they were making a fuss about nothing. His only concession was that he agreed we would tie it back during woodwork, when the school reckoned it was dangerous. As the rest of the boys of our age seemed to think it was cool to be scruffy, the headmaster took his point.

Clothes were a constant preoccupation. Mum gave us a clothing allowance from the age of eleven onwards. She gave us £20 a month, which was enough to keep us in the styles we enjoyed, because you could buy a good jacket for £30. By the time I was twelve or thirteen I had a couple of suits and loads of tops and trousers. I spent most of my spare time, when I wasn't rehearsing with the band, working to earn more money.

Tony was running a property maintenance company again, and I used to do some work for him. I remember when I was thirteen spending a large chunk of my summer holiday plastering the Inland Revenue office at Victoria and then, because Tony was again having financial problems, never being paid. I had to lug huge bags of plaster up to the top floor. Granddad was helping as well, and he was never paid either: we still give Tony a hard time about it. When, in later years, the Inland Revenue began pursuing me for money I liked to think about how I gave them my services for nothing.

I also had a weekend job at a garden centre: hard, heavy

work unloading paving stones for £5.75 a day. After cycling a few miles to get there at seven thirty in the morning and back again at six in the evening, I was completely exhausted, and the payment was sheer exploitation. Later on I had a Saturday job at a hairdressers. It was originally arranged by the school, for work experience, and I stayed on doing a couple of evenings and Saturdays after that. I put down 'hairdressing' as my work experience choice because I had visions of spending a week in a trendy London salon, running my fingers through the beautiful blonde locks of some real stunners. Instead I ended up in a village shop in Windlesham, shampooing the blue-rinsed hair of the elderly clients. It was a unisex salon, and I remember a weird experience washing the hair of a bald man, which I know is a contradiction in terms. I can remember my thumbs skidding across the frictionless surface of his bald crown, and him wriggling in his chair as if he were enjoying it. It must have been the shortest shampoo on record. But I managed to save enough money to trade in my electronic drum kit for an acoustic one.

By the time I was fourteen I knew that I was going to give the music business a very serious try when I left school. We were rehearsing five nights a week, and I'm afraid homework always took second place to drums. I thought that if I didn't make it in the music world I could always study later. Needless to say, my school reports were littered with remarks like 'could do better' and 'needs to try harder'.

I was happy enough to go to English lessons, but that was because the teacher was pretty. There was another teacher who was really tasty, the music teacher. I used to look at her and wish I was a few years older. It worried me though: fancying a teacher seemed a bit kinky, almost a perversion!

Matt – at this stage of his life everyone called him Matthew, except for me and I called him Maffy – and I were often in trouble for childish pranks, pathetic little rebellions against the mindless authority of the school regime. Years later, when we were famous, the school asked if we would go back there to perform: I wouldn't go back there for any money. They did nothing to encourage me and I can actually remember a chemistry teacher laughing with contempt when someone said I wanted to make records when I left.

There was one thing about school I enjoyed, and that was running. I was county standard at cross country and 1,500 metres, and every afternoon after school I would change into my running gear and do an eight-mile run from Camberley to Frimley and Lightwater and then back home. I was ridiculously fit. Matt was more interested in athletics, and always did well at long jump, high jump and triple jump.

After Caviar I was invited to join another band called Hypnosis, with another couple of brothers. They were a class above us, but by this time I had a reputation as one of the best drummers around the area, for my age. I did a couple of gigs with them and they were keen that I should stay. I insisted that Matt also be allowed to join, as a singer. They agreed, and that was Matt's first taste of singing in public. Everyone always assumes that Matt was the instigator of our career in music, but it was actually the other way round: at that age it was me who was paving the way for him.

Meanwhile, though, he was more interested in a career on the stage. He took drama as one of his optional subjects at school, and his teacher, a lovely lady called Jane Roberts – one of the few teachers you could really talk to – recognized his potential and gave him the starring role in the school production of *Cabaret*, in which he played the German Master of Ceremonies. He was brilliant: he got tremendous reviews. The actress June Whitfield was in the audience, and so were some senior members of the Royal School of Ballet, friends of the drama teacher. They all said that he had a real talent and should go to drama school.

All the family came to see the show. Mum was very proud, and even she admits she was surprised how good Matt was. Dad said he was bowled over: it took him a few minutes to realize it was his son up there speaking German and performing so brilliantly. I had a small one-line role as a sailor in the same production. I thought it would be good fun and I got to miss a few lessons for rehearsals.

After playing with Hypnosis Matt and I broke away and started rehearsing just with Craig. We didn't really have a name, but we played a few gigs in clubs and discos, with club owners paying us in Cokes. We were happy to do it for the experience. We were writing our own songs, but they were not what the punters wanted to hear, unfortunately. I remember one evening we played at a working men's club, and we'd run through lots of stuff before anyone even started tapping their feet. That was when we played 'House of the Rising Sun'. I hate that song, but it always gets people going.

Afterwards the barman asked how old the drummer was, and said he thought I would go far. I have always put everything into my drumming, even in a place like that where they were definitely there for the beer, not the music. You see some drummers performing as though they are half dead, with a cigarette balanced on the edge of their kit and a cup of tea to hand. I can never play like that: for me, it's all or nothing.

*

When I was twelve I met a whole new branch of my family. After Dad's mother died he contacted the people in her address book, to let them know. One of the names was a sister of her first husband, Dad's real father. There had been no contact between them since Dad was a baby, but the letter to his aunt triggered a feeling in her that Dad might like to meet that side of his family. He travelled up to St Anne's, near Blackpool, and stayed with his father and a stepmother he had never met before, and also met two half-brothers and two half-sisters for the first time. He found the family very warm and welcoming, and after he had established a good relationship with them he took Matt and me to stay with them. It was a lovely experience, they were friendly and easy-going. My step-grandmother was gentle, homely and kind to us, and cooked us huge breakfasts in the mornings. Unfortunately, Dad's wife Margaret was with us and, as had become her habit, she tried to impose her standards of behaviour on us. She insulted me by asking me if I had washed my hands after I had been to the toilet, as if I was a tiny child.

Dad enjoyed his new family for five years, until his marriage to Margaret broke up. Then, tragically, his father and stepmother decided to side with Margaret, who had told them a highly coloured version of the marriage breakdown. It was she who left Dad – not the other way round. Dad is philosophical about it. He still keeps in touch with his half-sisters although he has no contact with the rest of them. He says that his stepfather, Denis Weston, was the man who brought him up, and he is still very close to Denis, who he regards as nothing less than his father.

I have no sense of loss through not seeing them any more as they never figured in my childhood; but I do know how important my father has been in my life, and how vulnerable I am sometimes because of the times when I felt rejected by him, so I have a lot of sympathy for his difficulties with his own father.

Throughout my early teen years, my relationship with Mum, Tony and Dad was fraught at times – and with my stepmother Margaret I ceased to have any relationship. She objected to the way we dressed and did not want to be seen with us. It reached the stage where we only wanted to visit their house if we knew she was not going to be there. Dad admits that he wasn't too keen on our taste in clothes (he says we both looked like the Thin White Duke, dressed all in white with long blond hair), but he took the line that we were well-behaved, polite and had never given him any serious cause for worry, so he was not going to make an issue over the way we dressed.

The first time that we came face to face with Margaret's rejection of us was when we were going with Dad to a Divine concert at the Lyceum. It's hard to know how to describe Divine: he was a fat, camp entertainer whose very bizarreness accounted in part for his success. Another large part of his success was that he was managed (until his death in 1988) by Bernard Jay.

Bernard has been a friend of Dad's (and Mum's) since Dad was first a bobby on the beat in the 1970s. Bernard was general manager of the Mermaid Theatre, and one day Dad popped into the theatre, in uniform, to get out of the rain. He was on duty escorting the Lord Mayor of London to the College of Arms, and was not needed again until it was time for the Lord Mayor to leave. Bernard took pity on him and plied him with coffee and brandy, and while chatting discovered how hard up Dad and Mum were. After that, he took the trouble to invite them to every first night party at the theatre.

They both appreciated it: it was a sparkling break from the routine of bringing up two small children on a tight budget, and the only problem they had was finding suitable things to wear. Everything else was laid on free for them.

Bernard has remained a fixture in our lives since then. We were never christened so we don't officially have a godfather, but Bernard has always been like one to us. After he took over management of Divine he invited us to the show at the Lyceum, and we were thrilled to accept.

I was genuinely upset when Dad told us that Margaret had decided that she preferred not to go if we were going to be there. Although Matt and I did not get on with her, we were sad for Dad's sake that this night out became a showdown, putting him more or less in a position of having to choose between us and her. I'm glad he stood up to her and chose us that night; it was a breakthrough, as though he were saying 'She's not going to stand between us any more, guys.' I remember feeling so happy that he had made a move for us.

Dad thinks that we were feigning being upset at Margaret's absence, but that is not so. We felt hurt at the rejection, even from someone who we knew did not like us. I always hoped, while Dad was still with Margaret, that for his sake she would try to rebuild a relationship with us, but she never did.

Her absence did not stop us enjoying the show. We shared a box with Su Pollard and her husband. I have never met Su since, and she probably has no idea that the blond twins whose hair she ruffled grew up to be Bros, but we all had a really good time that evening, thanks to Bernard.

'I'm ashamed to admit that I did not stand up to Margaret enough,' says Dad now. 'But I'm pleased with the fact that ultimately, when push came to shove, I chose to spend time with the boys.'

From that day on our relationship with Dad, though not

perfect, was much better. He's the sort of father who has found it much easier to get on with us as we have become young men: he would probably admit himself that he never had much idea about being a father to little children, but that he started to appreciate us as individuals when we reached our teenage years, and began to realize what he had been missing out on.

I've always been very proud of him: he's good-looking, cool, he dresses very well. I can remember seeing him in a suit and a Crombie overcoat and feeling that he looked so much better than most other kids' dads. He's been in the police for over twenty years now, and more than ten as a detective, so he's pretty streetwise. He took us to trendy restaurants like Joe Allen's, which other people's parents would never have heard of.

I think he was embarrassed by us when we were little, and I'll always be hung up about that. I still feel I'm striving to make him proud of me, even though I know he is now. There were times in my childhood when I tried to be defiant about him, thinking 'Sod him, I don't need him.' But that was only to cover my deep longing to be an important part of his life. The day he stood up to Margaret, something fundamental changed.

As we hit our teens, though, we ran into more trouble with Mum, especially me. I was never around: I used to disappear after school and she would be going mad not knowing where I was. She'd end up driving around the streets looking for me and I'd be at a mate's house or trying to learn the art of chatting up girls. There were plenty of rows about me never being home: if I wasn't with friends I was out working, trying to make money.

Matt was much more of a homebody so he wasn't in as deep as me. One day I wound Mum up so much that she

hit me and broke her wrist. I was twelve or thirteen, but
a lot taller than her, probably five inches. It's pretty stupid
to try to punish someone that much bigger than you by
hitting them, there must have been some better way of
getting at me.

Tony never had any problem about treating us equally:
I'm sure he disliked both of us at this stage, although he
denies it now. He thought, with some justification no
doubt, that we were a couple of little sods – or not so little,
as we were towering over him by the time we were twelve.

'Fathers just don't get on with teenagers, and that's all
there is to it,' says Tony. 'Teenagers are strange and difficult creatures. I didn't have it any easier with Carolyn and
Adam, except that I wasn't there all the time to be aggra-
vated by them. We had all the normal problems: girls,
staying out late, not letting their mother know where they
were going after school. And you can't have a son in the
house with a drum kit without some noise problems.

'I was concerned about the effect on their mother,
because she worried so much when Luke went missing.
So I ended up telling him off. But because I am only a
step-parent, he resented it more than he would have done
if I had been a natural parent. I don't think I would have
behaved any differently if he had been my own son. Yes,
there was plenty of friction, but looking back I don't believe
it was any worse than any other household with two adoles-
cents around the place.

'Luke thinks I disliked him at this stage, but it's not
true. There was plenty about him that I disliked, but it was
all to do with his teenage behaviour, not his personality. In
actual fact, I admired him a lot. Luke always took the
attitude that if he wanted something, and it cost money,
he would go out and work for that money.

'I like to think that in some way my example helped.

However hard up Carol and I have been, and however disastrous my business ventures, I have never claimed state benefits and never sat around feeling sorry for myself: I've always tried something new. Luke, more than Matt, is the practical one, the one who sees that something needs doing and gets on and does it.'

Tony's attitude and example have certainly helped me, in all sorts of ways. The lack of continuity in our lifestyle as children has helped me cope with my own erratic working life, and I share his attitude of refusing to roll over and die just because something has gone wrong. I was always willing to get my hands dirty if I needed to, to make a living, and I would do the same today.

His working life has given us all a few laughs, as well. There was one scheme he embarked on when he decided he would import all sorts of goods from all over the world. He sent off for masses of samples, and for a while it was like Christmas every day at our house, with mystery packages arriving from exotic destinations. Tony, Matt and me used to fight to open them: he was just as much a kid as we were. I particularly remember some headbands with visors that had a tiny radio concealed in them – Matt and I would have died for them. Some of the other things were really boring, though, like plant thermometers.

Tony was always on the verge of breaking through to a great success. One of his projects that we all thought would be a winner were some gadgets called 'buffet mates', which helped you hold a glass and a plate in one hand by clipping them together, so that the other hand was free to use a fork. We could see a great future for them. Tony wrote to the Royal Navy, to the very top, and suggested they buy a consignment because they were always having cocktail parties on board their ships. They sent for a couple of dozen. We sat back and waited for the huge order to roll in, which never came. But it taught me that you should never be frightened of going straight to the top.

I've always liked girls. I like their company and, from early adolescence onwards, I knew I liked them in another, more significant, way. But like most schoolboys I didn't have a clue what to do about it: there was a lot of fumbling and embarrassment in store for me before I reached the stage where I could really enjoy that wonderful little game that keeps the human race going.

Nature doesn't make growing up easy. You don't wake up one morning and find that you've acquired a generous helping of manhood: it's a gradual process that leaves you wondering if you are ever going to be normal. I think I expected to acquire body hair as easily as growing mustard and cress seeds at school: one day nothing, the next day a fully sprouted crop. Instead I watched for months as one wispy hair followed another. Embarrassment and self-consciousness must be the best contraceptives ever: I'd have died rather than let any girl have a good laugh at my expense.

I remember watching a film, *Bird on a Wire*, starring Mel Gibson and Goldie Hawn, in which Mel Gibson's character talked about going without sex while he was in prison: 'Mr Wiggly's been on bread and water for three years,' he said. I was intrigued by a super-looking grown-up guy having a nickname for it: for months afterwards Mr Wiggly was my euphemism for the part of my anatomy that I was inspecting daily for signs of change.

When Matt and I were about thirteen we discovered a treasure trove at the bottom of Tony's wardrobe. We were on the hunt for money: our pocket money invariably seemed to run out about halfway through the week. Rooting through the pockets of Tony's jackets sometimes turned up the odd fifty pence piece or two. But on this day we found something far more valuable: a pile of girlie magazines. There were about fifty of them. We sneaked them out, one at a time, and back in the privacy of one of our bedrooms thumbed through them appreciatively. Unfortunately, Tony walked in and caught us both peering open-mouthed at an astonishing centrefold. He snatched it from us and threw the lot away: we always reckoned he punished himself more than he punished us!

Despite my worries about my anatomy, I lost my virginity at an early age to a girl called Dawn – an appropriate name, because puberty was only just dawning for both of us. We were upstairs in my bedroom playing Monopoly when she started asking a few inquisitive questions about my physical development, and I certainly had a passing interest in hers. One thing led to another and before long we were doing more than comparing notes. It wasn't exactly the romantic build-up you get in a Mills and Boon novel, nor was it an earth-moving, time-standing-still tender experience. In fact, it was over by the time we passed Go and before we got to Pall Mall! I was more scared than exhilarated afterwards, and it took me another three years to get round to repeating the experience.

As I got a bit older I had other girlfriends and a lot of fumbling and groping went on, me trying to pretend that I was more experienced than I was. Tony once caught me in my bedroom, fooling around with a girl. I tried to be cool and said, 'Hi, Tony.' He didn't bawl me out, but he called me downstairs and explained that he didn't mind what I did, but he didn't want me doing it at home. I thought that was perfectly fair.

Sadly, many of my memories of school and my early romantic encounters have been polluted by the number of people from that time in my past who have sold stories about me – and about Matt – to the newspapers. Every time someone did that, it was as though they robbed me of a section of my own memory. They took whole chunks of my life away from me, ran them through a machine that distorted and cheapened them, and then fed them back to me. But by then they were no longer anything to do with me. We wrote a song, 'Treasure Memories', about the pleasure of shared memories. I'm afraid that is a pleasure that has been denied me for that time of my life: the past is clouded, and all the nice things that happened, in a very normal adolescence, have been soured.

CHAPTER FIVE

Chocolate in the Box

There was no rite of passage about leaving school, I felt no sense of loss, nostalgia or regret. I was just excited at the prospect of being able to rehearse full time, five days a week, instead of cramming in as many hours as possible after school. By this time Matt, Craig and I were together as a group. Because Craig was younger than we were, we had to wait a year for him to leave school before he could join the band properly: his parents had divorced, but they were both keen that he should pass some examinations, and he himself was less committed to a future in music than we were. He wanted to be a bank clerk.

Mum and Tony, like all parents, would have liked to see us become doctors or lawyers, but they were realistic enough to see that we weren't going to go for that. They looked at us and knew that we were dedicated and passionate about music, and they were sensible enough to see that we would do it anyway, and that we would do it better with their support than without it. Tony made it clear that once we left school we could not ponce off him and Mum, but we had no intention of doing that.

'They were already showing very, very considerable talent,' says Mum. 'They were writing, singing, playing and arranging their own music, and they were so excited about it all the time. We couldn't have stopped them if we'd tried.'

Dad was more inclined to think that we should be looking

for nine-to-five jobs, but he, too, could see that we were not going to be swayed. He was amazed by the perseverance we had already shown and he took the line that we should give it our best shot for three years, and if it had not worked out by then we should have a serious re-think.

My first venture into the big grown-up world of work was to sign on at the employment exchange for a couple of months. It was not a good experience: it made me lazy and did not do a lot for my pride. I can see that people who are forced to sign on for a long time could reach a stage where they feel at ease about accepting benefits, and that is dangerous. It destroys any need to work and it breeds contempt in other people. Luckily, I never grew to feel comfortable about it. When the clerk at the employment office asked me what I wanted to do, I said I wanted a record contract, and he studiously wrote that down on my form. I wasn't sure whether I was taking the piss or he was.

After a few weeks of that, I found myself a job valeting cars for £120 a week, which did not go very far as I was the only band member earning a wage, and was having to pay for any equipment we needed as well as making a contribution to Mum's budget.

I found the job through a girl I was going out with whose brother ran the valeting company. She wasn't a serious long-term girlfriend: none of them were. I'm not experienced enough to generalize, but at that time I found younger girls more difficult to get on with than older girls: probably because they were as self-conscious and inexperienced as I was. Older girls were kinder, they were polite enough to pretend they'd enjoyed it, even if they hadn't. Someone once asked me why I preferred older women and I joked, 'They fake it better.' But there is an underlying truth in it.

As well as girlfriends who were three or four years older than me, I also had some teenage experiences with much older women, women in their late thirties and early forties. I don't think I was unique: in a suburban area like Camberley there are probably lots of young guys learning the ropes with bored housewives. In my case it was usually the mums of my friends. You'd be sitting watching TV at their house and all of a sudden there would be a hand creeping on to your knee, and you took it from there. You always waited for them to make the first move. I never went out looking for it, and I would never have had the confidence or the nerve to start it, in case I got a smack on the head. But when it was being offered, I wasn't about to say no. It was great fun.

There are a lot of fit and attractive women whose husbands just don't make the effort to appreciate them, to make them feel special. They roll on them and roll off them once a week, and snore the night away afterwards. So when a young guy comes along they make a play for him.

It was through a girlfriend that I met our first manager, Bob Herbert. Bob was an accountant who at one time had handled the affairs of the Three Degrees, so I was pretty impressed by him. I met him at a party at his house, and I met his daughter Nicky at the same time. She became my girlfriend soon afterwards. Bob fancied the idea of managing his own group, and we were delighted at the idea of 'professional' management, so we became his band, his one and only band at that time.

He let us practise in his summerhouse during the day, and for a time we called the band Summerhouse. But we soon changed the name to Gloss. Bob found us very little work. His investment in us included paying for some photographs to be taken, some demo tapes to be made and buying a £400 PA system which he let us use. Bob gave lots of parties and liked to introduce us to people as his band, but after nearly a year with him we terminated the contract because we weren't going anywhere. We will always be grateful to him for giving us the time and the space to improve, but I believe we would have done that anywhere. The summerhouse, which was really a games area in the garden of his huge house, and included a pool table, a swimming pool, a sauna and a bar area where we rehearsed, was more comfortable than the garages and spare rooms we had been squeezed into before, but I don't think that affected our music. We improved because we were able to put in many more hours than we had when we were at school, and we would have done that anyway.

Bob had nothing to do with our image. Our clothes, our hair and our style were nobody else's but ours. Looking back, I'm horrified by it, but it certainly got us noticed. We were well known in the Camberley area long before we became famous. Mum spent hours sewing ruffles on to shirts for us, making cummerbunds. Craig was virtually part of our family, he spent so much time at our house, and Mum made his clothes, too. We went to clubs and discos in London from the age of about fifteen onwards, so we knew the looks that were in, and what suited us. We cared about our appearance and took time over it: my granddad, who says he's not old-fashioned but is, used to fall about laughing at us doing our hair. It was long at the time and Matt used to dangle his head over the back of a chair to brush his. Granddad, whose short back and sides is only a fraction of an inch away from a skinhead, thought we were weird.

As far as our music went, there were naturally plenty of influences, but Bob wasn't one of them. Matt was very into

Michael Jackson and Stevie Wonder, while I prefer blues and real rock stuff, although not heavy metal. I like the tough, bluesy sound of people like Joe Cocker. We both liked Police, and as far as drumming goes my idol was Phil Collins. (I have since met him and he was very offhand, which was terribly disappointing. Even though we were at the British Pop Industry Awards receiving an award and we were very big at the time, I was a dedicated fan, and I do not believe you should ever treat genuine fans badly.)

Matt and I collaborated perfectly writing songs. He always preferred to write the lyrics, and I didn't mind that. Craig joined in with the song writing when he was there, but obviously Matt and I did most of it because we had much more time. Life in the summerhouse was not luxurious. We had a sandwich toaster, and every day we would buy a loaf of bread and something to put on it: that was our staple diet. I would run the two miles from our home to Bob's house and back every day, as part of my fitness plan but also because we could not afford any other type of transport. Luckily, neither Matt nor I have ever smoked, so we didn't have an expensive habit to maintain. I once went out with a girl who smoked, and the smell of cigarettes from her got on to me and I was revolted by it. As for drugs, I tried grass once, but it didn't do a thing for me.

After a few months Bob Herbert bought a derelict house in nearby Lightwater. It was a property investment, but he said we could use it to rehearse there. The derelict house was something else. It had been gutted and it was freezing cold, with no windows. I had to play drums in my jacket and wear really thick socks. Mum came and saw it once and threw a wobbly about us spending our days there, and we didn't like it so we moved back to Bob's summerhouse.

We would get there about lunchtime, because I would

probably have to do some car valeting or other casual work in the mornings. Then Matt and I would write songs and hang about until Craig arrived, straight from school. When I look back on that year, it seems to have been spent waiting: waiting for Craig and waiting for our manager to set something up for us to do.

We thought we were worth more and that our career should be moving faster. We were with Bob for a little over twelve months and so little happened that I would find myself thinking, 'So this is what I couldn't wait to leave school for?'

During this time I was still going out with Nicky, Bob's daughter. I am reluctant to even write her name now, but I cannot deny the relationship happened. The reason I feel so bitter about her is that when we became famous she sold an astonishing, garbled, inaccurate account of our time together to the *News of the World*. It was a load of old bollocks, so far from the truth that I could not even recognize myself.

In retrospect, Nicky Herbert was not an important part of my life; she was just one of a run of girlfriends I had at this time, and even saying that much is dignifying her with more importance than she deserves. Ironically, she probably ended up with more money out of Bros than I did! Perhaps everyone reading this can think for a moment how they would feel if one of their very early girlfriends or boyfriends decided to make up stories about them for money. Wouldn't anyone feel cheated out of something that should have been precious, a memory of happy, youthful days?

There were plenty of other acquaintances who were prepared to make up tosh to sell to newspapers. I roared with laughter at the so-called schoolfriend who said I used to wear women's clothes and that I shopped at the make-up counter in Harrods. Harrods was a little bit out of my class while I was at school and the only reason we ever visited the make-up department was because a girlfriend worked there! As for the drag act, I did once buy a couple of women's vests, because they were skinny. But they were completely plain, not girlie looking. As for my wardrobe full of sequined evening dresses and stiletto heels ...

Then there was another story about me bonking loads of girls, sometimes two or three at once. Well, I wouldn't have minded a chance at some of the things I'm now reputed to have done! Let's face it, every young guy of that age does whatever the girls will let him get away with, and in every other case the girl forgets about it as soon as the guy does. But when you go on to become famous, they all suddenly have brilliant memories about every kiss and cuddle you ever gave anyone – and what they don't remember, they make up. I was just normal, active and enjoying myself.

We learned to ignore 90 per cent of what we read about ourselves in the papers. But there were always some things that hurt. Before we were famous we shared a flat with a couple of girls who were also twins. They were friends, really good friends, but we weren't romantically involved with them. When they sold a story about us we felt betrayed.

And later, when one of Matt's personal assistants – a guy we both liked and enjoyed working with – sold some pictures of Matt in the bath, we were mortified. It makes you very cynical about any kind of friendship. You learn to distrust everyone and that's an unhappy lesson.

The one important thing that Bob did towards our success was introduce us to another Nicky, Nicky Graham, a freelance record producer who worked with us on our demo tapes. The tapes were sent to various record companies and we were on the verge of signing a deal with Arista Records. They were going to take us all out to dinner to celebrate the contract, but at the very last moment they pulled out. You can imagine how shattering that was for three desperately keen seventeen-year-olds. I took great delight a couple of years later, when our records were walking into the charts without any help from anybody, in meeting one of the top Arista Records executives and saying to him, 'Hello, mate, you win some, you lose some.'

Nicky Graham was impressed by us and advised that we should get a more professional manager. With a bit of help from Tony, who is no fool, we were able to end our contract with Bob easily: because we were under eighteen the contract was technically with our parents, anyway. Later, when we were big, Bob sent a letter demanding money for what he claimed to have invested in us, but that was soon sorted out. He had over a year in which to launch us and, if he had played his cards right, make a fortune out of us. It was not our fault that he failed to do it.

Nicky Graham set up a meeting for us with Tom Watkins, who at that time was the manager of the Pet Shop Boys. We went to his flat in Blackheath in Nicky's new Renault 5, which impressed us. We were even more impressed by the reek of wealth from Tom's place: it was stuffed full of antiques and he proudly showed us a Picasso plate on the wall. Tom himself was a fat, flamboyant homosexual and both he and his apartment were obviously in a different league to anything else we had seen. Today I would think it ostentatious: as a naïve seventeen-year-old I thought it was class. I can remember thinking, 'Wow, this is the big time – we've made it.'

*

When I was seventeen I discovered one of the greatest love affairs of my life: cars. I was always desperate to drive and I passed my test about five minutes after my seventeenth birthday. Matt wasn't interested in driving at that stage (he later had to take driving lessons with a mob of girls round the car), and although Craig also passed his test when he was old enough, he was never a keen driver.

My affair didn't start with a brand-new, top-of-the-range sports car. My very first mechanical mistress was a £50 Fiat which you started by pulling a switch. Matt was driving it one night in the snow and whacked it against a lamp-post. He wasn't qualified to drive at the time, so we legged it: it would have cost more to get the wreck towed away than I paid for it. What's more, the lamp-post was leaning perilously at an angle of forty-five degrees.

Next I bought a Datsun Cherry 120E, S-registration plate. It was so rusty you could poke your finger through the sides. I paid four hundred carefully saved pounds for it, and I was devastated when the tracking rod snapped as I went round a bend. My sister Carolyn was with me; we were just out driving around and I was showing off my car to her. We slid round the bend and into a grass verge at a speed of about ten miles per hour, but the bodywork was so spent that even a collision at that speed caved it in. The car was a write-off.

My next car was even cheaper and even older: an N-reg Golf. You practically died of carbon monoxide poisoning from the fumes that came up through the floorboards, it was such a pig.

Then Tony and Mum took pity on me and bought me a Fiat Mirafiori for £700. I was driving home along the A30 dual carriageway to Camberley after visiting a girlfriend's house. I hadn't gone far when there was a massive bang and then a very peaceful sensation. There was no other traffic on the road in the early hours of the morning and I could hear the wind whistling past me as I cruised along. It was like being in a glider. It made a Rolls Royce sound as rough as a diesel. As I gradually slowed down I realized why: the massive bang had been the engine falling out, or at least part of it. The huge lump of metal lying in the road behind me was the piston, which had shot out of the oil sump. I had to abandon it and go back to my girlfriend's to get a lift home. Tony has always had terrible luck with his own cars and he didn't do any better choosing one for me.

My next car was a good one, a new Suzuki jeep. It was the first and best thing we bought when Tom Watkins arranged a recording contract for the new group that was about to be born: Bros.

CHAPTER SIX

When Will I Be Famous?

Tom Watkins sat on the other side of the desk in his lawyer's office, which was as opulent as his own, and the two of them exuded confidence which hit us like a drug. The talk that whizzed around over that polished table-top blew my brains. Tom was offering us a contract and his attitude was take it or leave it. He gave us the impression that he didn't need us and if we weren't prepared to accept his terms, that was it. He was the top London management guy, we were the kids from the sticks, and that was the card he was playing. He had gone from being Mr Nice Guy when we first met to Mr Cool Businessman: as soon as we had signed he was Mr Nice Guy again.

The signature I put on the contract on 8 December 1986 marked the start of a roller coaster ride to fame and success. We were advised not to sign by the lawyer we consulted about the contract. But choices are fine when you have them: when the only option in front of you is playing in a summerhouse in Surrey without an audience, or signing with a successful top London manager who can fix you up with a deal with a record company, what real choice is there? Which eighteen-year-old would not sign? It is also true that lawyers and accountants have to advise clients not to sign for all sorts of reasons – not least to cover their own backs – when they realistically know that the deal will go ahead. I'm not suggesting that our solicitor was only covering himself against future comeback: I think he genuinely had reservations about the contract. But I daresay that even if Matt, Craig and I could have peered into a crystal ball, we would still have gone ahead and put our names on that dotted line. I had been dreaming about a career in music ever since I first picked up my own drumsticks, at the age of twelve, and the small print was the last thing on my mind.

We knew that the management company had the right to take 20 per cent of everything we earned, but that did not sound unfair. If I made £100, I thought, I'd be happy for them to have £20. I had no idea about money: when the most you have ever earned is £120 a week from car valeting and someone starts talking in hundreds of thousands of pounds, you are out of your league. In those days I thought £100,000 would be enough to keep me for ever.

What was never explained to me in those heady days, and what was to be the hardest and bitterest lesson of my life to learn, was the difference between two little words: gross and net. I think I'll have them inscribed on my tombstone. My epitaph will be: *Luke Goss, he finally knew his net from his gross*. When we signed a contract that gave the management company 20 per cent of our gross earnings, we naïvely thought we were giving them 20 per cent of our own wages, the money that would end up in our wallets. In fact, we were giving them 20 per cent of everything we generated regardless of how much it cost us to make it. The dictionary says that gross means 'earned before deduction of expenses'. Net is 'the profit left after all operating expenses have been deducted from the gross profit'.

Let me give you an example. If a guy selling flowers by the roadside takes £100 a day from motorists who forgot to buy their wives' birthday presents, or want to say sorry for getting home late, that £100 is his gross profit. But it cost him £80 to buy the flowers from the market in the first place. So his net profit is only £20; that's what he has made for his day's work. If he has to pay commission to an agent (and flowers-sellers everywhere should be grateful they don't!), and the commission is 20 per cent of the gross, then he would have to pay £20 – which would completely wipe out the money he made for himself. He would have worked all day for nothing.

Let me give you another example. If a band plays a concert at Wembley Stadium, they don't expect to make much money. One-off concerts never do: it takes six weeks to rehearse, paying backing vocalists, musicians, lighting and sound engineers, etc. – we usually had a crew of between fifty and sixty people, all on our payroll – plus all the costs of the set, the staging, the hire of the stadium. You make money by doing a series of concerts, so that all the costs are shared over several nights of actually taking ticket money, not just one.

So a one-night Wembley Stadium show is a bit of a loss leader. It may make some profit, but usually it will just about break even. It's worth doing for the prestige and the subsequent record sales, but it's not in itself a huge money-spinner. Let's say it costs a million pounds to put it on and you take a million pounds in tickets and merchandising. There's nothing in it for you, the band. But when you then have to pay your management company £200,000 in commission because, remember, they are taking their commission on your gross earnings (the million pounds you made in ticket sales and merchandising), you are actually in for a substantial loss. And all because the guys who are supposed to be working for you, supposed to be managing your career, are taking from you money

that you never made. Even if you make a small profit, their
commission knocks you into the red.

A contract that says you have to pay commission on your
gross earnings regardless of your expenses, in a business
like the music industry which involves very large costs, is
iniquitous and, from the artists' point of view, unworkable.
When we signed our contracts with 3 Style Ltd, the company run by Tom Watkins and his partner Mick Newton,
we signed away any chance we ever had of substantial
earnings. We were doomed, from signature onwards, to
never make big money, and to frequently find ourselves
working for a negligible amount.

But, wide-eyed, inexperienced and interested only in
getting up on stage and making music, we had no idea
what was in store when we signed. To us, we had made
it. We had found rich, successful managers in Tom and
Mick, we were going to get a recording contract, we were
going to be stars. And we were very, very young.

Our dealings with Tom started before we were eighteen,
and therefore not legally old enough to sign our own contracts, so initially he met up with our parents; by the time
we actually signed Matt and I were just eighteen. Tom
had originally heard the demo tapes produced by Nicky
Graham and then he wanted to see us to cynically check
out if we were a bunch of good-looking guys he could
market. I don't believe he ever, even from those earliest days,
had any thought beyond a couple of years of instant stardom
and a quick killing for him, even though he was signing us
to him for five years. But I admit we were not thinking of
long-term strategy, career-planning, all that stuff, ourselves:
we were just desperate to get on with it. The average eighteen-year-old doesn't see much further ahead than next
month, never mind next year or the next decade.

We did have some other interest in us at the time that Tom was courting us. Denis Inglesby who, ironically, is now involved in my new management team, came to see us and talked to our parents about signing us. His approach was much more low-key than Tom's; we had already started down the road of negotiating with Tom and we felt that Tom would push us harder.

It's a very difficult decision to take and I'm the first to admit that we were seduced by the show of wealth and success that Tom put on for us. We were invited to dinner at his home and there were lots of important people from the music industry there, the talk of antiques and fine wines.

It was an unsettling time, especially for me, because I also had to finish with my girlfriend, Nicky Herbert. I did not think that either of us was mature enough to deal with our relationship after the split from her dad, and besides, the affair had run its course. There were bitter feelings and it was an emotional, uncomfortable time for me. It was exciting, but it also felt that it was a huge change all at once. Still, I never expected to be able to jump from one building to another without getting slightly hurt, and it had to be worth it. We now had managers with a posh office in a prestigious part of London, Welbeck Street, W1; they were not just playing at it like Bob, they did it full time for a living; and they had a track record with the Pet Shop Boys.

Although Tom openly admits he is homosexual and his style is outrageously camp, he never, ever made a pass at us. I'd have belted him if he had. He was paranoid about letting people know that he didn't make approaches to us. At his first meeting with my mother and Tony, in his office, he said, 'Don't worry, I have nothing but professional interest in these guys.'

Mum wasn't worried.

'If Luke and Matt had been timid virgins I might have felt differently, but I knew enough about them to know that they were happy with their own sexuality,' she says. 'They had met plenty of gays before, they weren't sexually naïve. I thought Tom had courage to say it to me and I appreciated him reassuring me. My worries about Tom were not to do with him being gay.'

Mum and Tony both had reservations about Tom, but not enough to make them persuade us not to sign: we were headstrong and determined and we would have ignored them anyway. Tony noticed that when they met Tom he made a fuss of Mum but ignored him, and he remarked afterwards that he felt Tom was out for himself. But, after all, we didn't expect him to be in it altruistically, and even Mum and Tony could see that Tom had the expertise to launch us well.

After we became famous Tom loved to see himself referred to as our mentor, our Svengali, our guru, the man who created us. His willingness to claim this ground helped to create the popular myth that grew up about us: that we were a totally manufactured and hyped group, that we did not even play our own music, that we did not write our own songs. It was untrue and unfair.

But I will admit that, with a great deal of subtlety, Tom helped to change our image in the early days, immediately after we had signed to him. I think he saw us as out-of-town boys. Although we'd been haunting the London clubs since we were fifteen and thought we knew what was going on, we had never been to real scene clubs. Tom retained a girl called Toula from a PR company and Toula showed us London from street level, not the gimmicky scene of the Hippodrome and Stringfellows. She took us to clubs like Go Global and Delirium, and we began to get into buffalo fashion. When we wanted to get our hair cut, Toula took us to Cuts in Soho, and when we wanted to get new clothes she knew where to take us, to places like American Classics.

Both Tom and Toula have since presented it as though they sat down and decided on an image for us and went out and bought it. It was not like that. Nobody has ever told me or Matt how to have our hair, what clothes to wear. Tom may have manipulated us by getting us to go about with Toula and see a whole new scene, but I'm sure he realized from the beginning that he could not give orders. He may have told Toula to make us more 'street', but it was a matter of persuasion and subtlety that did it. We went new places, we liked what we saw, we thought it would suit us. We tried having our long hair bobbed, but eventually we decided to have it all cut really short. We were never handed clothes and told we must wear them: we chose everything ourselves. Later on, when we had no time for shopping, we might get a stylist to bring bags of clothes for us to choose from, but that's as near as we ever got to letting anyone decide how we would look.

Tom started to get a promotional package together for us. We had some demo tapes. He organized a photo session with Neil Matthews, the guy who does *The Blues Brothers* calendars, and who subsequently took the most famous of all the Bros pictures. We were thrilled to work with him: the last pictures we'd had taken had been in a local wedding photographer's studio near our home in Surrey.

The name Bros came out of a session where we all kicked names around in Tom's office. I can't remember who actually suggested it, but we all liked it. Then we had a logo designed – a black label with BROS in white on it

– by Mark Farrow, who worked in Tom's office. Tom ran other companies, and one of them was a design team. He believed in keeping as much as possible in the family: he used to pay his own company, out of our money, to do work for us.

It was unusual to have a logo before a record deal, but it helped sell us to the record companies. Tom had black boxes made up, so that they looked like boxed sets, and inside each was a tape. Until the box was opened, nobody knew what we looked like.

I'm sure the fact that we are twins, and looked OK in pictures, helped sell us, both to Tom and then to the record companies. Matt and I never consciously used it, but I know we were aware of the advantages. Looking back now, I can only see disadvantages: it may have made our acceptance a bit quicker, but it was always for the wrong reasons. Like being remembered by the teacher in class because you are twins, not because you have done well. We were taken for our looks, not our music. If you are young and you look reasonably good in pictures, you may as well start getting used to the idea that nobody is ever going to take you seriously, and you are going to be pigeon-holed into the market for ten- to fourteen-year-old girls.

If you are good-looking it is also assumed that you are thick, a male bimbo. I can really sympathize with fabulous-looking girls who complain that nobody takes them seriously. I can remember chatting to Terry Wogan once, after we'd appeared on his programme, and I said something that made him look surprised. 'That's an intelligent perception,' he said, as though he didn't expect anything like that from me.

The choice for who we signed our first record deal with was between CBS and EMI. Tom negotiated it and Tom made the decision to go with CBS. It was a good deal:

RIGHT As you can see, I was always a cool dresser – here I am, aged two.

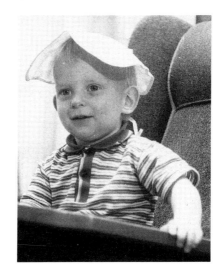

BELOW Side by side, smiling at the camera – good practice for all those publicity shots later on.

I've always loved and watched over Matt – even though he was better looking than me!

Mum and Dad before they were married, looking the way I'll always think of them.

Happy families?

LEFT On holiday in Majorca – Arnold Schwarzenegger, eat your heart out.

BELOW We could have done with these later on in life to keep our heads above water.

RIGHT I didn't know it at the time, but it was more than a farewell to Spain.

BELOW Summer fun in the garden at Mitcham.

RIGHT Mum and Tony
on their wedding day.

RIGHT Adam, my
brother, looking a bit
of a hunk.

Matt playing the Master of Ceremonies in our school production
of *Cabaret* – he was brilliant.

ABOVE A loving look – Tony and Carolyn.

LEFT A man who means a lot to me – my grandfather.

£260,000 to make an album. It sounded an enormous sum of money to me, but I had no idea how much it actually cost to make an album. And, of course, Tom's company took £52,000 in commission. A sum of £60,000 was held for completion of the record, so it ended up with me, Matt and Craig getting about £25,000 each, which Tom's company paid to us at the rate of £50 a week. Life did not suddenly change.

It did mean, though, that we were able to buy a Suzuki jeep as the band vehicle. Craig had passed his test but did not like driving in London, and Matt had not qualified as a driver, so although we jointly owned it I was the one who had the most pleasure and use from it.

Our days were spent travelling to Nicky Graham's house in Wimbledon to write songs for the new album. Nicky had a studio in his attic and we all trooped up there every day. It was a strange period: Nicky was very dictatorial in the studio, very opinionated, and obviously much older and more confident than we were. He had worked with the Nolans – not really the same scene, but he was very professional. Nicky and Tom took all the credit for writing the songs on the first album. The album sleeve said 'Songs by The Brothers', but 'The Brothers' was just a publishing name set up by the two of them. We did not realize we would not be getting a share of the publishing money, which turned out to be very large, as the first album sold three and a half million copies. We spent days working on the songs, improving them, changing them. Although Tom originally wrote our first hit, 'When Will I Be Famous?', it was very camp and much more of a simple chant: we made serious changes. I think a fair split would have been for the three of us, me, Matt and Craig, to have had a third of the publishing money between us, and Nicky and Tom to each have had a third. I was genuinely shocked that we got noth-

ing for all the work we put in, but of course we did not think
to ask questions about that sort of thing at the time.

Recording the album was even more of a shock. I had
always played live drums on demo tapes we had made
before, but now we were moving into the sort of class
recording where the drums are computer programmed,
because it costs too much money and takes too much time
to do it live. I did not have the first idea how to use the
computer, and there were days when I'd arrive at the studio
to find Nicky had already programmed the drums. Instead
of taking time to show me how to do it, he just got on with
it. I didn't have the confidence to argue. I was worried and
insecure: I used to listen to it and it sounded great, and I
did not think I could do it any better. So I'd go home and
literally burst into tears. I began to doubt my own ability,
and I felt useless and uninvolved. Craig was in the same
boat, because the bass was also programmed, but I don't
think it affected him as deeply.

Matt was OK. He was singing: they can't get a computer
to do that. And he was getting lots of support and feedback
because everyone was telling him what a brilliant voice he
had. Whenever I said anything about my doubts everyone,
including Matt and Craig, would tell me it was for the
good of the album. Already Tom and Nicky saw me as the
problem, the one who wouldn't roll over and play dead for
them. I can see it from Nicky's point of view: he'd recently
spent a lot of time learning to do computer programming
with lots of sophisticated equipment, so he had something
to prove. Perhaps because of that, he was never willing to
allow us to grow or develop, especially after he believed
he'd found a winning formula for us. I owe Nicky a lot,
he introduced us to Tom and found us professional management. But he also laid the foundation stones for some
of our later problems.

I was worried and upset. But set against that was the album, which was very exciting, very professional, so far out of the league of anything else we had ever done that we couldn't sleep at night for thinking about it. I had no idea if anybody would buy it, or what kind of people would buy it. I knew nothing about marketing strategies – I'd probably never even heard the phrase. But in retrospect I know that CBS and our management company together planned from the word go to chuck us right down the middle of the pop scene.

We had a collective brainstorming session to think of a name for the album. Everyone loved *Push*, and we could see the potential for having stickers for record shop doors with *Push* on them, complete with our name and logo. It was a very clever marketing idea.

The first single that was released from the album was 'I Owe You Nothing', which came out in August 1987. It went to number seventy-something in the charts, but it did quite well in the clubs. The video was very arty, with us surrounded by about thirty models, lots of dry ice and spooky lighting. (When 'I Owe You Nothing' was released again ten months later it went straight in at number one, and stayed there for two weeks, the only number one record we have ever had in Britain.)

When the single didn't make it into the top forty on the first attempt, the crucial top forty, I thought our whole pop career might collapse. But the record company had invested a lot in us and they were prepared to give it a much bigger go than that. They released 'When Will I Be Famous?' three months later, with a very street cred video of the three of us mooching through Soho.

'When Will I Be Famous?' was a cheeky title, a great gimmick, and it did the trick. When the mid-week chart position came in, it was at forty-one. We knew that if it went up we were going to be OK, but if it went down we'd got something to worry about.

I remember sitting on the settee at Mum's and Tony's house listening to the Radio One Top Forty chart show. A new chart entry was announced, in at number fourteen – it wasn't us. I nearly died, I was so despondent. And then Bruno Brookes announced there was a new band that might go places, just in at number thirty-nine. It was us. I exploded. Matt was upstairs and I thought he was asleep, but he suddenly screamed downstairs, jumping around and going mad. It was the most amazing feeling as we hugged and laughed and cried. That first break into the charts was the greatest buzz of all, much more buzzy than going straight in at number two with our next release. To hear the name of your band on national radio for the first time: wow!

We got our first real hot promotion when Cathy Gilbey, the producer of *Going Live* on BBC 1, booked us on to the Boxing Day programme. We were still total unknowns, just creeping in at the bottom of the charts, so it was a great spot to get and we owe a lot to her for backing her hunch.

The next day I got my first taste of fame, my first reaction from a fan. I was on Waterloo Station, about to tuck into a hamburger at Casey Jones, when a girl screamed at me. I was so freaked out I nearly screamed back. I looked behind me to see if there was anyone famous there. It was very weird and I was as shocked as she was.

Life was never going to be normal again.

But the great thing for me was that I had already met someone to share it with, someone who would, throughout the madness of the coming years, be my drip-feed of reality: Shirley Lewis.

CHAPTER SEVEN

Madly in Love

I was standing in the control room at Hot Nights Studio, Fulham Broadway, where we were making our first album. On the floor, recording the backing vocals for us, were three girls. I ran my eyes along them. I admit now that I'd set out for the studio that day with the express purpose of checking out these girls, top quality singers who had worked with people like George Michael and Elton John. I was impressed by their professional background – we'd never been in the league to use this class of backing vocalists before – and I wanted to know whether their looks would match up. It was the casual, chauvinist attitude of any eighteen-year-old guy, but I was soon shaken out of it.

When my eyes hit Shirley on the right of the line-up, it was like a jolt of electricity going through me. She was wearing tight jeans tucked into her cowboy boots. She's not particularly tall, she's got a great body and a fabulously pretty face. The other two girls, her sister Dee Lewis and her friend Helena, were also both attractive but I never gave them a second glance after I clocked Shirley. I couldn't take my eyes off her. I wanted her from the first moment I saw her.

I stared at her throughout the session, trying to force her to look at me. She knew I was looking at her and the harder I stared the more determined she became not to look at me. If she caught my glance she looked away again, quickly. At some point something amusing happened in the studio and we both laughed, and I caught her eye then, and for a moment we exchanged a smile that was nothing to do with what we were laughing at, it was a smile just between us. But for the rest of the time she did her best to avoid my eyes and I did my best to make her look at me. The sexual tension between us, before we had even spoken to each other, was explosive. I felt like a schoolboy falling in love for the first time.

When the session ended Helena suggested that we should all go to a nightclub, Brown's, together. She and Matt were obviously getting on rather well, and wanted to get on even better. Dee had another session to go to, so she could not come. I looked around and said, 'Where's Shirley?' She'd gone – I was devastated. But when I climbed into our jeep to drive off I saw her getting into her own car. I stopped and told her where we were going and she said she would come along. Matt went with Helena, and I had Craig in the jeep with me. I remember thinking all the way there 'Oh, God, I hope she turns up.'

When we got to the club we ordered beers and Helena asked for a Kir Royale. Shirley arrived and asked for a Perrier. I thought that was really nice, because we had very little money at that time; we were living on £50 a week each. I was wearing a buffalo jacket, covered with chains, and Shirley really loved it. She asked if she could wear it, so I put her girlie jacket on and we danced – we were both laughing a lot. When we sat down Helena was asking for sandwiches, which cost £30, but Shirley was still on her first Perrier. I've learned since that she can drink like a fish, but I was very grateful to her that night for not embarrassing me with expensive drinks and food.

We sat on stools, Shirley, me and Craig. Shirley and I were facing each other, very close, and we kept staring at each other. Her leg was in between mine, but not touching, except occasionally when one of us turned, when our legs would brush together – as if by accident, but all deliberate on my part. Every time we touched it was like another electric shock. Because Craig was there we didn't make it really obvious that we fancied each other: I wasn't even sure that she liked me. We flirted, but in a very subtle, restrained way, which made me desperate for her, but also desperate not to do anything to spoil the delicious flirtation.

We talked all night. We talked about sex, what we liked and what we didn't, and it was very suggestive and exciting, but still very understated. I felt she fancied me, but I knew this was something more than a normal pick-up and I wasn't going to risk it by making a move. Shirley was so classy I couldn't believe I had a chance. I was very surprised when she told me how old she was: twenty-seven. She looked gorgeous and although I knew she was obviously older than me I didn't think the difference was nine years. She also told me she had a three-year-old daughter. I felt that all this took her out of my league: she was a mature woman with a life of her own.

At the end of the evening she wrote her phone number down and gave the piece of paper to Craig, saying that if ever we were in town we should give her a call. I didn't know at the time, but she handed it to Craig because she did not want to seem too obvious. I was really miserable, I thought it meant she liked Craig. I'd felt more for Shirley in one evening of talking to her than I had felt for any other girl I had ever met, and I was desolate to think she preferred him.

I had been going out with a girl called Amanda for three or four months, but the next day I finished with her. I couldn't bear the thought of being with any other girl apart from Shirley. I realized how superficial my relationship with Amanda was: I'd talked more to Shirley in one evening than I had to Amanda in all the time I'd been seeing her.

The following day, in the studio, I plucked up the courage to ring Shirley. Craig made me do it: he said it had been clear to him that I was the one she fancied. I remember thinking, 'I'll ring her, and if she's offhand it will be terrible but at least I will know.' Sod it, what was there to lose except my pride? You only get one go at most things in life and I decided I wasn't going to pass Shirley up for fear of rejection. When I got through to her number there was an answering machine on. With butterflies in my stomach I left a message. 'Hi, Shirley, it's Luke. I just called for a chat. Take care. Bye.'

I deliberately did not leave a number for her to get back to me. I thought, if she's interested, she'll track me down. She did. She told me later she was really frustrated that I didn't leave a number, but she rang Helena and found out from her the number of the studio.

When Shirley rang I thought 'Wow'. I felt as excited as a kid at Christmas, but I managed to stay quite cool on the phone. We had a chat, but nothing went down about seeing each other. Then later that week Helena asked if we would all go over to her flat and she asked Shirley to go too. Craig was with us and when she walked in Shirley greeted all of us with a quick kiss. I was very confused, and again I thought she did not particularly like me. I realized later that I was just immature: I wasn't used to a sophisticated lady like Shirley, who did not want to make anyone uncomfortable by making her feelings too obvious.

Although we were still living in Camberley at this time, when we were recording we often stayed in London overnight with my mum's sister Sally. Craig was staying there too, and because he was tired he didn't want to remain at

Helena's for long. I ran him home in the jeep and Shirley
came with us. We decided to get a Chinese takeaway on
the way back, so we stopped at a restaurant in Bayswater.
We were laughing together and chatting. There was nothing on the Chinese menu that we liked, so we ended up
buying Kentucky Fried Chicken.

When we climbed back into the jeep, we both leaned
over at the same moment to put the bags of food on to the
back seat. For a few seconds, as we turned, our faces were
only a couple of inches away from each other, and I was
longing to kiss her more than I have ever longed for anything – I wanted her so badly. We gazed into each other's
eyes and then I forced myself to turn away and start the
engine.

Back at the flat Matt was 'indisposed'. He and Helena
had vanished into the bedroom without waiting for the
food. Shirley and I switched the TV on, settled down on
the sofa and, somehow, even now I'm not sure how it
happened, I suddenly had her in my arms and was kissing
her. We didn't bother with the food, either. It was the most
mind-blowing night of my life. It was brilliant, absolutely
brilliant. When we finally touched each other, all the pent-
up longing came out like steam from a safety valve. It was
so special, so different. I had no idea that you could feel
so much emotion – as well as physical pleasure – making
love to someone.

When she had to go, in the early hours of the morning,
I put the light on and I could not get over how gorgeous
she looked. Most girls look wrecked after a night of passion: Shirley looked incredible, just as beautiful as the
evening before.

She was completely in my head after that night. My
stomach churned like a tumble dryer whenever I thought
about her, and I couldn't stop thinking about her. It was

almost like a pain, gnawing away inside me. I had never felt like that before, it was so intense.

I'm glad we didn't fall into each other's arms the first time we met. The start of our relationship was slow and romantic, not tacky. I was in awe of her, because she was older than me, a successful professional with plenty going on in her life. I thought she was beyond my reach and it has been the greatest thing in my whole life that she wasn't.

It was a very physical relationship from the word go. We could not get enough of each other. But the amazing thing was that, when the sex stopped, we had so much to talk about. We were on the same wavelength and everything about her was everything I'd ever wanted.

Shirley was born in Forest Gate, East London, in 1960, the fourth of six children. The oldest of the family is Linda Lewis, who was a successful rock singer in the seventies and who got Shirley started on a career in music.

Shirley's mum Lil always wanted to be a singer, but wasn't allowed to – her dad, Shirley's granddad, said it would turn her into a 'hussy'. Both Shirley's grandfathers were black, from the West Indies, and both her grandmothers were white.

Shirley's dad was a bit of a jack the lad and when Shirley was quite young he ran off with her mum's friend. Even before that, he had never been around much so Shirley didn't really miss him. She thinks she's probably got a clutch of half-brothers and half-sisters somewhere, but she doesn't know for sure. She never saw her dad again. She isn't hung up about it: some of the older ones in her family are, but Shirley reckons she was protected by being so young at the time and having older ones around to look after her.

Her mum worked as a clippie on the buses and later as a ticket collector at the barrier on the London Underground. Because money was very tight, she used to work in the evenings as a barmaid, so Shirley was virtually brought up by her gran. For ten years Shirley's mum lived with Roy, who had been a bus driver on her route, and they ran pubs together. But by the time Roy arrived in the household, Shirley was about fifteen and already launched on her singing career.

She started singing professionally when she was fourteen, doing backing vocals for her sister Linda. Linda is ten years older than Shirley, and Shirley remembers doing a concert with her at the Royal Festival Hall, arriving home at three in the morning, and then having to get up for school the next day. Shirley hated school and never bothered to go much after she was fourteen: her mum didn't mind because she helped look after the two younger children and did the housework.

Her real surname is Fredericks, but because Linda was already established with the stage name Lewis, and because Shirley became known in the business as Linda's sister, it was assumed by everyone that her name was Lewis too. Now their youngest sister Dee, who was at the recording session where I met Shirley, is also known as Lewis.

Shirley is a natural-born great singer, she's never had a lesson in her life. She was thrown in at the deep end and found she had a good ear for melodies, and although at first she found harmonies difficult they are now second nature to her. With backing vocals you get work by word of mouth: when the word goes round that you are good, everyone wants to employ you. Shirley very quickly developed a great reputation. She has done an eighteen-month tour with Elton John, she's toured with George Michael, and she's sung on their albums; she's worked with Spandau Ballet, Billy Ocean, Curiosity Killed the Cat and loads of others.

Her first tour was with her sister, Linda, and then at seventeen she went with Bonnie Tyler to tour Asia. She was desperately lonely. The other girl backing vocalist had a boyfriend among the musicians, so Shirley was left on her own a lot and spent a fortune calling home and crying down the phone.

She met Jim Wheatley, the father of her daughter Carli, when she was fourteen, when he came to live just down the street from her. She didn't go out with him until she was sixteen, and when she was eighteen they moved in together. She was still living in the same house as him when I met her, although the relationship had broken down and they had separate bedrooms. The thought of her going home to him caused me a lot of problems, I was incredibly insecure over it.

Shirley says that when she was young, Jim was a very cool person to hang out with. He was six years older than her and knew his way about the East End. But as she became more and more successful they grew apart, and she had various other affairs and relationships. It was easy and convenient to keep Jim in the background, and there was nobody else who mattered enough for her to end it with him. She now regrets using him, but until she met me she had no idea that a deeper, more intense love could exist.

They lived together in a council flat but after Carli was born, when Shirley was twenty-three, she decided to buy a house. The pregnancy was a mistake, but Shirley does not believe in abortion – at least, she believes women should have the right to choose, but she was not happy about abortion for herself.

Jim did not have a regular job; he was a bit of a wheeler-dealer, buying and selling cars, that sort of thing. Shirley was earning very good money, anyway. He was delighted that she was pregnant, and it was settled that after the birth Shirley would go back to work and Jim would look after the baby.

Shirley did not see herself as very maternal, and she hated the pregnancy and the birth. But after Carli was born she fell head over heels in love with her. When Carli was six months old Shirley went away on an eight-month tour with Spandau Ballet, and she was knocked sideways by how much she missed Carli, even though Jim brought her to visit several times.

'I've never, ever felt like that before,' says Shirley. 'It hurt so much being away from her. I would imagine her, the things she would be doing, how she would toddle round the bed. Sometimes I could almost feel her in my arms, I was missing her so much.'

I know that, God forbid it ever happens, if Shirley were forced to make a choice between Carli and me, Carli would come first. I had to do a lot of rapid growing up when I got involved with Shirley, and one of the things I have had to come to terms with is that a mother's love for a child is stronger than any other.

The Spandau Ballet tour earned Shirley a lot of money as she was being paid £1,700 a week and all her hotel bills and expenses were taken care of. She was able to save almost all of it and that's when she bought a house in Chigwell. She and Jim were no longer a couple, but she was pleased for him to live with her because he was the best person in the world to look after Carli when Shirley was working. At that time, she thought they would always stay together – not because there was any great love between them, but because it was so comfortable.

*

Shirley remembers the date that she and I met. It was 10 June 1987. She had a phone call from Helena, a singer she had met on the Elton John tour. Helena asked if she would join her doing backing vocals for a new group called Bros. Shirley was very tired and didn't feel like it, but Helena persuaded her, and Dee as well.

'I was the first to arrive at the studio,' says Shirley, 'Then I met Matt, and Nicky Graham, the producer. I already knew Nicky: when I was fifteen I released a record with a friend of mine, Debbie. We called ourselves Domino. The record was released by CBS and produced by Nicky Graham – so my first record company and my first producer were the same as Luke's.

'Matt was trying to flirt with me, which I now know he does with everyone. I thought he was good looking, but I didn't fancy him at all. I told him he would like my friend Helena when she arrived, and he did. I remember thinking that Matt was really old-fashioned in the way he was dressed, with a James Dean sort of haircut and a jumper that looked like a schoolboy's: Luke told me later that it was me who was old-fashioned, and I was so far behind that I did not recognize how trendy they were!

'We were singing when Luke and Craig walked in, and I remember thinking how cool Luke looked. His hair was spikier than Matt's and he had a great jacket on. I knew he was staring at me, but I wouldn't look at him. It felt exciting. When we went to Brown's in the evening I remember telling myself that he was far too young for me and that I should be sensible and not allow myself to fancy him. But it was too late. I really enjoyed his company and he seemed much older than his age. After he left the message on my answering machine it was me who suggested to Helena that she should invite them all over to her flat.'

Helena's flat in Ladbroke Grove became a regular

meeting place for Shirley and me when we started seeing each other. We were still living in Camberley and she was going home every night to Jim and Carli, so it was an odd existence. I can remember driving home at four and five in the morning, absolutely exhausted and struggling to keep my eyes open. The jeep went at a flat-out sixty-five miles per hour, and more than once I had to pull over and sleep by the side of the road.

For quite a long time we used to book into hotels for the night, and because I was so broke Shirley was the one who had to pay. I remember being very nervous the first time, as we booked into the Royal Garden Hotel in Kensington, but Shirley thought it was all great fun. One night we looked out of our bedroom window and across the way, in another hotel room, we could see a couple making urgent love, and we collapsed laughing.

What developed between Shirley and me was a real friendship, and it was something I had never had before. It was like pressing the fast forward button on the video, we reached a stage of really knowing each other so quickly. Every one around me knew I was bowled over by her, and my friends who met her all agreed she was gorgeous. I am always aware what a very sexy lady she is and that has added to my insecurities. I knew that if I fancied her that much, other guys would, too.

I was self-conscious about my lack of money and about not having my own place. It made me feel so young. But Shirley never once made me feel that it mattered and she has never mentioned it since.

We got serious very quickly. Because Shirley was older, because she had a child, we needed to know where we were going quite soon. She wasn't looking for an affair on the side and I knew that you didn't prat around with a woman like her. We were both enjoying it, having fun, but she wanted to know the score. I never had any doubt that I wanted to be with her full time, but there were times when I found it very hard to cope with her having another life. I hated it when she went home after a night together, and I wasn't sure that she wanted to be with me all the time.

She always made it plain to me that she was a package, that she came complete with Carli. I was scared stiff of the responsibility – I had my nineteenth birthday three months after we met, and taking on a child seemed a very seasoned, mature thing to be doing. But I was scared stiff of losing Shirley, and she made it clear that as far as she was concerned it was take it or leave it. Without Carli, no Shirley.

I knew that if I gave her up over that, my love for her would be very shallow. And if I issued an ultimatum that she had to put me first, she wouldn't have it: and if she did agree, she wouldn't be the sort of woman I thought she was. So I told her that I was prepared to take everything that came with her.

Shirley says, 'I knew I was in love with Luke, and our times together were great, very romantic and lovely. But when you are having an affair you don't talk about the problems, and there were very big problems for me. I wanted him to understand what was involved, not just for me but for the others in my life. Carli was very happy and Jim was the best person to look after her. I didn't want to leave Jim and disrupt everything, unless I was sure my relationship with Luke would measure up to a full-time commitment.'

After three or four months, I met Carli. It was a weird experience, but I was completely bowled over by her. She was so gorgeous, so pretty, so cute, with long curly hair and a little high-pitched voice. It made me even more jealous of Jim. I knew then that whatever I gave to Shirley, however much I loved her, I could never give her her first child. I could buy her a Rolls Royce, but it would mean nothing compared to the living flesh of her own daughter. I knew that the little person in the back seat of the car was the greatest thing she would ever have, and I was not a part of it. Carli was the living proof of Shirley's relationship with Jim. It was a strange and sad feeling, and I ached to be the father of her child. It was hard to get my head round all that, but Shirley understood when we talked it through.

We agreed by this time that we wanted to live together all the time. I wanted to wake up in the morning next to Shirley, not see her rushing out of the hotel room to be home before Carli woke up. I wanted to do ordinary things with her: sit and watch TV together, eat meals together without going to fancy restaurants, be together twenty-four hours of the day, not just in snatched hours.

Shirley was doing a tour with Jennifer Rush in Germany, and we agreed that she would tell Jim when he went over to take Carli to see her. Because of the expense, I knew that they were all three of them going to share a twin room, and that was the hardest time of our whole relationship. I had agreed that I would not call, I would let Shirley handle it her own way. She felt she owed Jim an explanation because, after all, they had been together for ten years.

I was in agony that night, absolute agony. I wished I had the money to fly over there and be with her. I'm a very jealous, possessive person. Even now, after all our years together, I am only 98 per cent sure of Shirley – the other nice little two per cent of doubt keeps me on my toes, stops me taking her for granted, means that I will always work at our relationship. I don't want to get lazy and think

'OK, she loves me.' It works for her, because she gets better treatment as a result. If I don't give her romance and roses, I'm scared that somebody else will.

I also give her the freedom to be a baby with me. She's strong and capable and I know that if I wasn't here she'd run her life well, but sometimes I like to let her curl up with me, like a little girl, and let me look after her. We've both learned to cherish our relationship.

But in those early days I was one big walking mass of insecurities. Shirley knew how I felt, because I took the time and trouble to explain it to her. I think one thing that goes wrong in so many relationships is that people only see things from their own point of view, they don't think how it would feel to be their partner. She knew how I felt about her and Jim.

I only went to Shirley's house once, when Jim wasn't there. I went in and out very quickly: it felt wrong, disrespectful to Jim, to be there. I now know Jim, we've got to know each other over the years because of arrangements for Carli. We get on well and we trust each other: he trusts me with his daughter, which is an honour I appreciate. But even then, before I had met him and when I was crazy with jealousy over him, I felt it was a violation for me to be in his home.

By this time, Mum and Tony had sold their house in Camberley and moved to Peckham. They moved partly for us, because we were spending so much time travelling, and Mum was worried about us driving home late to Camberley. Craig moved in with us. The three-storey town house needed work doing on it, so during the week Matt, Craig and I shared one bedroom, taking it in turns to sleep on the floor. We were like brothers, we were so close during that time of our lives, and Mum treated Craig like another son. I spent so much time with Shirley that he and Matt usually got to sleep in the beds, anyway!

Shirley stayed at the house with me a couple of times, but it was not a comfortable situation. Mum had lots of reservations about her, and Shirley thought it was weird that I had to ask Mum and Tony whether we could stay there. She'd left her mum's home when she was sixteen and was used to making her own decisions about things.

In the end, Shirley and I found a flat together. I never formally announced to Mum that I was leaving home, and I don't think to this day she has ever fully forgiven me for that. I just drifted away and stopped going there, except of course to visit her and Tony.

Shirley did not have an easy ride with my family. Just as I found it difficult to deal with her having Carli, she found it hard coming to terms with how close I was to Matt and Mum. She said she was shocked how much I told them about our lives, and how if I had an argument with her I would tell them about it. She had never had a really, really close relationship like that with her mum or with any of her brothers and sisters, and it irritated her. I, on the other hand, had always been so close to them that it was natural to share things with them, especially Matt. I don't think he and I have ever lied to each other or ever kept a secret from each other in our lives.

But my family's minds were being poisoned against Shirley by rumours and innuendoes that were circulated about her in the music business, making her out as cheap and a bit of a tart. I didn't give a rat's arse about anyone else's opinions, and Mum and Tony knew better than to try to interfere because they know how strong-minded I am. Their actions and attitudes showed how they felt, though.

'I was mortified when Luke took up with Shirley,' says Mum. 'She was so much older than him, he was only eighteen. She had a child and as far as I could make out she was still in some way involved with the father of her child. I was very worried because he was so serious about her – he had hardly started out in life, and I didn't want him tying himself down. I think other mothers will understand that.

'I also found their physical relationship a bit embarrassing. They'd sit there with their legs wrapped around each other, even in front of people like Luke's granddad, who was too old to understand modern behaviour.

'Matt and Craig were both worried that he was too involved. We were all being fed a lot of anti-Shirley propaganda by the rumour-mongers. They suggested that Shirley would have a fling with him and then ditch him.

'When Luke left home I didn't see him for six months. We kept in touch by phone, but I cried myself to sleep at night worrying about him. I used to look at him on telly, and I was sure he was getting thinner and didn't look well or happy, which increased my bad feelings towards Shirley.'

Tony admits that he and Mum resented the fact that Shirley had a strong influence over me, and that like all parents they would have preferred me to be with someone nearer my own age. Both Mum and Tony now love Shirley and know that they were wrong about her.

'We are now very good friends, and I could not wish for a nicer, better, more generous person to share Luke's life,' says Mum.

'I'm not too proud to say I was wrong, totally wrong,' admits Tony.

As Bros became more and more successful, Tom saw Shirley as a real threat. He didn't want one of 'his boys' tied down with a steady girlfriend, because he didn't think it helped our image. He viewed us only in terms of record sales and fans. I was one third of the fancied equation, and he didn't want anything to interfere with that. He once said to me, 'If she gets in the way of my fucking boys, I'll fucking get her run over.' Even though it should have been obvious to me that he didn't mean it literally, in the heat of the moment I went for him and I had to be held back by the other guys who were there. He was saying that about the person I loved; he didn't give a damn about how much pleasure we had together, all he cared about was the image.

On one occasion Paul Russell, managing director at CBS, called me into his office and had a roundabout sort of chat with me on the problems of me having a girlfriend. He didn't tell me to split with Shirley, but he said that it was damaging to girl fans for me to be constantly photographed with her in the press, and that I should cool it a bit.

It took Matt about a year and a half to really get on well with Shirley. At first he, too, put her down: or rather, he put us down as a couple. Because our lives were so public, everyone seemed to think they were entitled to pass judgement on us. It was like giving people free tickets to the cinema: let's all go and look at Luke and Shirley and give our opinions about them. Their opinions were accumulated from crap in newspapers, but that didn't inhibit them. I've often seen mates of mine – even Matt – with girlfriends I rated as cows, but I was never rude enough to tell them. Everyone has to work out their own private life, but nobody extended that courtesy to me – they all felt they had the God-given right to put their oar in.

Matt realized eventually that Shirley and I had something very special going for us. He also realized that she would never criticize me, or stand around listening to anyone else criticize me. They gradually built up a good relationship: they tease each other, occasionally they have real arguments, but underneath it all they are very fond of each other.

My dad went to see Tom Watkins soon after we became famous. He had found out, through his job as a detective, that there were pirate tapes of our *Push* album being bandied about. He met Tom for the first time and they had a good talk about our careers. Then Tom digressed on to the subject of Shirley and told Dad in brutally harsh terms what he thought of her.

'Just because Luke's got his first bit of black arse, he can't see the woods from the trees,' he said.

He told Dad that I was neglecting my work with the band to be with Shirley, which was absolute rubbish. Dad admits he was impressed by Tom's business experience, by the way he presented himself, and felt that if Tom said I was throwing my chances away because of Shirley there might be some truth in it and he should talk to me about it. Luckily, he talked to Matt first, and Matt put him straight. Although Matt was perhaps a bit jealous of the amount of my time that I gave to Shirley, he certainly knew that I wasn't neglecting the band.

Dad said nothing to me. Today he says: 'I'm very glad I did not try to interfere. It was none of my business, and I should have known that. Shirley has turned out to be a delight, a really lovely lady, a down-to-earth person who has got no side to her. She has improved Luke's life a lot. She is the best thing that could have happened to him.'

I can't argue with that.

CHAPTER EIGHT

Too Much .

If there was a handbook on how to live your life, I'd have a copy in my back pocket at all times. But there isn't, you have to make your own rules as you go along. Besides, the kind of fame that hit us, and washed over our lives like a giant tidal wave, was so unusual that a book on how to cope with it would have a limited market. There are other people, especially in the music industry, who have had to deal with a similar brand of instant success: but ours was bigger, wilder, more out of control than anything Britain has seen before. At the height of our fame there were 40,000 paid-up members of our fan club, the biggest fan club in Europe, probably in the world. Everywhere we went, hundreds of them would be there, screaming at us, pawing at us, demanding a part of us.

It was exhilarating, exciting, enjoyable. It was also freaky, weird, unsettling. It was the dream I had dreamed when I formed my first band at the age of twelve: it was also the nightmare of a life without privacy, without rest, and dangerously close to being without sanity. I don't have a lot of time for actors and film stars who complain about fans invading their private space because, after all, we go into any branch of showbusiness hoping the public will like us, will become our fans. But the mania that pursued Bros was much harder to deal with than someone coming up to you in a restaurant for an autograph, or following you round a supermarket. We literally could not move outside our homes without bodyguards to scythe a way through the clamouring girls. Our houses and our cars were constantly daubed with love messages, our neighbours were subjected to seeing their streets become as crowded as football terraces, my girlfriend was abused and threatened.

Wherever we went, there were photographers on our tails. Even when Shirley and I thought we had shaken everybody off, and were enjoying a quiet meal together, a flashbulb would pop in our faces. Or we would think we had not been spotted, only to see a picture in the following day's newspapers. It didn't take me long to wonder whether I was in the right job: I remember admiring a beautiful Porsche outside a restaurant when we arrived for a meal one evening, only to discover it belonged to one of the paparazzi who was following me all over to take pictures of me. He probably made as much out of Bros as I did!

We read stories about ourselves in the press that were so bizarrely inaccurate we could only laugh at them. Not only were Matt and I not twins, we were not even brothers: 'It's amazing what you can do with make-up,' said one article.

Mum remembers a group of fans telling her all about our birth. When she said they'd got it wrong, they argued with her: as far as they were concerned, they'd read about it in a magazine, and they were the authorities on our lives while she was only our mother!

Even when the newspaper stories were true, they were frequently so trivial we could not believe any newspaper would print them or any reader would want to read them: Luke from Bros left his bath running and it overflowed. The *Daily Express* actually ran that. Who cares? The *Sun* ran one of their regular '20 Things You Never Knew About . . .' columns on Bros, and there were at least three things on the list that even Matt, Craig and I never knew before. And when two rival magazines in Australia fought over the privilege of giving away our unwashed bed linen as prizes for readers, I really did wonder who was loopy, me or them.

It would have been very easy to become a head case. We were only just nineteen when the mania hit, and the transformation in our lives was so fast that it was hard to believe it was actually happening. You suddenly start getting treated well in restaurants. You drive into a garage to put petrol in your car and you feel so damned ordinary, but then someone comes up and asks for your autograph. They probably feel silly doing it – but you are thinking 'Who am I? What have I done to merit this?' You feel sillier than they do.

Then you are suddenly performing for the Royal Family, headlining at gigs with other bands who have been your idols since you were a kid, being invited to open things and being handed awards – and still, inside you, you are thinking 'Who am I? What have I done to merit this?'

When our second hit single 'Drop the Boy' was released in March 1988, we were booked to sign records at the HMV record store in Oxford Street. Four thousand fans turned up, and caused a massive traffic jam that took six hours to clear. We had to be sneaked out the back way in a police van, while three other people climbed into our limo. The doors of the limo were ripped off, and we weren't even in it. It took a hundred policemen to control the crowd, and one fan ended up with a broken leg from the crush. When we were the special guests at Radio One to launch their new stereo broadcasting, the whole of the West End of London ground to a halt.

We were working so hard that we did not have time to sit back and think about what was happening. Our management were determined to capitalize on our success, and we were too inexperienced to know it could have been done differently; if we had the chance to do it again I would insist on everything being paced more sensibly. Tom Watkins believed we should commit 100 per cent of ourselves to everything that was offered, that we should do all the TV programmes, all the press interviews, all the public appearances we could cram in. When you are paying men in suits a vast amount of money to run your affairs, you assume they know best. But Tom had never heard the saying that 'less is more'. He believed all publicity was good publicity, and he'd encourage the planting of made-up stories about us in newspapers and magazines.

So we were caught up in a frenetic whirlwind of activity, and we were desperately short of hours in which to sleep, let alone spend time thinking about it all. Looking back to those days, I see nothing but a blur of travelling, performing, giving interviews, doing TV shows (we did fifty in two years), and desperately trying to squeeze in a private life. Trying to sort out in my mind what happened, I sometimes find myself flippantly wondering, 'Was I actually there?'

There are a couple of moments that stand out clearly as times when I rocked back on my heels and saw the whole thing in some sort of perspective. When our album, released on the back of 'Drop the Boy', went straight into the charts at number two I remember thinking, 'What the hell is going on?' It went gold on the first day, platinum by the end of the first week. OK, I knew it was a good album and I was proud of it, but I also knew it was going in so high, so fast, not because it had earned its place, musically, but because by that time we had armies of fans who would have bought it whatever was on it.

On another occasion I switched the television on in a

hotel bedroom, and it was the celebrity quiz programme, *Blankety Blank*. One of the celebrities made a joke about Bros and the whole audience laughed and clapped. That was when I knew that we were really famous, not just idolized by thousands of very young girls. The audience for *Blankety Blank* were hardly young trendies. It is strange to think that practically everybody in the country knows who you are.

It is also weird getting to grips with the bullshit. I was at a video shoot once, when we were making the video for 'Drop the Boy', and I was drumming so hard that one of my sticks caught me just below the eye and I started to bleed. I did not realize until I stopped that there was blood running down my face. Everyone came rushing around, making a fuss. I said, 'My looks are ruined. That'll cost me a few fans.' There was consternation on everyone's faces until I laughed. Once they realized I was joking, they relaxed and laughed. Up to that moment they thought I was really pissed off about it, and they were all going to stand around making soothing, clucking noises. Over one small cut.

From the moment the records started making it, we had to start touring and promoting them. There was a British tour that sold out in forty minutes, as fast as they could hand over the tickets at the box offices, there were tours in Europe, a world tour. You never get the chance to appreciate the places you go to: one posh plastic hotel is much the same as any other, one mass of screaming girls is much the same as any other, one stadium is much the same as any other, one TV studio is much the same as any other. And at that stage, all journalists asked much the same questions, whatever the language.

Here's a typical day from our schedule at that time.

Up at six in the morning, wakened by my personal assistant and my bodyguard, who would have stayed at my home the night before. We each had to have a personal assistant to cope with the pressure of our engagements, and a bodyguard was an absolute necessity, just to allow us to move. They were both very expensive items on our budgets, but we could not have functioned without them. My regular bodyguard was Kelly Samuels, one of the best, and a good guy to have around.

Getting up was always a nightmare, as I had probably only had four or five hours sleep. People will think it sounds lazy, to have someone there to wake me and run my bath, but I needed every minute in bed that I could get.

The first hour was spent getting ready: having a bath or shower, washing my hair, getting dressed. It is drummed into you that you are a pop star: you cannot walk out of your front door into a horde of fans looking like a slob. My case would have been packed the day before, with perhaps six outfits for four days. Breakfast between seven and seven thirty, and then into the chauffeur-driven car at a quarter to eight. If we were promoting a record, the record company would provide the car.

We would drive to Heathrow. Just before we reached the M4 I would ring Shirley to tell her I loved her, even though I had only left her less than an hour before: I hate aeroplanes and have a superstition that if I die in a crash I want her to remember that the last words I said to her were 'I love you.'

At the beginning of the tunnel approaching the airport we would pick up a police escort. The police would make a decision about whether or not we were going to pass through the airport: if there were only two to three hundred fans there, they would let us go through, but usually if

there were more they would have us driven straight round
to airside. Then we would have individual passport checks
and the whole thing would be relatively hassle free. If we
had to go through the airport if would always be difficult.
When we first started flying – and remember, I'd only been
abroad twice in my life before we were famous, so it was
all a novelty to me – I used to love going to the duty free
shop, but that soon became too difficult. Even when we
were beyond passport control, we would be besieged by
other travellers wanting to take our pictures and autographs.

Most of the airlines were very understanding. We travelled so frequently that we got to know the staff on British
Airways and Virgin flights. The stewardesses would spoil
us: I'd end up getting an extra breakfast and Matt would
always be asking for 'biccies'. We would often be invited
up to the front to meet the captain: pilots have daughters
who want autographs, too. One British Airways chief stew-
ard really cheered us – and the rest of his passengers –
when he made the routine safety announcements at the
start of a flight. He said, 'There are fifty ways to leave your
husband, but only thirteen ways to leave this plane . . .'
Then when he was announcing the movie he read out the
names of the stars in it and added 'and Matt Goss'.

We had one run-in with British Midland, when they
refused to shelter us from fans in their lounge which was
reserved for travellers who had used the airline frequently.
We did not qualify, but it would have been far more sensible to let us go in there than bring the rest of the place
to a standstill. We were so annoyed, and so hassled, that
we checked off their flight to Paris and on to a British
Airways one.

We stopped travelling long-haul flights in first class with
British Airways because they try to make everyone have a

sleep. They would put the lights out and tuck everyone up with blankets: Matt and I are insomniacs, we find it difficult to get to sleep at the best of times, but you felt you had to be quiet because all the other middle-aged first-class passengers were taking their naps. It drove us mad.

On the plane we would all drink, partly to get over our nerves about flying. The rest of the musicians would travel first class with us and we would fairly get stuck into the free champagne they handed out. At the other end we would be met by a couple of people from the record company, and we would all pile into the chauffeured Mercs and head for the hotel. We would be booked into huge rooms, usually suites, with bedrooms as big as a living room. In the early days it was a matter of dumping our bags and getting straight to work, maybe doing eight interviews with journalists on the trot. I'd be sick of hearing myself speak.

You think your own life is really uninteresting: you cannot understand why anyone wants to know all the details of it. What colour is your favourite? Have you got a lucky number? All that for the fan magazines, and more personal stuff for the newspapers and general magazines. You've got to keep a sense of proportion, or you end up believing your own myth. You end up thinking it really matters what you had for breakfast.

When you get really famous you can eat before you work: that's a difference we all noticed. The record company lays on lunch and restricts the interviews until after you have eaten. Then it's rehearsal, gig, collapse into bed, up at six in the morning to move on and start again. People who have never travelled much think it must be wonderful to stay in four- or five-star hotels all the time, with everything laid on. Well, the novelty soon wears thin. Sometimes I'd have give anything for a massive scoff: three slices of toast, baked beans, crispy bacon and mayonnaise. Instead we got those silly little sandwiches with the crusts cut off and a cocktail stick holding them together. I never learned the knack of eating them. Sometimes I'd be so hungry I'd stick them in my mouth, stick and all, and nearly gouge my gums out, and other times I'd take the sticks out and the whole sandwich would disintegrate. I think they're meant more for decoration than satisfying hunger.

There were times when I would have given anything for the freedom of being in my own home. I don't expect people to feel sorry for me. I learned pretty quickly that I liked good food, and I'd now list smoked salmon, caviar and lobster among my favourite tastes. But I also like to sit down to ordinary meals at home, or do something really slobby, like going to bed with a cup of tea and a packet of biscuits and dropping crumbs in the bed.

It also sounds a bit precious to always insist on having a suite in a hotel. But if you just have a room, you find yourself lying in bed in the morning, and the sheets have slipped off and you're naked to the world, and there are three or four maids coming in carrying one cup of tea. Because of who we were, we always got a lot of attention from the hotel staff, but there were times when I'd prefer not to have it. In a suite, my PA could handle the staff.

It's easy to sound a complete brat. But it is very lonely, living your life in hotel room after hotel room. I'd often wake up in the morning and smack my head on the wall, because the bed wouldn't be where I thought it was, because I wasn't at home – nor even in the same hotel room that I'd been in the day before.

There was also a strange unreality about the hours we lived, because we would finish a gig and be all hyped up – you can't just put your head down and go to sleep ten minutes after getting back to your hotel. It was hard to unwind. We'd have a meal, try to come down to normal, but inevitably it would be the early hours of the morning before we were able to sleep. Sometimes we'd play very silly jokes on each other, just to lighten up the atmosphere. We once stripped Craig naked and sprayed shaving foam all over him and locked him out of his room, then called for the hotel porter.

On another occasion, in Manchester, we sprinkled chocolate laxative all over a chocolate mousse that John Buckland, who was a personal assistant shared by all three of us in the early days, was about to eat. We had already covered his loo with clingfilm, and put a red dye in his shower. You can imagine the mess he was in. We'd sprayed his phone with Deep Heat, a treatment for aches and pains, so when he picked it up his ear was burning. On top of that, his bed was full of condoms filled with toothpaste and water. The following day he walked everywhere with a huge bottle of kaolin and morphine, and on a forty-minute flight back to London he went to the loo six times. Amazingly, he stayed friends with us all. We had the safeguard of knowing that none of our crew could do the laxative trick on us, because we had to appear on stage.

It sounds terribly childish, but we were only nineteen, we were on the road and bored, and we would do practically anything for a laugh. At least we never trashed any hotel rooms!

Matt and I always travelled with a bag full of computer games to while away the hours. We are both terrified of flying, but he is worse than I am. Being with him helps me, because I have to concentrate on helping him. We hold hands at take-off and landing, and I usually do something stupid to distract him and make him laugh. We were once flying to Paris when our plane was hit by lightning.

There was a huge thud and a jolt that terrified everybody, and increased our paranoia.

On any plane journey we'd always get plenty of approaches from fans sitting in second class. We would usually ask the stewardess to collect all the things they wanted signing, and we'd sit for half an hour just doing that. If there were real, dedicated fans back there we would send them champagne. We soon realized it was a mistake to go back and see them. It was all right walking down the aisle to get there, but by the time you turned round to go back you'd find your face was three inches away from somebody's home video camera, and you were doing an Eskimo kiss with the lens. You couldn't tell them where to stuff it, because that wouldn't look too good when they showed it to their friends back home, so you had to smile and pretend you didn't mind. They'd often thrust a message into your hand that they wanted you to read to the camera, sending your love to all the folks back home. Only usually you couldn't read the writing. There must be some very odd home movies of me dotted about Britain.

Then as we tried to get back to our own seats we would be besieged, just as though we were doing a personal appearance. Everyone, it seems, knew someone who would want our autographs. It was better if we were flying by a foreign airline, because then it would only be the kids who knew us.

The press made a great deal about us having a hyped image, but there was certainly no great strategy behind it. We wore Levi 501s that were big and baggy, plain white tee shirts, big belts and Doc Martens – it was a very accessible style, one that thousands of people adopted without ever knowing it was influenced by us. Obviously, to go on stage we needed extras, like incredible jackets. But it started out very simple, very affordable, very unisex. The girls who followed us, Brosettes as they came to be known, often wore leotards instead of tee shirts with their 501s, but essentially they dressed like we did. It wasn't necessarily a very flattering style for hordes of dumpy little twelve-year-olds, but their parents should be grateful that it was at least a very clean style, and that their feet were not being squeezed into narrow, uncomfortable shoes.

Because our fans were so young, we felt a tremendous sense of responsibility towards them. Every time we gave an interview we felt we had to say sensible things. We are against drugs and we don't smoke, so that part wasn't difficult. But it was hard not throwing in the odd swear word, and I won't pretend that we never drank anything stronger than milk shakes. We soon realized that everything we said, even if it was meant to be a joke, would be taken up and repeated, so we had to guard ourselves very closely. On the one or two occasions we relaxed with journalists, we lived to regret it.

I understand what makes kids into fans. It's just puppy love. Most people have puppy love for someone down the road, someone older than them at school, or someone famous. The common factor is that it is someone unattainable, a love that you can't do anything about, probably because you are not really ready to do anything about it. When I was really young I had crushes on Lena Zavaroni and, later, Blondie – although I was never so smitten that I would have stood outside their houses for half an hour, let alone months on end. Fans are very different from groupies, who get their kick from doing something about it: our band image was so young that our fans didn't fall into that category.

There's obviously a nice feeling of companionship if they share their puppy love with several thousand other girls. They can join a club, hang out together, be together in it. At the time, they really do believe that they love you, but gradually they stop thinking about you twenty-four hours a day, they grow up, build their own lives, and maybe you will always be a sweet memory for them, but that's all. There are lots of middle-aged women walking about today who screamed for the Beatles, the Stones, Cliff Richard. It hasn't stopped them leading full and happy lives, but they still have a soft spot for the entertainers they loved as kids.

But I have to admit, for those on the other side of the equation, fans can cause a few problems. From the moment the second single hit the top there were never less than six hundred girls outside Mum's and Tony's house in Peckham. To this day, Mum has mirrored glass on her windows, so that from inside you can see out but from outside you can't see in. It was the only way to preserve any privacy in there, but it's very odd. Normal people don't live like that.

Mum and Tony coped with it very well. At first they were very excited and proud, but it did get difficult for them. They'd wake up in the morning and Mum would pull back the curtains and a loud 'ooooh' would go up from the girls on the pavement outside, who had either been there all night or had arrived very early. Girls would scrawl their names and love messages all over the front of the house, on their cars, on the steps. Fans have absolutely no regard for property: they would write with a permanent marker all over anything. The jeep had a convertible roof which had to be scrubbed with turps to get the fans' signatures off. They might write 'We love you Luke' but it never seemed like a gesture of love, giving us all so much extra hassle to cope with.

Mum says she remembers the first time the girls turned

up thinking how odd it was that they were there to see her sons.

'At first it made me laugh. I love Luke and Matthew dearly, but it's hard to accept people who are very close to you as sex symbols,' she says. 'But after a while it stopped being funny. The girls climbed over the back garden wall, peered constantly through the letterbox, made a lot of noise and litter in the street. Every morning Tony and I would go out with a brush and a dustbin, sweeping up the mess: that's hardly the glamorous life of a pop star's mother, is it? But we believed the people living near us had enough to put up with, without the mess too.

'The neighbours were wonderful: the people of Peckham never blamed us or took it out on us that their lives were disrupted. When Luke and Matt lived in posher areas, they had lots of trouble from the neighbours; ours were brilliant. On some days you couldn't get down Commercial Way, because the traffic was stopped because of the girls.

'The local police had a bit of a nightmare coping with them, but they told us that crime in the area went down. How can anyone break into a house when there are three hundred girls in the street?

'The boys had to pay for us and our neighbours to have iron railings put up instead of our fences, which gave way under the pressure of all the fans leaning on them. There was a constant knocking at our door, and if you didn't answer they'd scream abuse at you through the letterbox. It often started as early as six in the morning. Our front path and the whole of the front of the house were covered in writing, messages from fans. It looked awful.

'Most of the girls were lovely, although they were very demanding. They wanted me to stand and talk to them, even though I obviously had my own life to lead. Some of them still come back to see me, but now they bring me pictures of their boyfriends, show me their engagement rings, show me their wedding pictures and even one or two of them have brought their babies.'

Even my granddad found himself a star attraction with the fans. How many other over seventy-year-olds were being asked to sign their names on the legs of young girls? Luckily, he never had more attention than he could cope with: he's pretty good at telling them to go away when he wants to be.

We had a core of about forty or fifty fans who were always there, who I got to recognize and know by name. At least, they were always hurt when I couldn't remember their names, but there are only a certain number of Clares, Jackies, Julies, Tinas and Debbies you can sort out in your head, and I'd often get them mixed up. We were genuinely fond of them: you appreciate someone who will stand out-side in all weathers just to see you. We were also genuinely worried about them: they came from all over the country and would sleep rough to be outside our house. There were stories of fans being mugged, teachers being upset by the number of girls playing truant, parents wanting their daughters back home. We were forever telling them all to go home, reminding them to at least ring their families.

There was trouble, inevitably, from neighbours and from innocent people who were stopped from going about their everyday lives because of our fans. I felt sympathy for them: but as I said at the time, I did not personally send out invitations to five hundred girls with a fiver inside each one to persuade them to turn up wherever we went. Half the time we never knew how the girls found out where we were, but they always did. While some of our neighbours were great, others were really snotty about it, they seemed to disregard the fact that we had rights as human beings, too. But others could see that we were as much victims of the fans as they were.

Not all the fans were lovely. Some would be very abusive: if Mum said we were not there, they would not believe her. And from the very beginning we suffered from the envy of young guys, who would throw stones at the Peckham house and hurl abuse at us and our families. Even to this day, I cannot walk down a street in London without some bloke or other making a rude gesture or calling me something choice. I never got to understand why guys hated us so much, why complete strangers felt they had the right to spit at us, or to wind the windows of their cars down when we were in a traffic jam next to them and call us obscene names, often in front of Shirley.

It was hard to always remember that the girls at the door existed on every crumb that we threw to them. If it was cold and raining and I didn't want to stand around chatting, they'd get very upset. They'd make up stories about us. They'd hate as fast as they loved, because such young girls are very fickle.

We got plenty of hate mail. One letter that really spooked us threatened that either Matt or I would be killed – but we were not going to be told who. The writer said we would both suffer: the one who was killed and the one who was left behind to grieve. It takes a particularly unpleasant, vicious sort of mind to dream up a letter like that, and there were things in it that showed the writer knew a fair bit about our movements. We handed it over to the police.

Another letter said that Shirley and Carli would be cut up and posted back to me in little bits, and Shirley came in for a lot of verbal abuse. 'Black cow' would be one of the more repeatable names she was called.

There was one particular girl who caused us a lot of

bother. She and her mates were dubbed the 'Peckham Posse' by the press, because they used to go around threatening the other fans who turned up on our doorstep. I think she was actually mentally unbalanced: that's the most charitable opinion I can give. She would shout abuse at all of us, really nasty, horrible stuff. My bodyguard had to hold Shirley back one time, she was going to kill her. The ludicrous thing was that this girl claimed she was in love with Matt, but she called him names, too. Her timing was impeccable: she knew just what to shout to cause the most hurt. The police were called several times, but there wasn't much they could do except move her on, and she would be back the next day. I used to wish she would turn into a guy for five minutes so I could beat the brains out of her.

Tony probably suffered financially more than anybody from our fame. When we moved to Peckham he had started his own property business, using our home phone number. The girls got hold of the number and the phone rang every ten seconds, completely wiping out his business. If we went ex-directory nobody looking for Tony's business would be able to find us, if we took the phone off the hook for peace his contacts could not get through. Not surprisingly, the business failed.

Tony, being Tony, picked himself up, dusted himself down and started all over again. He phoned a friend, our neighbour when we lived in Camberley, who had a chain of travel agents, and asked for a job. The man said he didn't want to give Tony a job because it might ruin their friendship. Tony offered to work free for a week, to demonstrate how good he is at selling, and if at the end of the week our neighbour could see he had made a difference, perhaps he would employ him. He got the job. He's gone on from there to form a partnership with another friend in two travel agencies of his own.

Mum and Tony both went through health problems at this time and the constant presence of the girls and pressure from the press did not help. Mum had to go into hospital for an exploratory operation and came out to find the headline 'Bros Mum Fights Cancer' spread across the paper. She had reporters knocking at the door saying that unless she told them what was really the matter, they were going to print that she had had a mastectomy. Tony told them that was not what was wrong with her, but he insisted that Mum be allowed the privacy of not having to make public announcements about her health. At the same time, Tony's arthritis had become much worse, and he had to go into hospital for a hip replacement. As Tony was born with dislocated hips he has always been in pain.

My dad didn't have quite the same problems with our fame. At this time he was working in the CID HQ, dealing with fingerprinting and photography. As he has had a life-long interest in photography, the job suited him perfectly. He'd been through his own personal problems, because in 1986 his second marriage broke up when Margaret left him. He was devastated. He had thought it was a happy marriage, despite her refusing to be involved with his sons. When she went he was desolate. Years later he was able to say to Mum that he finally realized what he had put her through, all those years before.

He'd followed our early career with great interest. When our first single, 'I Owe You Nothing', came out, he rushed out and bought a dozen copies, and got us to autograph them for his friends and family. When the next one, 'When Will I Be Famous', went big he was very proud, but deliberately didn't boast about it at work because he felt it didn't go very well with a career as a CID officer.

'When it did become known,' he says, 'I never had one nasty remark, one jealous remark. I had a few more friends and acquaintances seeking me out to get the boys' autographs, but as it was impossible to see Luke and Matt when they were so busy, I disappointed lots of people. I went to Liverpool on a course at the height of their fame, and it wasn't until the very end of the course that the other people there realized I was their father, and then everybody was terrific about it.'

One thing our parents really suffered from in those early days of fame was an inability to make contact with us. We were surrounded by other people. So many fans, nutters and business contacts were trying to get through to us and our management, it was impossible for anyone else to get through.

In the end we had to devise a system of codewords, so that Mum could convince our security people of who she was when she phoned.

We were also just so busy and so tired that I'm afraid we forgot to keep in touch as much as we should have done. We were travelling the world, never getting enough sleep, never sure what day of the week it was. But Dad did get really hacked off after not hearing from me or Matt for nine months: when I rang him he tore me off about it and I could see from his point of view that we shouldn't have let things slide like that. I never let it happen again. It was ironic to me that he should be so upset, when I thought back to the misery he brought into our childhood by not contacting us.

Dad finally understood what our lives were like when he came backstage at one of our concerts.

'Until I saw them working, saw how much was going on around them, how little time they had to themselves from waking up until falling asleep, I had no idea what it was like,' he says. 'I didn't like it when they weren't in touch, I didn't like it for my sake and theirs when people asked me about them and I had to say I had no contact with them. But I understood why, when I saw what their working life was like. They were never off duty, never able to relax, never able to get away from what they had become.'

For the first eighteen months of our fame, we enjoyed it. There were problems, but the good things outweighed the bad. You are on a real high, happy and excited much of the time. It is great to feel successful at anything in life, you get a tremendous buzz from it. You also feel as we did – wrongly, as it turned out – that you are making lots and lots of money. I don't believe that wealth is the most important thing in life, but it sure helps. As someone once said, being rich may not make you happy, but being poor is guaranteed to make you unhappy! And we also enjoyed a lot of genuine companionship and good fun together on the road.

Being famous also gets you out of a lot of chores – I always tell people if they never want to go to Tesco's again, all they've got to do is release a hit record!

But you can forget any idea of a normal private, family life, as Shirley and I soon found out.

CHAPTER NINE

It's a Jungle Out There

Shirley and I started living together before I was famous. But as soon as Bros hit the big time, there was a lot of sniping from fans, music industry people and the press that she was only with me for my money. We were always able to laugh about it: Shirley says that if I was fat, ugly and old, maybe people could be forgiven for thinking that. But I'm young, I look OK, and anyone who has been around us for five minutes knows that we love each other and care about each other. Why shouldn't she be with me?

Shirley was my saviour during the mad years of fans and fame. She has been around the music business for years, she knows the way it works and the way people in the industry work. She was wise to all the bullshit and the games that go on, and she slammed reality down my throat from day one. If I was behaving like a prat or an arsehole, she told me. She never let me become an airhead, and if I ever tried to pull the wool over her eyes she would say 'Don't take the piss, Lukie', and bring me back to earth. I like to think I would have been strong enough to have survived the last few years without becoming a basket case anyway, but having Shirley with me made it so much easier.

Matt became the most glamorous member of the group, mainly because he was the lead singer but also because he didn't have a girlfriend and was therefore obviously 'available' for the fantasies of the fans. But I felt very sorry for him: his was a very lonely life, with nobody to turn to or confide in. He also never knew why any girl he dated went out with him: was it because she really liked him, or was it because he was Matt Goss of Bros?

Occasionally I envied him: when we were away on tour he didn't have to rush away from the dinner table to phone home, and he could disappear off to a nightclub to let his hair down. But Shirley and I had a pact that we would always ring each other, every evening, wherever we were in the world. Because she goes away on tour, too, and because she is surrounded by other musicians and works in a mainly male world, I have had to learn to cope with my insecurity and jealousy. She felt the same about me so we decided that, whatever else, we would always put each others' minds at rest with a call.

That one little phone call can make the difference between pacing the floor with butterflies the size of pterodactyls in your stomach, and settling down for a good night's sleep knowing that your lady loves you. Sometimes it would be a drag: I'd be having a nice meal, beginning to unwind after a gig, and I'd have to leave the table to ring Shirley. But it was always worth it and it is a rule we both live by: a relationship has got to be worth a few missed dinners. We often ended up waking each other at stupid hours of the morning because of the time differences round the world, but I didn't mind missing sleep for Shirley, ever.

Life together was not easy, and for the first couple of years we rowed a lot. In the first year of living together, I was actually at home with Shirley for eight weeks, and that's if you count every evening as a full day. It created tremendous pressure, although it also meant that the fire and the passion was kept well and truly alive. Absence certainly does make the heart grow fonder. When we saw each other after a few weeks apart we would rip each other's clothes off two seconds after getting inside our own front door.

Our first home together was a flat in Regents Park, which we rented for £50 a week from a friend of Shirley's. It was a beautiful three-bedroom flat that would have fetched £400 a week commercially, but we were allowed to use it as a favour. The problem was that it was only semi-furnished, if that: there was a sofa and a chair, and we had a TV sitting on top of a pile of telephone directories. We slept on the floor, like squatters, for the whole six months.

There was a washing machine, and Shirley used it to do our laundry. She's not very good at washing, and all my white tee shirts came out a pale grey colour, and jumpers would be shrunk small enough to fit Carli. I'd go to a recording session and there would be Matt and Craig in brilliant white tee shirts that my mum had washed for them, and mine would look even worse by comparison. But it was lovely of Shirley to do it for me: I didn't demand it or expect it. It was just such a sweet gesture. I'd wake up and she'd be getting my breakfast and ironing my jeans and I'd love her so much that it was like a sharp pain that took my breath away. It was a side of her that nobody else ever saw. She was predictably referred to in newspapers as a 'dusky beauty', which always made us laugh because the journalists obviously never had the imagination to find any other words, but she was a sophisticated, professional lady: nobody would ever imagine her doing the washing.

Since those days, she hasn't. She admitted she was no good at it, and we've used a laundry ever since. As for ironing, whoever needs something to wear irons it, although I must admit I sometimes get round her and persuade her to do it for me.

Life at the flat in Regents Park was a complete contrast

to the rest of my existence, being whisked about in limos between five-star hotels. I'd give Shirley a big hug before climbing into a big black Daimler, leaving her in that empty flat, but I'd keep a picture of her and the flat at the back of my mind all the time: they were reality, the rest was bullshit.

Matt and Craig were still living at Mum's house, and I think I toughened up faster than they did because I was away. I look back now and I think I loved Shirley as much then as I do now, though perhaps that is only because I love her so much now that I remember it that way. But there was definitely a specialness about our first home together, and I know that I loved her very, very much.

Carli did not live with us at first. Our lives were very unsettled, and Shirley felt that Carli was better off at her own home, in familiar surroundings, and with Jim, who had looked after her from birth. Jim had taken the split badly, and pleaded to be allowed to have Carli with him. Shirley later regretted this decision: she now thinks she should have had Carli with her all the time, however difficult it was. But I wasn't mature enough to share Shirley from the very beginning. I needed some time on my own with her. Carli used to come to stay at weekends, and I would find myself feeling very tense about that, especially if that was the only time I was around, too. I wanted to have the freedom to make love whenever and wherever we wanted to, to go out for meals together and not just to hamburger joints with a kid in tow, to stay up as late as we wanted without having to worry about getting up in the morning with the child.

I know it sounds very selfish, but I think it was also very sensible. Natural parents have nine months of pregnancy to adjust to the idea of having a child around: I could not go from being an 18-year-old bachelor into fatherhood without a falter in my step. Today, Carli lives with us and it works out well; I think if she had lived with us from the very beginning it would not be so happy now. But I do realize what a tremendous sacrifice Shirley made for the first two years that we were together, and what an impact that has made on her whole life.

It wasn't a great shock to Carli, because Shirley's life always involved being away from home for long stretches. She'd been on tour with Elton John for eighteen months and only seen Carli when she managed to get home, or when Jim brought her to visit. So it was not as though she was going from being a stay-at-home mum to not being there at all.

After six months in Regents Park we had to move, because we were only given a short-term let. We found another flat in Wimbledon, again belonging to a friend of Shirley's. This time it was fully furnished – oh, the bliss of a mattress under us at night – and very comfortable. But I was famous by then, and it did not take the fans long to track us down, to the annoyance of the neighbours. It never took the fans long to find us: the *Sun* had an irritating habit of printing every address Shirley and I moved to. Irritating is an understatement: each time I heard that they had done it was such a disappointment, because I knew that life would become a nightmare once again.

It was a basement flat. I remember one morning when we were enjoying a few loving moments in bed together and Shirley suddenly said, 'Luke, Luke – look at the window.' I turned and saw eight eager faces peering in at us. Somehow the fans had got across the gardens and round to the back of the flat. See what I mean about no privacy?

They could also hear from the front of the flat whenever Shirley and I had a row, which we did quite a lot at this stage of our relationship. Usually they would side with her

– when she went out the girls would say things like 'Luke had no right to speak to you like that last night.' There I was, trying to find my way through a new and very precious relationship, and I had two hundred Claire Rayners on my doorstep! The woman in the flat upstairs also heard us, and she'd stop Shirley on the stairs and ask if we had managed to sort everything out.

Looking back, both Shirley and I think it was a miracle that our love survived this part of our lives together.

'It was not a nice period, we were under so much pressure, and Luke was working so hard,' says Shirley. 'I never saw him, then when I did he would expect full-time attention even if it was the weekend and I was seeing Carli. They did not get on well at that time: Carli is also very demanding. It was complete murder, I'd dread it. They'd both compete for my attention, and I felt dragged between them. Luke was also under pressure from those around him to get rid of me, which I did not know about until later.

'I had my own record coming out and my record company was insisting that I did lots of interviews to promote it. But every time I spoke to a journalist all they ever wanted to know about was Luke – and what I didn't tell them, they made up. It was claimed in one paper that Luke was shocked and horrified when he found out about Carli: in fact, I told him about her the first day we met. Another interview made out he was my toyboy and I had taught him all about sex: that's ridiculous. It was lucky that he had already found out how some unscrupulous journalists operate, otherwise it could have caused great problems if he believed I had really said those things. We laughed about them, but you do feel tarnished by them.'

The fans forced us out of Wimbledon, and for a while we lived like gypsies, never putting down any real roots.

We found a flat in Maida Vale, but only stayed one night. The place was crawling with cockroaches. I rang the landlord next day and said, 'I'm paying £500 a week to live here – how much are they paying?' We had another flat for a short time in St John's Wood, and again the fans found out where we were. The neighbours were not sympathetic: they were rather well set-up middle-class people who resented a young working-class guy having the money to move into their posh area, and they made a lot of fuss about the girls being there. Time and time again both Matt and I encountered the same problems with neighbours: we could put ourselves in their shoes, and we genuinely felt very sorry for them. But they never put themselves in our shoes, they blamed us personally for what went on. It became a regular refrain of mine: I didn't send out personal invitations to the girls to be there, I didn't want them there, and I didn't encourage them. Yes, I spoke to them: we soon learned that it was better for us and our neighbours for me to give them a smile and a few words than to ignore them, because they were quieter and better behaved when they were happy, and they were also more likely to go away, although that was a forlorn hope.

It was hell for us. The phone rang constantly and if we put the answering machine on the whole tape would be full of messages from girls, sixty or seventy of them. Some of them would be creepy and horrible, usually threatening what they would like to do to Shirley. Family and friends would try to call and constantly get the engaged tone. We changed our phone numbers all the time, and yet within two days the girls would have it. Shirley's sisters said if they had a pound for every new number we had, they'd be rich.

In desperation we lived at the Mayfair Hotel for a time, which was a crazy extravagance, but we needed to get away from the mob that pursued us everywhere. It was costing £250 a night and we were eating at Langan's brasserie, just around the corner, three or four times a week. Langan's is very popular with show business people, and I know to most people it must seem a bit posey to go there. But the reason it's popular is that they look after you well, keep the photographers at bay, don't fawn over you but don't set out to be deliberately rude and offhand, either, which some restaurants do. The kind of money that was changing hands over the Bros phenomenon made me feel I could easily afford to be extravagant.

It was at this time that our management decided we should all buy a flat together, me, Matt and Craig. It was a crazy idea: who would imagine that three guys who worked together all day wanted to live together? Or that three healthy red-blooded guys would want to settle down in a bachelor pad together? We all got on well and we'd shared a room before, but that was only temporary and convenient. It was a fantasy of the management's: they could project to the fans a picture of us, like three college students, all rooming together happily, sharing japes and jokes. They also wanted us all in one place: again, they were viewing us as a market commodity, not as three individual human beings. I never moved in, but I did become a one-third owner of a flat in Maida Vale found for us by our management company.

The flat was in Clive Court, a handsome mansion block, and it was a beautiful flat, very light, white and airy looking. There were three bedrooms, three bathrooms, a large living room and a kitchen. Not only did the management find it, but they also decided to do it up for us; as well as 3 Style Ltd, Tom Watkins was involved in other companies, one of which was an interior design business.

Tom told us he was going to turn the flat into a

showplace, one of the most dazzling bachelor pads ever created. We were away working at the time, so we had to leave it all in his hands. Although I figured it would not cost more than £30,000, it ended up costing us that much *each*. It was very over the top, very camp – and very, very expensive. The final bill was £91,000. There were glass shelves in the bedrooms, recessed wardrobe space that had blinds in front instead of doors, three huge sofas in the lounge and a built-in lighting system that caused nothing but problems. The whole flat was rewired for a 12-volt system, but the transformer kept blowing, which cost a fortune every time it happened. The lights, which could be moved about on tracks by remote control, were great fun when they were working, but a great pain when they weren't.

The carpet throughout the flat was handwoven, for God's sake. That's only for the mega-rich, and to be honest I don't think any of the three of us really appreciated the difference between that and machine-made carpet. As long as it was comfortable and looked good, we would have been happy.

When it was finished, it looked like a posh hotel suite for a Japanese businessman, a cross between a home and an office. I preferred it before they started on it.

Because we were touring while the work was being done, we were not often consulted and we had no day-to-day control over it. Tony and my granddad went over there one day, without the management company knowing. Tony went home and said to Mum: 'I've just seen the biggest waste of money of all time.' He's been a builder, an estate agent and a property developer in his life, and he knows a bit about the business. So does Granddad, who was a building foreman before he retired, and blunt with it. He told one of the decorators working on the flat that he wouldn't let him decorate his lavatory!

'A brand new kitchen was ripped out, simply because it was the wrong colour. And the new one was inferior to the original one in quality,' says Tony.

'I looked at that flat and every bone in my body said it was wrong for them. It was the wrong flat, in the wrong place, and with a fancy design being installed at enormous cost. Who would ever think of putting three young pop stars in a block of flats mostly occupied by affluent retired people? The boys were completely blameless: they were busy out there making the money to pay for it all. I made a lot of noise and eventually found out what the cost was running at.

'It was hard for us to get hold of the boys while they were away. But in the end I managed to get through to Craig and told him what was happening at the flat, and what it was costing: Craig spoke to the other two and they called a halt to it.'

It was while we were away on tour that I rang Shirley and told her to find a decent flat for us to live in, and she found one in Fulham where we stayed for a year It was a better place for us, because it was in a large complex with security gates, beyond which the girls could not get. The complex had a swimming pool and gym and other amenities, but we never used them.

Because it was a large complex, and I was hardly ever there, I never got to know my neighbours. So I was astonished to read a front-page headline in the *People* which said 'Exposed! Heroin Dealer in Bros House' and another headline which said 'Bros and Heroin Henry'. From that you would imagine that I actually had a heroin dealer as a lodger, whereas in fact he was just another tenant in another flat in the same block. After all we had said about being anti-drugs it was a major blow. We had given so many interviews condemning drugs, condemning pushers and condemning acid house parties where young kids were being seduced into experimenting with drugs, and from reading that headline it looked as though we were the biggest hypocrites out. Our lawyers said we should sue, so we did – and we won a huge apology and damages.

We had never challenged a newspaper before, not for all the hundreds of misquotes and inaccuracies and made-up stories about us, even when they had been personally very wounding. But this time we felt we had a duty to get the record straight: if thousands of very young fans hang on every word you say and try to emulate your lifestyle, right down to dressing the way you do, you can't run any risk that they think you are into drugs.

While we were living at Fulham Shirley and I had a huge row and split up. It is possible in the pop business to get eaten up by your own fame and start playing by the rules other people think you should – as stars – follow. You are expected to go to the right places, be seen with the right people. I remember going to the *Batman* premiere and everyone was jostling in a not-too-obvious way to have their photographs taken, because if the photographers weren't after you, you were nobody.

Celebrities are funny creatures, they greet other stars like long-lost friends, even though they have never met them before. There is a shallow camaraderie of the famous, but there is no genuine support for each other. There are lots of snobberies and divisions within the music industry, and lots of cutthroat rivalries. I was part of it. Nothing that I was living amongst did anything to make me a better person: stardom doesn't show you how to behave, what to value, what to aim for. You live in Ostentation City. There is no freedom to move into any other world, because you are hemmed in by the fans, the management people who plan every minute of your day for you, and your own sheer exhaustion. You start to get a very two-dimensional picture of yourself, almost as though you believe the rubbish the newspapers keeping writing about you.

The years of our fame were the years that most young people do a lot of growing up, finding their role in an adult world, establishing themselves. They do this by mixing with different people, making judgements about the sort of life they want to lead, the friends they want to have. We were denied, because of the pressure of our work and our inability to move around normally, any chance to mix with anyone other than those in the music business.

My relationship with Shirley almost became a casualty of all this. I started to take her for granted. I ignored the fact that she had the same headaches and the same craziness caused by the fans as I did. She sums it up by saying, 'I wasn't getting enough respect. Luke was surrounded by people who told him all day long how wonderful he was, and he stopped hearing my voice trying to bring him down to earth.'

There are plenty of things for any ordinary couple to row about: we had all those plus a whole bag more. The first five years is the most testing for any relationship, and it's always a miracle when a couple get through it. If you think of all the normal problems and multiply them by four, that's what we had. Everything we did was under a spotlight, every suspicion we ever had about each other was stoked up by malicious press stories. I know it comes with the territory, but it was still bloody hard to get through.

We split up when I flew to Australia for the world tour.

I was going to be away for three months, which would be the longest we had ever been apart, because when I was touring Britain or Europe Shirl would fly to join me every couple of weeks. We had a massive row the day before I left. I can't even remember what it was about, but Shirley says it was because I would not even discuss marrying her, which she wanted. Shirley told me she would not be there when I got back.

We parted from each other without speaking, but I thought about her all the time on the twenty-seven-hour flight. I stuck it out for two weeks, and then I called her at her mum's house. She was being really tough and didn't want to know me.

For about a month I didn't call her again, although I was longing to. Then one day I did, and although she didn't say everything was all right, she agreed to meet me at the flat when we got home.

I went to a lot of trouble to impress her. I didn't go straight there from the airport, I went to Matt's flat to get changed. I put on a new Comme des Garçons suit, and I turned up driving my new car, a Toyota MR2. I went to the door with a bunch of flowers in my hand for her. She'd never seen me in a suit, and I could tell she was impressed. She looked gorgeous. I took her to the car and we went to the San Lorenzo, Princess Diana's favourite restaurant, for a meal. In the car I handed Shirley a green box and said, kissing her lightly, that it was something I'd bought for her. When she opened it she saw a beautiful Rolex watch with diamonds, which had cost me £3,000. The look on her face was worth every penny.

We sat in the restaurant, drinking wine and gazing at each other across the table. I hope Princess Diana gets better service at the San Lorenzo than I do: every time I have been there I have had to wait for ages for my food. That evening we had to wait for thirty minutes, pretending to be cool and civilized. At last the meal came, but after a couple of mouthfuls I said to Shirley, 'Do you want to stay here?' She shook her head. I paid the bill, we drove home and fell on each other passionately. We did what we had both wanted to do from the moment she opened the door of the flat to me. It was wonderful, and I swore that we would never let this business come between us again. She knew then that I loved her, I showed her that I did that evening, and I promised never to take her for granted again. We ended up having takeaway hamburgers – much, much later.

Shirley has always been a fiery lady, with a lot of temper to go with her passion. If she thinks I'm getting out of line she wallops me: she just cranks her fist back and drives it into me. In the early days she did that a few times, but she never hurt me enough for me to retaliate: I'd just take hold of her hands and she'd get even more furious.

She wanted to get married from the beginning, but I wasn't keen. Now I'm older I would like to marry her, but I want to be able to do it in style. In those days I was very worried that marriage would change the relationship we had, and I didn't want that.

Shirley says, 'I think I wanted Luke to marry me as a gesture to the world that I was important to him. After all, I was getting lots of stick from the fans, the press, his management. I wanted to metaphorically put two fingers up to them all. And also, because I'm older than Luke and had been in a long relationship before, it was important to me. But I realized when he was away and didn't ring me how silly all that was. It was not worth being apart and unhappy, when we could be together and happy, even if we were not married.'

We've always been straight with each other, which is essential. If Shirley disagrees with something I say in public she won't put me down by saying so there and then, but she'll always let me know what she feels later on.

You know what Paul Newman said, 'Why settle for a

burger when you've got steak at home?' That's how I feel
about her, and even at this time when we were rowing and
things were bad between us, I knew that I was certainly
never going to find anyone better. I'm always grateful that
I had girlfriends from an early age: it meant that even
though I was very young, I knew the grass was definitely
not greener on the other side of the fence.

Buying things for Shirley was always a lovely way of
expressing my feelings. I had money, but I think even if I
hadn't I would have loved finding little things that were
special for her. At one time she had about twenty-five
expensive bottles of perfume in the bathroom, which I
brought back from trips. I discovered early on that you
really can say it with flowers: girls are suckers for them.
One day when Shirl and I had had a row I found a card
with a picture of a little man crawling out of a kennel, and
it said 'I'm in the Doghouse'. I sent it to her with a large
bunch of flowers and a message that simply said 'I love you,
darling'. She rang me straightaway, and all was forgiven.

The best thing I ever bought for her was a car, a Golf
convertible. She was doing a video shoot and I turned up
outside with the car, with a huge pink ribbon round it, a
bottle of champagne and two glasses. She couldn't believe
her eyes. It was a great buzz for me. It was a lovely day,
so we cruised around with the top down and I kept thinking, 'Wow, I just bought my missus a car.' Cars have always
been my one true extravagance – but I got a greater thrill
out of buying one for Shirley than any of my own. Had I
known then the true state of my finances, I'd have settled
for something less, but I had no idea I couldn't afford it.

It dawned on me one day that what I really wanted for
me and Shirley was a proper home of our own, somewhere
we could really be private and secure. I wanted a house.
By this time Craig had left the band, and Matt was living

on his own in the flat in Maida Vale, so he bought out my share for £50,000.

This gave me the deposit to put down on a house. With a mortgage of £200,000, I had a quarter of a million pounds to spend. It sounds like a lot of money, but this was 1989, when house prices were ridiculously high, and that kind of money certainly didn't buy anything very swanky. We found a bungalow in Frimley, Surrey. Because my accountant advised it, we took the mortgage out over ten years, instead of the usual twenty-five. This meant our repayments were £3,000 a month. I didn't mind, I wanted to get the debt cleared off as soon as possible.

We had to have nine-foot high electronic gates and video security cameras installed. Again, our neighbours did not like the constant presence of the girls, with their noise and litter, but there was not a lot I could do to help. It was the usual scenario: middle-aged, middle-class people who had lived in the area for thirty years feeling resentful about an upstart like me. Dad talked to the local police, and I always had a very good relationship with our beat bobby, but he could not be based there permanently to move the girls on, day and night.

The police have a difficult job controlling fans. It is very hard to deal with a hundred young girls: harder than a tough crowd of soccer hooligans in a way, because it has to be done so delicately. Although I did not have the problem in Frimley, in London both Matt and I were not always treated well by the police themselves. Sometimes they seemed, like the neighbours, to blame us personally for the girls, and on a couple of occasions Matt was actually manhandled by police outside his flat, and they were abusive to him. In the end it was Dad, himself a very experienced policeman, who said to us: 'You are no less a citizen than your neighbours who are complaining about you. You have no more power than the police themselves to get rid of the girls, and you cannot be held responsible for their conduct, nor can the police treat you with less respect or attention to your needs than they treat any citizen.'

He was angry and said if Matt was abused again he would arrest the police officer who did it. More diplomatically, he set up a meeting with the residents in Matt's block. The Chief Superintendent from the local police station attended, Dad took a day off work to be there as our representative, and Tom Watkins was supposed to send somebody from our management company. The Chief Superintendent, presumably busy enough with other things needing his attention, managed to be there, with a secretary to take notes. Dad lost a day's pay to be there. The residents were there. The management company were not: half an hour before the meeting they sent a message that they had nobody free to attend. It may only be a small thing, but it is an example of how the company were simply not interested in us as people. Matt's relationship with his neighbours and the local police was not going to make any money for them, so they did not bother to attend.

I loved doing up the bungalow. It had four bedrooms, but we converted one into a dining room, and I did the interior design myself. I hate cluttered interiors and I love modern furniture. I had sunken lights fitted, with blue stained-glass filters over them, and wall lights that were carefully moulded into the walls. There was an electric blue carpet throughout, and the furniture was black and chrome, with a black leather Giorgio Armani suite. I had a pool table, and a big stone-built barbecue at the back with a roof over it. We loved entertaining friends and family at weekends. It was my first proper home, and I was very excited about it.

Shirley and I went on a £58,000 spending spree to get all the furniture for it, but we were literally starting from scratch: we needed everything from beds right down to knives and forks. We enjoyed it, but we didn't always agree. I put a deposit down on a green suede bed, which at the time I thought was wonderful. Shirley took one look and said that if I wanted to sleep in that, I would be sleeping on my own, and we cancelled it, thank God. I don't know what came over me – it was horrible.

My excitement about the house was smashed to nothing the day before we moved in by seeing the inside of my new home splashed all over a Sunday newspaper. The pictures showed the place before any work had been done on it, with an awful brown bathroom and a naff serving-hatch and tacky wallpaper. But it was still my new home and I felt very intruded upon, as though there would never be any little bit of privacy for me and Shirley. I had never allowed a journalist or photographer inside any of the places we lived because I always wanted a secret life, away from all the publicity, so it was horrible seeing my first proper home exposed to the world.

In seven days after we moved in we blitzed the place, there were about ten workmen there every day. Shirley's brother Keith is an electrician, and he had a team of six men there from eight in the morning until ten at night. There was another team doing the decorating. I was going away on tour, so I was a slave-driver: I really wanted to see it all finished and looking lovely before I left.

On the day we moved in I got stuck in with them. Scott Davidson, a keyboards player who was my great friend at the time, and I actually painted all the radiators black ourselves. What we didn't know was that while we were rubbing one of them down, out in the garden, me wearing a very fetching and trendy pair of overalls, a photographer was hiding somewhere over the back fence with a zoom lens on his camera, taking pictures.

We lived at the bungalow for two and a half years, and I loved the place. During this time Carli came to live with us permanently. She had come to us before, but hadn't liked her new school and moved back to Jim. But then she came to us for good. Shirley knew that she had reached the stage where she really needed a mother. She wanted her hair doing nicely, her toenails painting, all sorts of things that a dad on his own can't cope with.

At first, I didn't feel like her stepfather – and I've never, ever tried to take the place of her father. Jim will always be 'Dad' and I will always be 'Luke' to her. As a stepchild myself I knew the dangers. You've got to take it easy, take it slowly, gradually build up a relationship. One of the important things is to have some authority: Shirley has always appreciated that. It's a crappy feeling not being in charge in your own home – like owning a power cruiser and sitting in the cockpit, but not being allowed to drive it.

There are times, especially with a young child, when you need absolute authority. You can't argue about it. You don't say 'Excuse me, I think you're going to burn your hand' to a child playing with fire. You yell 'Don't touch that!' But it only works if the child is used to you having authority and will obey you. Shirley has always been very good, much better than my mother was with Tony, about allowing me authority, but she's not perfect. It is hard for Shirley or any mother to give a man power over their child, but it's the key thing in building a good relationship. If you work too hard, if the kid knows you want to be their friend so much that they can get away with anything, then you compromise your position, you accommodate them to the point where you turn yourself into a punch bag for them. The rules are very delicate: you can't be overly strict, but you can't buy a stepchild either. It's a mixture of authority, friendship and eventually, in its own time, love.

Then you get the rewards. Occasionally Carli says to me 'Will you take me to bed?' which is what Shirley usually does for her. Then you know that you are getting there. She tells me she loves me sometimes, and it is spontaneous and nice. She always pretends she hates my cooking, but occasionally without thinking about it she will say 'That was lovely.'

As a step-parent you know you will always be second best. Everything her dad buys her is wonderful: I just support her, but she'll never give me credit for that. You have to be mature and accept things without saying anything, you have to swallow it. These were hard lessons for me to learn because I was only twenty-one when Carli moved in, but I've surprised myself.

Then again, I'd probably done more and seen more in my first twenty-one years than most people do in fifty, and I've had to do my growing up very quickly.

Chapter Ten

Sister

She was eighteen. Pretty. Very clever – she had passed ten O levels and three A levels. She had everything ahead of her, the world at her feet. She was a happy girl, a good mate, great fun to be with. She was popular with her schoolfriends and she was very generous, always fixing up stunts to raise money for charity.

And then she was dead. It was as sudden, as brutal and as unbelievable as that. It was Good Friday 1988, but there was nothing good about the day for my family. A drunken driver killed my sister Carolyn and her friend Emma as they drove home in Carolyn's car. The other driver died too, and in some ways I can only feel relieved, because if he had lived I don't know how I would have coped. I would have wanted to kill him every single day of my life, because there is not a day that goes by that I don't, however fleetingly, think about the destruction he wrought.

Her death was officially recorded at the inquest as 'accidental' because there were no witnesses to the crash. But the coroner said that, although he could not technically record a verdict of unlawful killing, he felt that Cas and Emma had been killed. Cas was a part of my life from the moment that her dad, Tony, moved in with my mum. There may have been no blood relationship between Matt and me and her and her brother Adam, but we were as close as many natural brothers and sisters. We played together, squabbled together, teased each other and were all very proud of each other. We loved each other. Cas was planning to go to university, but first she was going to Israel to work on a kibbutz for a few months. She wanted to travel, to see the world, experience new things.

We were at the height of our fame. Our single, 'Drop the Boy', was number two in the charts and our lives were crazily busy. My main regret now is that we did not have time to see as much of Cas in the six months before her death as we always had done: we didn't see much of any of our family in those mad days. But Cas was finding it hard to come to terms with Brosmania, she didn't like being labelled 'Bros sister', she was swamped by our success. To her, we were never big stars, just her brothers. She would hoot with laughter at the idea of us being sex symbols.

I'm sad that we didn't have time to show her the good parts of life with fame, to treat her and spoil her. But most of all I am sad for Tony and his ex-wife Pauline. She was their daughter, she was on the verge of becoming a woman. By now she would have her degree, have a career and, who knows, might even have settled down and started her own family. Tony and Pauline have been deprived of all that. I feel the loss of Cas like a cold weight inside me and tears well up into my eyes every time I think of her. It must be a hundred times worse for them. Tony has never really come to grips with it, and I don't suppose he ever will.

We did not hear about Cas's death until the day after it happened. Our personal manager Mark Evans, who was with us in Manchester when it happened, had a phone call late at night telling him about it. He knew that we could not get home much faster than the flight we were booked on the next day, so he decided not to tell us that night. The next day we both noticed that he was very subdued, but it was not until we got to the airport that he told us that instead of going to our own homes, we had to go straight to Mum's and Tony's. He felt it was not his place to break the news to us. I immediately knew that something very serious had happened, somebody had died. All sorts of terrible possibilities ranged through my mind: I never for one moment thought of Cas.

When we arrived at Mum's house after what seemed like an impossibly long journey from the airport, with Matt and I not daring to speak or even look at each other, there were the usual crowds of girls outside, but they were less noisy than usual. Even they sensed that something was wrong. As they tried to chat to us I brushed them aside, anxious to get into the house and upset with them for being in the way.

Inside, Mum asked us both to sit down. Her eyes were red and it was clear she had been crying. She and Tony stood side by side. I couldn't bear waiting any longer, I'd been getting increasingly wound up. 'Who's dead?' I blurted out.

Tears ran down Mum's cheeks again as she said, 'Cas was killed last night.'

'What do you mean, killed?' I yelled.

Mum told me she had been in a collision with a drunk driver, and that, worse, she had not died immediately. I have never felt such an intense hatred well up in me in all my life: if that driver had been alive I would probably have ended up in prison myself, for killing him. I was hysterical with grief but also with rage that any man thought he had the right to take our sister's life for the sake of a few drinks.

I could not believe it was Cas who was dead. Somehow, however much you love them, you are half prepared for the death of an old person. You grieve for them, you miss them, and you are no less miserable: but you know, inevitably, that one day you will attend their funeral. I never expected to attend Cas's. I never expected a girl who was a year younger than me to die, and especially such a vibrant, busy, cheerful girl, while she was still a teenager.

For a few moments all I saw before my eyes was a blackness. I punched out in my anger and put my fist right through one of Mum's doors. Matt reacted exactly the same. There was little we could do to comfort Mum and Tony, there are no right words you can say to somebody at a time like that.

We left them and had to fight our way back to our car. It took two minutes to get through the throng of girls, and I resented their presence more than I ever had before or since. Cas's death made my career seem so trivial and stupid.

But it wasn't trivial and stupid to our management company, who had agreed to us appearing on *Wogan* the following evening. There was a murmured suggestion by somebody that perhaps we wouldn't want to do it, but that was never a serious option. As far as they were concerned, it was good promotion for us and we had to do it. It did not even give us one day to ourselves to mourn our sister. We were to be presented with a gold disc by Terry Wogan, so we had to look pleased and happy, even though inside we were both numb with grief. Luckily, we were so used to television and public appearances by this time that we could do it on autopilot. Mum and Tony sat in the audience: they had planned to be there, and they were determined to go through with that to give us support.

Cas's funeral was a terrible nightmare, one of the worst days of my life. We appealed to our fans to stay away: we wanted to be there, but we did not want to turn the event into a circus. Rather than that, we would have stayed away, because the last thing we wanted to do was deflect attention from Cas. The fans showed a great deal of restraint and respect: not one of them turned up at the church. I wish I could say the same for the national press. I was crying as Matt and I walked side by side out of the church, in front of our sister's coffin, into a battery of camera lenses. There were at least twenty photographers there, all laughing and chatting away to each other as if they were outside a film premiere. As soon as they spotted us they started clicking away.

My anger overcame me and I told them to fuck off. It was a spontaneous outburst of real fury towards them. We may have been Bros, we may have been famous, we may have had thousands of fans, but on that day we were two 19-year-old boys who had lost their 18-year-old sister, and we had the right to be left in privacy. I understand that my anger should really have been directed at the newspaper decision-makers, who sent those men there to take our pictures. But 'I was only obeying orders' kept the gas chambers fully staffed. It is no excuse for losing your sense of common decency and humanity. I think if I had been a photographer asked to do that job I would have refused. Those who did do it should at least have shown the courtesy not to giggle and chat outside a church where a funeral service for a young girl was being held.

I regretted my outburst bitterly the next day, but not because I had changed my feelings towards the photographers. 'Bros in Four-Letter Fury at Funeral' said the front-page splash headline of the *Sun*, with a picture of me in tears. The memories of Cas's funeral that we all have will never be taken away from us, fortunately, by that crass treatment, but none the less – and not for the first time in my life – an intensely private moment was tarnished by their intrusion. My only consolation is that I believe most

people who saw that front page will have asked themselves
why on earth the cameras had to be spying on us, and most
people will have understood exactly how I felt.

The following year we released a record called Sister,
which we dedicated to her. Matt wrote the words. It was
our own personal tribute to her, in the only way we could
make it: through music. We both cried at the recording
session. The urgency of my grief for her has gone, I now
simply feel a great sadness when I think what might have
been. I still miss her, though not as much as at first: it is
funny how for months after someone has died you catch
yourself unawares planning to tell them something, do
something with them, and then you have to remind yourself
that they are no longer there.

My anger has never gone away. I would not drink and
drive before her death, now I will not even stand by and
watch others do it. I tell them that it's not themselves they
may kill, but some innocent person. I ask them how
they would feel, living with that guilt. Whenever I read in
a newspaper or see on the television news of someone
being killed by a drunk driver, I am ready to kill again. I
think penalties should be far stiffer, and random breath-
tests should be introduced: if people are innocent, they
won't mind taking the test. And if they are guilty, send
them to jail, even though they have not caused an accident.
Because the truth is that they could, and the next victim
could be your sister.

Within two weeks of Cas's funeral, and for no reason that
I can explain, I was thumped in the face by a complete
stranger. I know it sounds bizarre, but it happened. It was
part of the unreal reality of my life at that time: on the one
hand there was the ridiculous adulation of the fans, and
on the other we seemed to inspire complete and unmerited

hatred. The hatred that was felt for Bros was on the same level that people reserve for mass murderers or traffic wardens, and I have never understood it. We hurt nobody. If they didn't like our records, they didn't have to buy them. We didn't ask the newspapers to print far-fetched stories about us, but nobody was forced to read them. I could have understood indifference. I could have understood dislike: there were people who did not like our music, and that was their valid opinion. But hatred?

Anyway, the guy who clunked me in the face certainly felt pretty heated about me. I had never seen him or his mate before in my life, and I probably wouldn't know them if I saw them again. But I don't think they'll forget the encounter in a hurry. Shirley and I were driving along in the jeep, and a couple of guys in another car clocked us, and the driver kept trying to get me into a burn-up situation. I ignored him. When we got to the traffic lights near the Royal Albert Hall he got out of his car and started yelling abuse at me, and calling Shirley some not very pleasant names. I got out and went towards him, and he whacked me in the face. Before I had time to recover he did it again, and I fell backwards on to the floor. Shirley leaped out of the car, in a helluva temper. She smacked him in the face, and as I looked up from the floor I saw him thump her, hard. That was it, I lost control. I jumped up and lammed into him so hard that I'm sure I broke his nose: it seemed to skid across his face and ended up under one eye, and there was blood everywhere. His mate then got out of their car and came towards me. They were both big guys, in their late twenties, as tall as me and much broader. Instinctively I looked round, grabbed hold of a road works sign, and swung it at him. It hit him in the face. They both staggered back to their car and I pulled Shirley back into the jeep and drove round the corner into

Hyde Park. I pulled up and sat with my head in my hands. A crowd of fans had followed and there were twenty or so of them just standing around our car.

Then a police car zoomed up. They'd had a report that I had started the fight. I said, 'What do you think, officer? Two guys, both older and bigger than me, calling me a poof and a lot worse? Get real.' So they then asked me if I wanted to prefer charges against the men, but I could not be bothered with all that hassle. As I felt I'd given as good as I got, I reckoned they'd learned a lesson. It was only when I had time to calm down that I looked closely at Shirley's face: she had the beginnings of a beaut of a black eye. By the next day it was completely swollen. What sort of headcase, over six foot tall and weighing about fourteen stone, hits a woman?

Afterwards we heard a funny sequel to the incident. The American singer Jermaine Stewart is a good friend of our family, and he'd been to visit our mum that afternoon. On his way back in a taxi he saw the fight. By the time he'd paid off the taxi we'd gone, but the bloke who started the fight was still trying to start his car. Jermaine went up to him and thumped him. 'That's for hitting Luke, you bastard,' he said. It wasn't exactly a hard punch, because Jermaine is no street fighter, more of a token gesture. But at least that thug now knows what it feels like for someone to walk up to him and thump him out of the blue. That's exactly what happened to me.

It is only one incident, but it gives a snapshot of what our lives were like. Not every attack was like that, thank God: I was physically very shaken up, and frightened by what happened. It made me realize how close Shirley and I were to being really injured, and how close I was to seriously injuring someone else, even though they deserved it. Most of the people who hated us seemed to think it was open season to spit at us, give us rude hand gestures and hurl verbal abuse.

A week after this incident I was driving through London and I saw a poster that hurt me as much as the smack in the face from that thug. It was a crude drawing of Matt, Craig and me with nooses around our necks, and underneath the caption said 'Dross. Is This the Future?' On each of our tee shirts in the picture there was a different slogan: Robot-built for Robot Ears, said one; Death of Live Music, said another; Death of Real Bands was the third. The poster was apparently the work of an underground band trying to get themselves some publicity at our expense. It was sick – and it wasn't even witty. I'm happy to say the band have never been heard of since.

It was in October 1988 that we flew out to Australia for the start of our world tour, known as the Global Push tour. It cost about a million pounds to lay on, because we travelled with forty-seven people and eight tons of equipment. The equipment alone cost £60,000 to airfreight on the first leg of the tour, to Australia. The net profit on the tour was just over £100,000, not a very big cake to be sliced between the three of us, and a lot less than the £250,000 our management took from the tour. But we were oblivious to our impending financial problems, because at this time the figures quoted to us were gross ones, and we were all pretty impressed by those.

I was excited to be going. It was a tremendous opportunity to see the world, and it was going to show us whether our appeal was wider than just Britain. We knew we sold records abroad, but would we pull in crowds to our shows? We were curious to find out.

Australia was beautiful. The work was hard: we arrived after a twenty-seven-hour flight, had forty minutes at our

hotel to freshen up and then straight into ten days of solid
work. But the Australian branch of our record company
laid on a couple of great treats for us. One night they hired
a boat for a party, and we sailed under Sydney Harbour
Bridge and past the opera house. On another occasion they
laid on an afternoon of rest by the shores of a very private
lagoon. There was a barbecue with delicious food, but
you had to swim across the lagoon to get it. We were
well-protected by bodyguards wherever we went, and all
went smoothly.

After two weeks in Australia we flew to Japan, which
was a completely different sort of experience. We had a
huge following there, and we were amused to see a double-
page spread in one of their national newspapers with a
picture strip of twelve photographs, telling fans how to
blow-dry their hair like Bros. The really trendy TV show
out there was called *The Funky Tomato*. The name was in
English, because all the programmes aimed at kids have
English – or really, American – titles. When we arrived to
do the live show there were 2,000 fans there, and all there
was to hold them back was a little white rope. The Japanese
organizer of the tour said we wouldn't need bodyguards:
Japanese fans knew how to behave themselves in a dignified way, he said. He was wrong. When we arrived this
high-pitched shriek went up, as though somebody had
stood on the cat, or a lot of cats because it was very loud,
and suddenly we were in a rerun of every encounter with
fans we had ever had. In the end we had to be rushed out
of the building through a back door.

Our Japanese fans tended to be a bit older than our
English fans, and the girls were very cute. They would get
embarrassed, put their hands over their mouths and walk
up and down on the spot. They called us Matt-o-san and
Luke-o-san. Like fans the world over they bought us gifts,

but what gifts! We'd find Comme des Garçons shirts and Gaultier jackets delivered to our hotel.

I didn't like eating raw fish, and when you are on tour you have to be quite careful about experimenting too much with food, in case you get a bad tummy. So we lived on lovely little dumplings called shwai, which we ate with soy sauce, and our usual stand-by, the Golden Arches. That's what we always called McDonald's, just to make it sound slightly more interesting. We tried one dish at our Tokyo hotel which we really loved, but unfortunately we could only eat it once: when we discovered the price we had to give it a miss. It cost £100 per portion. It was called Kobi beef, and it comes from cattle that have been fed on ale and hops, and massaged with oil by monks. I don't know if it was the booze or the massage that did it, but the taste was amazing, and it was as tender as fish. When we got the bill for the meal we decided, regretfully, that we wouldn't be having it again.

We got used to unreal bills in Japan, though. On one occasion I ordered five coffees and five orange juices for a group of us in a hotel, and the bill came to £90. The hotel we stayed in was very stiff and traditional, and the Japanese certainly deserve their reputation for Oriental inscrutability. One morning at breakfast Matt and I showed up wearing black Samurai wigs with flowing hair and long sideburns. When the band walked in they cracked up, but the waiters didn't even manage a smile.

We travelled on the famous Bullet train at 200 kilometres an hour, visited Buddhist and Shinto temples, and rang the bell that hangs at the epicentre of the Hiroshima bomb. It was a tremendous two weeks, although I must admit I felt rather like an alien. All Westerners look odd in Japan but, being so tall and so fair, we stuck out even more than most.

*

It was in Japan that Craig's problems started, and we launched into the unpleasant episode that would end with him splitting from us, and Matt and me – particularly me – being made out as baddies, when all we were trying to do was keep the band, which was his band as well as ours, in business. Craig was exhausted, purely and simply. Matt and I were bigger and stronger than he was: Craig is not small, but he is more slightly built than either of us. I always felt very protective towards Craig. Just as I viewed Matt as my younger brother, Craig was my 'little brother' too. He'd been so involved with the whole of our family for so long that we really did think of him as a brother. I really loved him, and I would have belted anyone who said anything against him. He, for his part, could always make me laugh, and that's a great releaser of tension.

By this time Craig had a girlfriend, Kim Appleby of the Mel and Kim pop duo. We all met Kim at a birthday party for Tom Watkins: she was a shy, nice girl who seemed well suited to Craig. Mel tragically died of cancer in 1990. I know that Craig was missing Kim badly, but I was also missing Shirley, and Matt didn't even have a girl at the end of a telephone line to help him through the strains of the tour. Kim gave Craig some independence, and he was breaking away more from Matt and me. The public saw Craig as the underdog, but he never was. Outside Britain he and I attracted as many fans as Matt did: in Britain Matt, the lead singer, was seen as the main attraction of Bros. We never treated Craig as anything other than an equal, but in fact it was my idea to start a band, and from our earliest days Matt and I were always more dedicated than he was. We always defended him: we once turned down an advertising contract with BMW because they only wanted Matt and me, not Craig.

We were all suffering on that tour: for twelve months

we had scarcely had any time off, and the pressure of fans on the doorstep took its toll on all of us. But after Japan we had a week back in England before flying to Germany at the beginning of December, and I had hoped that Craig would see a doctor and get his problems sorted out. In Germany he said that he was too tired to stand up on stage, and he wasn't well enough to do the interviews and other promotional work that went with the tour.

The dramatic effect of the show was ruined with Craig sitting down. We had an expensive and spectacular opening, which had to be jettisoned. As the lights went up on the stage, a pod like a spaceship was lowered with Matt standing on it, and then two arms came down, one with me and one with Craig. As we reached the stage, we all flew up into the air on harnesses, did somersaults, came back down and ran backstage to remove the harnesses. It was a stunning few minutes. We felt that by not doing it we were cheating our fans. The whole show was a high energy production, with lots of running around. We were young, fit guys, and that's what our fans wanted to see. For Craig to sit down all evening meant that we had to tone it down all the way through. It was not the same show.

I felt very strongly that Craig should sort himself out. If he was ill, he should pull out. If he wasn't ill, and was just tired – as we were – he should make an effort for the sake of the band. I hated the uncertainty of not knowing whether he was going to do the full show, or this emasculated sitting-down version. And I was irritated by all the molly-coddling of him that was going on. He was resting while Matt and I were doing all the promotional work, and he was being pushed around in a wheelchair backstage. I didn't understand it: if he was sick enough for a wheelchair I felt he should have pulled out. If it had been me I would have taken action, got the problem sorted out, and been back, fit and well, as soon as I could.

One evening he was sitting in his wheelchair and I asked him, fairly fiercely, 'What's happening tonight? Are you standing up or sitting down?' He replied that he hadn't thought about it.

'What do you mean, you haven't thought about it?' I shouted. I was angry. 'It's our show – we're on stage in twenty minutes. What do you mean?'

I was raising my voice, and he started having a go back at me. In a fury, I advanced and pushed him, telling him to get his act together. He screamed back that I could only hit him because he was in a wheelchair. It was a ludicrous thing to say. If he had been a cripple I would have been bang out of order, and I would be the first to admit it. But he was a guy of the same age as me, my mate. He was rolling over and letting this illness thing take a hold of him, instead of fighting it, and it was making me mad.

My bodyguard grabbed me from behind, which made me even more angry, and as I swung my arms I clipped Craig, but only lightly. The bodyguard hauled me away and I was struggling to get free, and Matt was trying to help me, shouting 'Leave my brother alone!' Everyone else was fussing around Craig.

I could not believe that this was what it had all come down to. I had been working myself silly, and I was being treated as Mr Bad Guy, the sort of person who hits a man in a wheelchair. Yet I believed that if he had chosen to Craig could have stood up and squared up to me, I felt he wasn't disabled. I thought he should have levelled with us about his condition – whether he was ill or whether he wanted out – and we would all have known where we stood.

There were tears running down my face when the bodyguard released me, and Matt and I ran out of the stadium.

It was a big show: there were already 10,000 fans in their seats waiting for us. We had no idea where we were or where we were going, but we ran for about a quarter of a mile, and then sat down on a grass verge. We talked it through and calmed down, and walked back, with our arms around each other. One thing we realized that night was that the bond between us was as strong as ever, and we were sharing this problem.

There was a big hoohah going on backstage at the gig: the show was due to open and Luke and Matt Goss were missing. Our bodyguards were worried: they had let us run out on a winter evening in a strange city. We were so easy to recognize, it could have been dangerous.

After all that, it was inevitable that Craig would sit down on stage, so we were only able to deliver our tame half-voltage show. We went back to the hotel without speaking to him. The following morning Matt and I were scheduled to give a long interview to a magazine journalist who had flown out from England. As usual, Craig was excused this promotional work. While we were doing the interview we saw Craig getting into the tour bus and the bus driving off, but we didn't think anything of it. The bus was often used to chauffeur people about. It was only after the journalist had gone that our tour manager came to tell us that Craig had gone home to England.

We were gobsmacked. He hadn't even said goodbye to us. I know we had argued bitterly the night before, but band members, locked for too long into each other's company, often row – and that's true of most groups, not just Bros. Craig had seen Matt and me come to blows before. And considering how much we had been covering for him, we thought he owed us the courtesy of an explanation and a goodbye. Neither Matt nor me are the sort who bear grudges: we'd have given him a hug.

We were to see Craig just once more as Bros, when he left his sickbed to come to the British Pop Industry Awards, in February 1989, where we were presented with the award for the best British newcomers, voted by Radio One listeners.

After that, the next time we saw him was across the boardroom table in Tom Watkins's office, and both he and we were flanked by lawyers. I made a desperate bid then to cut through the appalling web of misunderstanding that had been woven between us. 'Craig, what's happening? Can't we just talk?' I said.

He looked at his lawyer and his lawyer answered for him, and I knew then that the lifts we had given him on the back of our bikes eight years ago, the fun we had shared rehearsing in the summerhouse, the mad times before we were famous, the stupid costumes my mum had made for us, the agony of gigging in working men's clubs where the last thing anybody did was listen to the band, the bedroom in Peckham where we had squabbled over the beds, the excitement of watching our first hit storm up the charts – all that, and so much more – all counted for nothing.

But before that, Matt and I were landed with pulling the rest of our European tour out of the fire. We decided not to cancel it after our management company passed on a message from Craig that he wanted it to go on. Guitarist Paul Powell flew out to take Craig's place, and we were able to get the show back to its original format. We had to cancel just one performance. (In our whole career we have only pulled out of two gigs: that one, and one in Vienna where the sports hall we had been booked into turned out to be totally inadequate.)

The rest of the tour went smoothly, apart from an orchestration of press criticism at home in Britain, saying we should not have done the show without Craig. At that point he could have put out a statement saying that he wanted us to go ahead with it, but he never did. We made many attempts to talk to Craig by phone, but we were always blocked. We had no more information about what was wrong with him than the fans did. We read in the papers that he had ME (myalgic encephalomyelitis), or 'yuppie flu' as it was nicknamed. ME is a controversial illness that leads to great debilitation, often lasting for years – controversial because many doctors don't believe it actually exists as a virus, but is just the result of the inevitable stresses and strains of twentieth-century life. We read at another time that Craig was being treated for a mental illness. We did not even know, for sure, where he was being treated. We were thwarted at every turn. Mum desperately wanted to see him: after all, he had been like a third son to her. But she had no more luck than we did.

We sent an acoustic guitar and flowers to the hospital for him. When we heard that he was going to appear with us at the British Pop Industry Awards, we bought him a new jacket and sent that to him too. But he still reckoned he wasn't well enough to play with us that evening, although he seemed relaxed and happy and we all got on well. It was tough on Paul Powell, who was booed by Craig's fans wherever we appeared in Britain, and Craig didn't put out any kind of statement thanking him for what he was doing, to take the heat off him. We still thought that it was only a matter of time before Bros were back together again, all three of us.

The day after the BPI awards the press coverage was full of emotive language about Craig. He was 'brave', 'close to tears', 'sensitive' – and by implication we were everything that he was not.

At no time did Craig ever ring us or see us to tell us that he no longer wanted to be part of Bros. We read it first in the *Sun*. The next communication that we had with him after the BPI awards was served on us by his lawyers: he wanted to negotiate a large settlement for leaving Bros, and that was how we found ourselves facing him across a desk with lawyers at our sides.

Our final agreement was that we paid Craig a substantial amount, which seems extremely large indeed considering the true state of our finances, about which we were still in the dark (in fairness, so was Craig). In retrospect we have ended up saddled with debts that are a legacy of the time when Craig was in the band. He got out before the financial bubble burst.

Every penny that Matt and I paid over to Craig came out of money on which we had already paid commission to our management company. He escaped from Bros without debt, with a very healthy bank balance, and with a great deal of public support. There had been a tendency from the first moment that his illness became public for the press to cast him in the role of victim, and Craig was more than happy to go along with that. He allowed the public and the fans to run away with the completely false idea that somehow we nasty brothers had railroaded him out of the band. From that day on, the amount of aggro Matt and I had to cope with from complete strangers trebled.

We were constantly jeered at for 'paying him off', and that was the phrase the newspapers used, too. I would not mind if it really had been a pay-off, but the fact is that it was he who wanted to leave. We did not want to part with him and we did not want to part with a large sum of money. I still fail to understand how someone can *choose* to leave and then get paid for doing so, and I fail to understand how, when we were splitting because *he* wanted to, we could come out of it as the bad guys.

Yet what had we done? We waited eight months for him

to leave school to join the band. We offered to cancel the tour. We were genuinely very worried about his illness and we did our best to make contact with him. Yet not once did he speak up in our defence. Nothing ever happened between us that can have caused him to hate us: the only bust-up we ever had was the final one, when we were all so tired and tense, and that could have been patched up. Craig felt very sorry for himself, but he more than anybody should have been able to see that everything he had been through, we had been through. The workload and the pressure that had made him tired and unwell had been just as great for us.

I know nothing about Craig now. If I met him, I'd hope we could say 'Hi' and be civilized, for old times' sake. But he is a stranger to me, and I would prefer not to meet him. There is now too much water under the bridge for us to put our arms round each other and share a laugh, like we used to. It is too late. I could never understand why he cut Mum and Tony so completely out of his life. OK, they were bound to be associated with us, but on the other hand they had done so much for him that he owed them a phone call, a letter. Mum was very hurt.

We have met Kim since we split with Craig, in an airport lounge in Germany. She was polite and friendly, and said that Craig was fine. We afterwards heard a rumour that Craig had been booked to fly with her, but had changed his flight when he discovered we would be there at the same time.

I don't want to go through my life nursing a grudge, and I hope I have now got my feelings about Craig into perspective. He cost me a lot of money, a lot of frustration and a lot of pain. He isn't going to cost me a lot of bitterness.

CHAPTER ELEVEN

Shot in the Back

Like practically everybody who has had a fairly ordinary, not-very-well-off upbringing, I used to feel a bit inferior to public school types. I naïvely thought they were better educated, better brought up, had better manners and were better behaved than council house kids from comprehensives, like me.

I now know I was wrong. I've mixed with enough of them not to feel at all over-awed by their cut crystal accents and their Sloaney slang. The only difference between them and poor kids is that mummy and daddy can pay to hush up their vandalism. Their 'boisterous good spirits' would land them in court, if a cop caught them at it on a rough council estate. But behind posh hotel doors, and with a hefty donation to charity as a licence, the Hooray Henrys think they can do as they please.

Matt and I were invited to make the prize draw at the Berkeley Ball in April 1989. Tickets for the ball cost £45 each, and all the profits were going to the NSPCC, a charity that does a great job for under-privileged kids. It was over-privileged kids who needed help that night. When we got to the Savoy Hotel we faced a loud and orchestrated barracking. 'We hate Bros!' started quietly, mingled with screams from fans who were glad to see us: it gradually built up, and within seconds the yobs-with-yachts brigade were pulling the table decorations to pieces and throwing them at us. If they had been flowers it might not have hurt so much: they were oranges, and most of them still had the pieces of wire that held the decorations together sticking out of them. When they hit you in the face, they hurt. I was hit a couple of times.

Boy George was in the audience, and whilst I don't know whether he started the chanting, he was certainly not very helpful. After a few minutes Matt and I were forced off the stage. Boy George then apparently jumped up and started saying some pretty obscene things, and he too was pelted with oranges. When we left, we were determined not to be beaten by these rich idiots. The Savoy is quite close to where the firm that provided our bodyguards is based. We nipped down there, and they happened to have half a dozen giant guys sitting around doing nothing. They all piled into a car and came back to the Ball with us. We marched through the audience, who were surprisingly quiet, and did what we had been originally invited there to do: we made the charity draw.

I felt very sorry for the woman from the NSPCC who was there, and I hope that at the end of the day she got a nice fat cheque for the Society's work. Then, at least, something good will have come out of those brainless idiots – although I suspect it will have come out of mummy's and daddy's wallets, not their own.

Recording our second album, *The Time*, was a lovely six-week interlude in the summer of 1989. Yes, it was hard work, yes, it was mentally draining, and yes, I was lonely because Shirley was not able to be with me all the time. But it was a nice change from being chased and mobbed by fans all the time, or the subject of unprovoked abuse.

We made the album at Miraval, in Provence. The recording studio is in a chateau owned by the famous jazz/classics pianist, Jacques Loussier, who rents it out. It is a very beautiful place, and private – well, almost. The chateau is surrounded by 300,000 acres of land, mostly vineyards, but with a mountain thrown in for spectacular effect. Apart from the peasants working the land, the only people we saw while we were there were the people we were working with – oh, and the thirty or forty dedicated Brosettes who somehow or another tracked us down. But as the chateau was a mile up a private road, they did not bother us; we had to admire their determination though.

The chateau itself is far from luxurious: the bedrooms are spartan, like monks' cells. But we found that very refreshing, after all the time we had spent in luxury hotels. I only wished I could have afforded to take a longer break there, without the pressure of work, just leading a very simple life.

There was not a great deal to do in our spare time: we didn't have a lot of time free, anyway. But we made our own fun. We had each been given a 350cc Yamaha quad bike. We had a sponsorship deal with Yamaha, and one day one of their executives handed us a catalogue and asked us to choose a bike each, so we picked the quads. They delivered them to Miraval. We also hired three two-wheeler motorbikes, so that the other musicians there could join us, and we used to career around on these things like wild kids. It was terrific away-from-it-all fun, a great way to unwind after a day in the studio.

There was one incident I will never forget for the rest of my life. We drove all the way up the mountain on the Yamahas, carving a way through trees and bushes and undergrowth. It was worth it: the view from the top was amazing. Matt and I were breathless looking at it. And then suddenly, miles away, we saw a flash of lightning followed by a crash of thunder, and we could actually see the landscape turn grey as the rain swept across it. The storm was coming towards us, fast. It took a moment or two to hit me, and then I realized we were on top of a mountain, sitting on metal bikes, with lightning getting nearer and nearer. I yelled to Matt and we tore off down the hillside, literally racing the storm, back to the chateau. Downhill we could really make those quad bikes shift: we got back filthy, scratched to pieces from all the bushes we had driven through, and completely exhilarated.

We had a few laughs at Miraval. Nicky Graham, who was producing the album, had his girlfriend – he's now married to her – with him for the whole six weeks. He likes sunbathing naked, so whenever you went to the pool you were confronted by the sight of a starkers Nicky. It's amazing how difficult it is to hold a conversation with someone who has no clothes on: despite yourself, your eyes can't help wandering to the bits you don't normally see. At the pool you could at least avoid him, but one day we turned up in the recording studio to see him sitting there, his legs and chest bare, with a clipboard on his lap. I assumed he was wearing swimming trunks, but when he stood up I was again confronted by the sight of his 'walnut', which is what we nicknamed it. We made lots of jokes about it, wrote a few rude slogans for him to find, and on one occasion dressed the studio monitors up with cones and tape in a crude model of him and his girlfriend. He laughed: the studio manager, who lives at Miraval permanently, was less amused.

We felt sorry for the studio manager's two teenage kids. They went off to school every day, but when they got home they were stuck in the middle of nowhere, with no mates around for miles. We used to let them play about on the quad bikes, and when we came home after completing the album we left the bikes – together worth about £5,000 – there for them. The kids were delighted.

We loved excuses to be kids ourselves. We were still very young, but we'd been expected to grow up so fast that when we got a chance to let our hair down, we were in there. Making videos was work, and meant we had to put in long, tiring, often difficult days, as anyone who has ever been involved in filming will know. But on the other hand, the videos gave us some fun. I always insisted on doing all my own stunts, although the film company offered me a stand-in.

We made the 'Too Much' video in the South of France, staying at Nice in the Negresco Hotel, which costs £1,000 a night. It was super-luxury, which we could afford because Yamaha were picking up the tab: we were filming an advert for them at the same time. I was disappointed to find that even at that kind of price they never got my breakfast order right! The 'Too Much' video told a little story about me being jealous of Matt and a 'girlfriend', and at one point he and the actress playing the part of the girlfriend had to run along a beach and kiss. I persuaded the director to make them do it five or six times more than they needed for the filming, because Matt was enjoying a good snog with this very pretty girl!

The stunts involved me driving a Porsche at speed along the winding coastal roads near Nice – I wasn't about to let any stunt driver do that! We also had to climb a rock face, and be whizzed away in a helicopter with the doors open. The helicopter pilot was an American stunt flyer called Joe Wolf, who did 1,000 hours piloting a helicopter in Vietnam, so I had plenty of faith in him.

The video I most enjoyed doing was for the second release of 'IOU Nothing', when I had to drive the Suzuki jeep pretty fast and skid it round on a tarmac road. Again, the film company offered a stunt driver, and I said no. After they'd seen me doing it, one of them suggested that if ever I wanted a new career, I could become a stunt driver myself! I really fancied the idea.

There was very little time in our schedule for holidays, and whatever free time I had I wanted to spend at home with Shirley. The only holiday we ever had was three days in Hawaii, and that wasn't a lot of fun. We booked a holiday in Maui, one of the Hawaiian islands, at the end of the Push British tour, and I was dreaming about it for weeks: we were tired, we needed a complete break, and we really thought we were going to spend a couple of weeks in paradise. What we didn't realize until we got there was that paradise is full of burger bars and fat American tourists wearing loud Bermudas.

The apartment we had booked, which we thought would have its own pool, turned out to be part of a complex of three hundred flats with three pools between them. There was so little of the original style of the island left: I was very disappointed. I was also homesick after the tour, so Craig, Shirley and I booked ourselves on to the first available flight home. Matt managed to switch to a better apartment and stayed on. The best fun we had was flying home with Cher, who was a great companion on the plane.

As time went on, although I wanted a holiday, I came to dislike the idea of travelling. Not only because of my fear of flying, but because some of the hatred that we experienced from guys in the street seemed to be institutionalized in the customs halls of the airports we passed through. Customs officials seemed to enjoy giving us a bad time, and I've lost count of the times we were strip-searched. I know rock bands are notorious drug users, but we had always stood up so tall against drugs that they must have guessed we wouldn't be carrying anything. Even if we were the world's biggest hypocrites and secretly taking every illegal substance we could get our hands on, would we be daft enough to walk back through customs with it on us?

We ended up in the cells once, when we came back into the country from Japan, where we had been doing some promotion. Sony, our Japanese record company (they subsequently took over CBS), gave us lots of presents just as we were leaving Japan, cameras and videos. We didn't declare them when we got back to England because we didn't know that you have to declare gifts. We went through the green channel and went home: we usually left our luggage to be collected by members of our staff, because there would always be fans waiting for us and we simply wanted to get through the scrum and get away. Not long after I arrived home I was ordered back to the airport. Matt and Craig were there, and we were all put in separate cells for four hours while everything was sorted out. I kept telling the customs officials that I didn't want the cameras: they could take them. But in the end we had to pay £1000 in duty and a £3000 fine. To avoid the same problem again, when we came back from our next tour the tour manager spent the whole night before we arrived home cataloguing everything we had bought while we were away. He did it all on a small computer, and he worked out the duty that there was to pay. We presented the customs people with a complete inventory, thinking they would appreciate it. No such luck: they insisted on searching all fifty bags of luggage, while we stood around waiting. The last thing they were going to do was hurry. Some people don't half like to make the most of their bit of power.

However much success we had – and if success can be measured in hit records and screaming fans, we had it –

we never had the one thing we craved and deserved: credibility. We were easily and readily dismissed as a manufactured and hyped group, as if we had been plucked off the street by Tom Watkins and were nothing more than a figment of his fevered imagination.

What price all those years drumming away in my bedroom till my fingers bled? I might as well not have bothered: the last thing anybody thought was that I actually played the drums.

Way back at the very beginning of our success as Bros, just three months after 'When Will I Be Famous?' was released, a newspaper article appeared that sowed the seeds of destruction for the band, although at the time nobody realized it. It was not an interview with me, Matt or Craig, or with anyone working for us. It was, astonishingly, with Shirley's sister, Dee Lewis. Dee sang backing vocals on the song, which was recorded eight months earlier, at the time that I met Shirley.

It was an interview which appeared on the 31 January 1988 in the *News of the World*. 'Pop Bros "A Bunch of Fakes"' said the headline. The story read:

> New pop heart-throbs Bros were last night branded a band of cheats. Session singer Dee Lewis claims the three lads mimed to HER vocals on TV's *Top of the Pops*. Dishy Dee, who has also backed Rick Astley and Wet Wet Wet, fumed: 'I sang the words "When Will I Be Famous?" on their single. I couldn't believe it when I saw the boys miming to my very female voice.'

The story went on to say that we had ditched Dee after recording our album, and that there was a rift between her and Shirley.

Nobody knows more than I do about the way newspapers

can take one small remark and build it up into something big, and even sometimes invent the remark in the first place. Dee was trying to promote her own record at the time, so she was happy to give interviews for publicity. But if she said the words attributed to her in that article, she was the one who declared it open season for knocking Bros. From that one suggestion, that we didn't perform on our own records, sprang the idea that we were a totally manufactured group, created and manipulated by our management, with session singers and musicians supplying the sound.

It became fashionable to claim that we were just pretty faces put together as a package. I'm not blaming Dee for all of that, but the fact that a singer, a fellow musician, had come forward and endorsed that theory gave it enormous credibility. People who didn't know us and had never seen us perform live passed judgement on us. I heard one story that went round that I was physically too small to even play the drums! For some reason, most people expect Matt and me to be short: it's a trick that television and photographs play. But in actual fact we're well above average height; and I'd have had to be a midget not to have been able to play drums.

Once stories start, it's almost impossible to stop them. Dee Lewis was a backing singer, she got paid for a job: there was never any question of ditching her because that's not the way backing vocalists are employed. Sure, she sings on 'When Will I Be Famous?', with Matt singing falsetto under her. Look at the words of the song and you'll realize it is meant to be a girl asking the question anyway. And yes, we mimed on *Top of the Pops*: at that time every band to appear on the programme had to mime to their own records, because there was no facility to allow them to play live. But no, we were not afraid of appearing live: at the

British Pop Industry Awards, the one where Craig put in a short 'reunion' appearance with us, we were the *only* group to play live.

Dee's interview was the first bit of bad publicity we ever had, and it was very, very damaging. If someone comes along and tells huge lies about you – like saying I lived in the same house as a heroin dealer – you can sue and you can get a big public apology to put the record straight. But if they just snipe at you by innuendo, there's nothing you can do. Elton John and George Michael use backing vocalists – have they ever been branded cheats?

If we had had a few hits behind us when she said it, we probably could have weathered it. We would have had time to establish our credibility. But on our first hit, and with the added disadvantage of us looking pretty, and with Tom Watkins more than happy to give the impression that he created us, we were perfect victims. Shirley and Dee have now patched things up, but I don't know if Dee ever realized the extent of the harm she did. It may sound silly to say one newspaper interview sparked all our problems, but I really do believe it did.

We also ran up against an influential critic. Jonathan King, who did a weekly column for the *Sun*, decided from day one that he did not like us. The fact that our name Goss rhymed with Bros was a bonus: the fact that it also rhymed with dross was yet another bonus for the headline writers. Jonathan King dedicated himself to being controversial. Like many column writers he realized that his value to the newspaper depended on stirring up a reaction from the readers, whether they agreed or disagreed with him. He always looked for the controversial ground: slagging off Bros, when he knew that so many young girl readers were our fans, guaranteed a huge postbag for him and justified his existence as a columnist.

From our point of view, it perpetrated the myth that we were talentless bimbos hyped to the top of the charts. His most damning piece about us came out less that two weeks after Dee's story. King said:

> I suspect they had little to do with the record. I suspect they can hardly sing. I can see they have NO stage presence, NO performing skill, NO charisma, NO looks, NO fashion sense and NO dance ability.

Not a lot left for a pop band to have, is there? On one level we knew that we had to take criticism, and we're the first to admit that we became better performers as we became more experienced. But that kind of blanket condemnation can only have been done for effect. It said more about Jonathan King than it did about us. But it gave ammunition to the kids – particularly young guys – who were looking for any excuse to attack a group that was big with the young, female market.

I'm not writing this as a whinge against King, but because I want to quote from another piece he published in the *Sun*, almost a year later. He wrote:

> I want you to sit down, take a deep breath. You are not going to believe this. I went to see Bros last week at Wembley and thought they were EXCELLENT! Pause for 12 million readers to pick themselves up off the floor in astonishment . . .
>
> From their spectacular entrance to the fireworks and explosions, they put on a wonderful show. Their sound is powerful and loud, the boys work hard, spinning and twisting and running round the stage . . . The fans had a marvellous time . . . Perhaps we are to watch Bros develop from a manufactured unit to a real supergroup. I hope so.

The dig about 'manufactured' was still there, but otherwise it was a complete turnround. The trouble was, it was too late. The damage had already been done. It didn't matter how good our music was, how spectacular and professional our shows were, the smart talk was always that we were a phoney group created by cynical old music industry hands in some smoky back room somewhere.

There were other newspaper stories that we could do nothing about that created a picture of us as arrogant brats – and our management company was happy to foster these. For instance, we were reported to have turned down a chance to do five nights at Wembley as support band for Michael Jackson. The story said we had rejected £500,000, even though Jackson had twice upped the money, and that we told Jackson's management that we would get in touch with *him* when *we* needed a support act. What a lot of rot: it had been suggested at one stage that we might be in the frame for the Jackson tour, but it was quickly abandoned when we realized that we already had heavy commitments at that time; we were going to be away on tour ourselves. But for someone 'close' to us, as the story put it, to suggest we told Jackson we would contact him for support was such crazy nonsense it was dangerous. It made us sound like a couple of jumped-up prats who thought we were better than Michael Jackson. (Jackson is Matt's all-time hero.)

Another story said we had been dropped from a concert in aid of the Prince's Trust at the Royal Albert Hall in front of Prince Charles and Princess Diana because we had demanded top billing, above people like Eric Clapton and Peter Gabriel. We were never going to appear! It would have been ridiculous for us to put ourselves above guys like that, who were our idols. And even if they had not been rock legends, we would not, at a charity event, have made trouble about billing. Once again, we were made out to be selfish, big-headed and arrogant, and there wasn't a lot we could do to correct that image.

We featured fairly constantly in stories about our body-guards 'beating up' paparazzi, the freelance photographers who hang around premieres, trendy restaurants and night-clubs until all hours of the morning in the hope of getting a picture of a celebrity a bit the worse for wear, or with a girl on his arm who isn't his wife. One snap of someone really famous doing something that the tabloids – with their strange set of double standards – think they shouldn't be doing, can make a guy like that a fortune. If the star is big Hollywood box office, or Royal, the man with the camera can pay his mortgage for a year. When times are hard and stars doing naughty things are thin on the ground, the paparazzi are not above making their own news. They would hang around so close that our bodyguards would have to push them aside. This was not done with their arms: the bodyguards were big guys who would stick their chests out and barrel their way through the scrum of girls and photographers, leaving a wake for us behind them. As soon as it happened, you'd get a photographer screaming that he'd been 'beaten up'. At first I thought they were the most awful wimps who wanted to work in the kitchen but couldn't stand the heat. But I soon realized it was a way for them to make a quick buck: they could sell a picture of me to a newspaper if they could tie it in with a story about my 'aggressive' minders. I've seen the same story hundreds of times since: Madonna's minders are always supposed to be attacking photographers. Well, I can't speak for the quality of her employees, but our minders were all professionals who would have regarded it as a failure if they had had to resort to hitting anybody, and they never failed.

Dealing with the press was a terrible catch-22 situation.

Occasionally I would hear through our fan club of fans who were seriously ill in hospital, and I would visit them. I always stipulated that I did not want publicity, but inevitably there would be some. If Matt and I turned up together, we weren't going to be able to walk in and out of a hospital without anybody recognizing us. And anyway, half the point of being there was to give the staff and families of the patients a boost, as well as the patients themselves. So, not surprisingly, it would usually leak out to the local press and then the national press that we had been there.

Then we would come in for criticism for only going in the first place in order to get publicity! We couldn't win, and in time both Matt and I became very dispirited by the constant carping. It affected our own attitude to ourselves: every time we were interviewed we were defensive, trying to justify ourselves – particularly, trying to overcome the allegations that we were talentless and manufactured. We were in a vicious circle.

Matt and I have both got a good sense of humour and we take the mick out of ourselves all the time. We don't mind being the butt of jokes: we really enjoyed seeing our puppets on *Spitting Image*, wearing nappies and singing 'When Will I Start Shaving'. We were pleased when we heard that Dawn French and Jennifer Saunders were 'doing' us in their French and Saunders series, and when they appeared on camera we broke up laughing. They must have been in the make-up department for hours to turn themselves into Bros. But then the sketch portrayed us as real thickos, with me as an absolute dunce who just said 'Yeah, yeah, yeah.' They'd researched the make-up but not us: any journalist who has ever interviewed us will tell you that I am the one who does the talking. Matt is more worried that he will say the wrong thing, so keeps quiet.

But compared to lots of people in the music business, we've both got something to say. We may not be well-educated, but we're not thick and we're both articulate.

Watching the sketch, I felt humiliated. I realized that a lot of people were tuned into that parody, people who knew nothing about me, and who would make judgements about me because of it. It is a very lonely, desperate feeling. If anyone has ever experienced what it is like to be laughed at by their mates, or by the people they work with, or even by their family, for something that is totally unjustified, perhaps they can begin to imagine how 'outside' I felt. It wasn't just a small group laughing at me, it was half the nation. I don't suppose comedians like French and Saunders go home and feel guilty about the unhappiness they cause, any more than the journalists who make up stories do. I know, too, that we are not the only people to have been hurt like this, but it doesn't make it any easier. I no longer watch shows like that as if I'm an ordinary member of the audience: I now find myself thinking all the way through about how their victims must feel. I do believe it is possible to be funny without losing compassion; humour does not have to be cruel. You can laugh *with* someone, you don't have to laugh *at* them.

One example of our no-win relationship with the press was our Wembley stadium concert. We played the stadium, the most prestigious venue in Britain, as a one-off show before leaving Britain to tour America.

One of the papers started a story that we had only sold half the tickets for the show. In actual fact we sold over 65,000, when the capacity was 70,000. Lots of really big bands don't even try to fill Wembley Stadium – they have a much bigger stage and therefore far fewer seats, sometimes down to about 40,000.

ABOVE Me, Matt and Craig, with our cousins, Darren and Daniel.

BELOW Me and Matt relaxing with Dad before our first hit.

ABOVE Shirley and Carli, the two women in my life.

BELOW Some people find milk bottles on their doorstep in the morning – this is what my mum found.

ABOVE Three mates enjoying a drink and a laugh.

RIGHT Grabbing a quick hug from my mum, somewhere on tour.

LEFT Wherever I went, Kelly was never far away.

BELOW Contrary to the press stories, our charity work was never intended as a publicity stunt. Here we are in Birmingham helping to raise money for a police minibus.

RIGHT One of the few pictures of me and Shirley together – she hates having her photo taken.

BELOW Here I am, at home and at my happiest.

One of the rare moments when I emerged from behind my drums and the fans actually got to see my legs!

Me and Matt before our show in Wembley Stadium, with one
pleased Dad.

It was a growing-up experience looking after Bros's financial affairs – David Ravden before and after his involvement with me.

But because one newspaper had said we had only sold half the tickets, the rest took the same line. Every time the gig was written about before we played it, the same thing was said; nobody ever bothered to check with the box office. On the night, the place looked full: a few thousand empty seats in that size of a crowd just does not show. We got very good reviews, but anyone who did not go would have got the impression that we were playing to rows of empty seats.

The following day we were due to fly out to start our twelve-week American tour – we were understandably nervous, because America is a difficult market to crack. The stadium show was a great success, and after it we thought our management company would have laid on a small celebratory party for us. There *was* a party backstage at Wembley: it was for 1,000 people, the vast majority of whom I have never seen before in my life. Matt, Shirley and I went, but we walked out after a few minutes because it really didn't seem to be anything to do with us. There were one or two of our friends there, but the crowd was so thick that we needed our bodyguards to help us move through it. That's not what you want at the end of an exhausting stadium show – the biggest show of my life, which went out live to millions of people on Sky TV.

We were booked into the Mayfair Hotel that night, because we were flying out the next day. When we got back to our hotel rooms we were still hyped up from being on stage, and we could not believe that nobody from our management team had laid on a meal for us, or anything. I really did think that we would walk into the hotel and find a surprise party had been organized, but nothing happened. It was a huge anti-climax. I expect everyone from the management company enjoyed the party at Wembley, which Matt and I were paying for.

We, in the meantime, were on our own at the hotel feeling miserable.

The American singer Debbie Gibson opened the Wembley Stadium concert. We were delighted to meet her: we were going to America as guests on her tour. Debbie is very young, very pop, very talented, but for Matt and me she would not have been first choice: we would rather have tried to break into the American market with an older audience. We didn't have a pop image out there. Our success in America had been limited to records doing quite well at the club/dance level: it gave us a chance to break in with a fresh profile. At one time it was suggested we should support the Bangles on their tour, or even Madonna, and we would have much preferred either of those. But our record company implied that if we didn't accept the offer to open for Debbie, they couldn't guarantee the success of our new album, *The Time*. The reality was that CBS was under pressure from America to get us on to the Debbie tour.

Our team made every effort to make sure she was looked after at Wembley. Her equipment was held up at the airport when she flew into Britain, but we did everything we could to sort things out. We gave her and her band one and a half hours on the stage to check that everything was OK, we laid on a limo to chauffeur Debbie about, and we gave her a superb dressing room. After all, we were big in Britain and we wanted to give her all the help we could.

We thought her team would do the same for us in America. We were wrong.

CHAPTER TWELVE

Cat Among the Pigeons

Less than forty-eight hours after performing in front of 65,000 screaming fans at Wembley Stadium, I was on stage in San Francisco in front of an audience of seven thousand, with an eight-year-old boy in the front row with his fingers in his ears. Half the audience were very, very young kids – even by our standards. The other half were their parents, many of them wearing bored expressions and earplugs.

So this was America. Our records had done quite well as club dance music out there, but we had never had a hit. This was our big attempt to break into the country. But from that first concert, we knew it was going to be a disaster. Not only was the audience completely wrong for our strong sound, but we were being treated very much as second-class citizens by Debbie Gibson's management.

It was the first time we had played live in America and we wanted to get it right. It is normal procedure for a band to be given at least three-quarters of an hour on the stage to check all their equipment. First you do a line check, when all the roadies make sure that the equipment is plugged into the right sockets, the microphones are not whistling, etc. This is followed by a sound check, involving the musicians. When you travel, as we did, with half a million pounds worth of gear, you don't want to plug into the wrong socket and blow everything. We hung around for ages waiting to be called for a check, but we were told we could not have one. We had been so used to running our own gigs – and giving any band appearing with us the courtesy of a good long check – that we were staggered by this attitude.

When we got on stage, the atmosphere was non-existent. People were wandering around buying hot dogs. There were a few claps when we were introduced, but most of the audience weren't even paying attention. Some of them didn't look old enough to be potty-trained. Our equipment was literally being plugged in as we went along, but I don't think anyone out front knew or cared.

Our sound was definitely too heavy and rocky for the kids: generally speaking we got a bit more reaction from the parents, but it was still a very lukewarm reception. On that first night we were so dispirited we only played three numbers. Back in the dressing róom, both Matt and I wept. We thought we had arrived in hell: thousands of miles from home; a gruelling twelve weeks of travel ahead of us; not even enough respect from Debbie's management to give us proper checks; and the prospect of playing in front of a lot more audiences who couldn't care less whether we were there or not.

Our tour manager had heated words with Debbie Gibson's tour manager, and after that first disastrous night we were given fifteen-minute sound checks at the other venues. Fifteen minutes is nowhere near enough, but it's a helluva lot better than nothing. We, and all our crew, found the way we were being treated was abominable. No big headlining band gives even the newest unknowns as hard a time as we had, yet we were supposed to be 'special guests' on Debbie's tour. We were being treated like dogs-bodies.

It is ironic that in Britain the quality of our lives suffered because we got too much star treatment – too many fans, too many photographers, too many demands – and in

America it suffered because we got none. It should have been great fun: going on the road as an unknown band again. But the conditions we had to work in, and the casual disrespect we were shown, meant that there was no fun left in it.

Worse even than the way Debbie Gibson's management treated us was the way our own record company behaved. They had promised that our single, 'Too Much', would be released ten days after the tour started. Every night on stage, in front of the little kids and their mums and dads, we introduced the number as our new release. Every day we waited for news that it was out; eight weeks later, it had still not been released. The only point of the tour had been to promote the record: we knew from the word go that the tour was going to run at a loss for us. It actually lost us over £40,000, but we had hoped that would be more than compensated by record sales and merchandising.

'Too Much' was finally released three weeks after we went home to England. Not surprisingly, it stiffed.

There was nothing glamorous about being on the road in America. We travelled in coaches, which admittedly were luxurious, but we spent so long in them that we grew to hate them. There were such distances to cover, that we drove through the night, every night.

We would leave the stadium by ten o'clock and the coaches would rumble off down the freeway. We had two, one for us and one for the rest of the crew, but we had the other musicians in with us to spread the load. For the first three or four hours we would play video games, have a drink, try to relax. Then at two in the morning we would pull into a truckers' café to eat. We'd find ourselves surrounded by real weirdos, night people who hang around places like that. Big guys with beer guts and beards would look at us threateningly when we walked in. At first, we'd be wearing our normal jeans and tee shirts and terrific jackets, but after a while we made sure we had changed into tracksuits and baseball caps, and kept our jewellery hidden. Sometimes one of the big guys would say, 'You all in a band?' but there was nothing nice in the question. In the end I would always answer 'D'you care?' because you knew they didn't.

I frequently rang Shirley from one of the phone booths around the counters of these truck stops, and I'd be aware of several sets of eyes watching me while I talked to her. It was creepy. The food wasn't great either: on the American tour I ate an awful lot of chilli at two o'clock in the morning.

Back on the bus we would climb into our bunk beds to sleep. The beds were very narrow, and the head clearance was so small that if you tried to turn over your shoulder hit the roof. There was a curtain across each one. We all had Gameboys with comm links, which are wires to link two machines together so that we could play doubles, and we called these wires out umbilical cords. We would go to bed linked up to the guy in the bunk above or below, and for an hour or more all you would hear in the coach was the electronic bleeping of the Gameboys.

The coach was air-conditioned, which meant that we had to wear our tracksuits in bed or we woke up cold and clammy, with the sort of fine layer of dampness that air-conditioning leaves. We took a consignment of Sergio Tacchini tracksuits on tour with us, which we all wore. We looked like clones with hairstyles from hell when we woke up. Matt and I would be stiff and sore because with our height our heads and feet touched the ends of the beds.

We would get up at about ten in the morning, and

sometimes we would have another eight hours on the bus ahead of us. Other times we would get to where we were playing and check into a hotel. Sometimes, if the bus arrived while we were asleep, we would be left on it in the car park. It was strange waking up, finding you were alone on the bus, and having to struggle off and look for the entrance to the hotel.

Life on the bus was very unhealthy. We ate out of boredom: salsa, tacos, tortilla chips. And we drank beer. I remember sitting across a table from Paul Gendler, who played guitar, and there were so many empty beer cans on the table that there wasn't room to put another one down. We all felt awful and looked awful.

We did not personally blame Debbie. She was only eighteen at the time, and her mother and older sister, both on the tour with her, seemed to us to rule her life. At one stage she was sleeping on a couch at night herself, and Matt actually told her to remind everybody that it was her tour, she was the star, and if she was going to look good on stage she needed a good night's sleep.

But life was made as difficult as possible for us, and our management should not have tolerated it. Petty problems came up all the time. We got a message one evening to say that Matt was not to go up on the rises, which were square black boxes at either side of the stage. He invariably leaped up there to try and gee up the audience. It was an uphill battle but we never gave up, and on some nights we actually did manage to breathe life into Frankenstein and get the crowd tapping their feet and cheering.

Apparently Debbie's team did not like this, and they wanted to restrict Matt. Sending us a memo was the best way to ensure that Matt leaped on to one of the rises within ten seconds of hitting the stage. Her tour management were fuming, but did not try to stop him again.

Debbie's band were on stage before us for sound checks, and they would always keep us waiting: after they'd played their set they would stay out there jamming, using up our time, without any thought for us.

The venues were often nothing more than a local games hall, and we would be given the locker room to change in. We would have to put up makeshift screens, made of wardrobe boxes, between the girls and the rest of us. At other times we would have a dressing room the size of a bathroom, for all the guys to use. We had to take it in turns. When we thought back to the effort we had put into making sure Debbie was comfortable at Wembley, we felt really hacked off. If she had been roughing it, too, it would have been different, but she always had a decent dressing room.

We covered a lot of America, but I'm afraid it is all one big blur. Looking out of the coach window, one freeway looked much like another. Eating at two in the morning, one truck stop was much like another. I saw enough to know that America is a very lonely place, peopled with cynics. Although they are outwardly very optimistic and friendly – 'Have a nice day' – they are deeply distrustful, always looking for the catch in everything. I think if you were lying in the street dying they'd be trying to figure out what your angle was.

I was annoyed to be told it would not be a good idea to take my regular bodyguard, Kelly Samuels, with me on the tour. Kelly's black, and I was told that if there was trouble in America I wouldn't want a black guy trying to sort it out. Yet when we got there and hired policemen as bodyguards – yes, you can actually hire cops out there to work for you – I got a sergeant from New York Police Department, and he was black. I was upset, because I thought I had been unintentionally drawn into racial discrimination.

The whole tour left a bad taste in my mouth. I had flu

and felt lousy for a lot of the time, which didn't help. Working the hours we were and living in the damp conditions of the bus did not help: I could not shake the infection off, and I'm sure it jaundiced my whole view of America. At one point I felt so ill that I wanted to take a night off, but Debbie's management said I would be in breach of my agreement if I did that, so I had to go on. A doctor came and gave me an injection of a white fluid, which I now think may have been an anabolic steroid; the Americans are very casual about using steroids.

The high spot of the American tour was our twenty-first birthday party, which was when we were appearing in Dallas. We were determined that the miserable tour was not going to stop us celebrating, and we wanted our family and friends with us. We paid for twenty or so people to fly out. At the time we thought we were close to all of them: today, none of them are in touch, with the obvious exceptions of our family, Mum and Tony, Dad and his girlfriend Alison. He's known Alison, who is also in the police, for a few years now, and she's a great lady. We find her much easier to get on with than Margaret, but then I suppose we are older and less troublesome. She's a very gentle person and very good for my dad.

Shirley was also on tour in America at the same time as us, promoting her single 'Realistic', which got into the top twenty in most states. She was able to take time out from her ten-week tour to spend my birthday night with me.

We hired the two-storey presidential suite at the Crescent Hotel to hold the party in, and there were smaller suites for Mum and Tony and Dad and Alison. When Dad was shown to his room he said, 'Son, you shouldn't have done this,' but when I saw his room I told him there was a mistake. He thought he was being transferred to a smaller one – in fact, the hotel had put him in a room instead of a suite. He was gobsmacked when he saw it. Mum and Tony were sure they had been given the wrong room, too: they thought their suite was so plush it should have been ours. We got a tremendous buzz out of treating them like royalty. Mum had never been to the States before, so it was really nice to be able to give her a holiday there. The whole party cost us £25,000, including the flights, but I have such good memories that we certainly did not begrudge it – at the time, remember, we had no reason to believe we were not making lots of money.

Debbie and her band were at the party and had a great time: it was a much more lavish affair than Debbie's own birthday party, earlier in the tour.

Matt and I gave each other expensive gifts. I gave him a Cartier Pasha watch with a red alligator strap, and he gave me a Cartier necklace. They each cost about £4,000. Tom Watkins and Mick Newton, who we had flown out, presented us with a blow-up jukebox and announced that the real things were back home: they had bought each of us Wurlitzer jukeboxes, worth about £5,000 each. They were not our first gifts from our management: Tom had given each of us a Rolex watch when our first album went gold. He later complained to a magazine journalist that we spent too much money and went 'from Timex to Rolex' in one step. I think he has forgotten that he, our 'mentor', was the one who gave us our first Rolex.

We had to leave the morning after the party to get on the damned bus again. The coach had a roof which slid back, and I sat on the top waving to Shirley and wishing I could stay with her. Instead I got drunk and played video games and watched films for the next ten hours. I missed her miserably.

We got a ten-day break during the tour, and Mum and

Tony stayed in America and met us in New York, where we performed at Madison Square Gardens. Dad was unable to take enough time off work to stay out there. Matt went to Los Angeles for most of the break, but Shirley was able to join us for several days. I had a few press interviews to do, but otherwise it was meant to be a relaxing time. The trouble for me was that I was so miserable about the whole tour that I found it very hard to relax, and when I'm miserable I overcompensate by spending money.

I bought quite a lot of new clothes, and I also treated Mum. She's a great one for searching out bargains, but I insisted she buy some really nice clothes. We went out for some good meals as well. The one that sticks in my memory is the one where Shirley and Mum both had too much to drink. They were knocking back cocktails called B52s as if they were lemonade. I don't know what lethal ingredients go into them, but they are certainly deadly. The combination of the cocktails plus the wine at the meal was disastrous: they were both wrecked. We drove back in a hired limo through Central Park, in lovely autumn sunshine, with horses and carriages trotting alongside us and the most beautiful view in New York stretched in front of us, and Mum had her head out of the window saying she wanted to be sick and Shirley was sitting on the floor accusing Tony of stealing her shoes. I remember saying to Tony, 'Look at our women, we might as well be in the Old Kent Road for all they care.'

We had to shovel them into the lift at the Parker Meridian Hotel, where we were staying, Shirley still without her shoes on. Upstairs I got her into bed, which is more than Tony did for Mum. She lay down on the bathroom floor, so he simply put a pillow under her head and left her there! She wasn't feeling too good the next day.

Apart from that, they really enjoyed their time in New

York and I loved being able to treat them. When I look back I wasted so much money on so many people who really didn't matter to me at all: I don't regret one penny spent on my family, who have been with me all the way.

There was only one other occasion when Shirley's tour crossed with ours. I was checking into a hotel late one night and there was a message from her, asking me to ring her. I saw that the dialling code for her number was the same as mine so I legged it up to the room and rang her. 'Where are you?' I asked, before she had time to speak.

'About fifteen minutes away from you,' she said.

I told her to get her ass over as fast as she could. I was so excited: it was four weeks since we had last seen each other. I could not believe it, and I was unable to sit down the whole time I was waiting for her. Then there was a knock at the door of my room and she was there. I could touch her, hold her, smell her. It was the most wonderful surprise and we had a very happy night together – or, I should say, a very happy four hours, because it was two in the morning when she arrived and she had to leave at six.

We worked ourselves stupid on the American tour. I wish all the critics back in Britain who sniped at us for being talentless and hyped could have seen us out there, in front of audiences who had never heard of us and didn't want to hear from us. Dad remembers watching us perform in Dallas:

'I saw my kids really work. The venue was half empty, some of the audience were wandering around outside on the grass buying hot dogs. They started to play, and they played their nuts off, and I saw people being pulled in from the grass by the sheer force of their music and stage presence. Before they had finished, they had got the bums on the seats and the feet tapping. Nobody can accuse them of not being able to perform, nobody.

'I saw Luke come off stage with blood streaming from his hands, he had been drumming so hard.'

My hands were always a problem. Bros shows were high-energy productions, with a lot of heavy rhythmical drumming. I would develop nine or ten blisters on my right hand, and five or six on my left. My wrists would ache like crazy, and for the first few weeks of any tour I would be in agony. The blisters would often burst, and there would be blood splattered all over my drum kit.

When Matt sang 'The Boy is Dropped' he did it alone on stage, without any instruments, so I would dash backstage where someone would have a large bowl full of ice waiting for me. I would plunge my hands into it. It was agony, but it eventually dulled the pain enough for me to go back on stage and carry on playing. Mel Gaynor, the drummer with Simple Minds, gave me some great tips when we met him at the Nomis recording studio near Olympia, and now I tape my fingers with thin gauze bandages. Over the bandages I wear golfing gloves, because they are skintight and don't limit my movements. They wear out pretty quickly, lasting about two shows. They are sold individually, not in pairs, and for a tour I would need about a hundred gloves, at £11 each. We tried to get the manufacturer to do a deal on them, but they replied that they were 'happy with the sort of business we have now'. In other words, they were too snobby to be tied up with a pop group.

What they didn't know was that I am genuinely a golfer. Well, I like playing golf, but I'm not terribly good at it. Matt and I were once on a golf course in Wales when some girls from a local school spotted us and chased after us: they were in a bit of trouble when their deputy head got them back into school, I believe. But in America we loved playing, partly because we enjoyed hiring golf buggies and riding in a huge convoy round the course. Matt and I spent £150 each on all the gear, the sweaters, shoes and caps. We looked like serious pros, until we tried to hit the ball. We ran into a bit of opposition when some women golfers complained that we were laughing and enjoying ourselves, and upsetting their game. The club where we were playing seemed to think we were really out of line, but we had done nothing except have a good time: we weren't vandals or anything. I occasionally get a good par three hole, but usually I'm two or three over.

While we were touring we met the Rolling Stones. They were appearing in Kansas and we went along to watch their gig. I didn't even know that they would ever have heard of us, but Ronnie Wood said straightaway, 'What are you bastards doing here?' with a big grin on his face. We played pool and table tennis backstage with him and Bill Wyman, and they asked us for signed pictures for their kids. I thought, 'Hold on a minute, this should be the other way round, I should be asking for this.' It was a very strange feeling. I think they were pleased to see another couple of English lads.

Matt was wearing a custom-made leather jacket with crystal studs, which cost him £1,200. Ronnie Wood wore it on stage for the first five or six numbers of their show, which we were watching from the sound recordist's box. Matt was a bit nervous when he whirled it round his head as though he were going to sling it out into the audience, but in the end he flung it behind him and Matt eventually got it back. At the end of the show they all signed it.

It was an incredible experience watching them perform. They've been at it so long, survived so many ups and downs, and they're so very, very good, that we were in awe of them. But they were very easy-going and Ronnie Wood said some very encouraging things to us.

It always seems odd, meeting your heroes. I remember

the first time I met Elton John, it was at a photo session with top photographer Terry O'Neill. Elton was wearing a huge square canary diamond. I'd never seen anything like it. 'Is that real?' I blurted out.

"Course it is, you stupid bastard,' he said, with a grin. I did feel stupid, but to me it looked like something you get out of a Christmas cracker, it was so big. We got on very well with him. We suggested he get a twelve-inch remix done of one of his records, for the clubs, and he did. Elton always said good things about us.

But in the meantime, we were having problems with our second album, the one we made at Miraval. We pleaded with the record company not to release it while we were in America, but they ignored us. We weren't around to promote it: by the time we were back, the impact of the release was over. It sold 1.2 million copies, which is not at all bad, but is only a third of what the first one sold. When I thought of all the packaging and promotion that went into making the first one a hit, I could not believe how careless everyone was with this one. Even the album cover was wrong: it was a terrific photo of Matt and me taken by Terence Donovan, but it was supposed to have been bleached out to give a very black and white over-exposed effect.

So the American tour screwed everything up, and was the beginning of the end for Bros. We went on the tour to promote a single that was not released, and while we were away our album was released in Europe and we could do nothing to promote it. If that isn't clever planning by the record company, I don't know what is. It was as though they were deliberately setting out to sell as few records as possible. It's hard to believe that they had a vested interest in us doing well. And our management company weren't much better. Tom was unable to achieve anything for us in America, and he, too, seemed to have lost interest in how the album release was handled back home. It was a mess.

I knew then that as far as Tom was concerned, we were past our sell-by date.

When you are young, famous and think you are rich, you don't worry about security. You spend your money on things that give you pleasure: and I got pleasure from cars and jewellery. Neither of those are very good investments, but I enjoyed them. It's no good filling your life with regrets. Sure, if I had my time all over again I would do a lot of things differently. But looking back I can see that when I bought cars and jewellery – and cars in particular – I was just living any young guy's fantasy. I'd been desperate to get mobile at the age of seventeen in any old banger, and as soon as I started to earn real money a decent car was what I wanted more than anything in the world. Because of my age and the kind of cars I loved, it cost a small fortune in insurance: £6,000 a year. But I thought it was worth it and, more to the point, I thought I could afford it.

The Suzuki jeep the band used in the early days was given away as a prize in a competition in the *Sun*. Our accountant at the time told each of us that we could spend up to £14,000 on a car, and my choice was a red Toyota MR2 T-bar, my first real grown-up car. I was thrilled about going to collect it – and horrified to find that somebody had tipped off a photographer who was waiting across the road. The *Sun* ran a huge picture of me shaking hands with the salesman before climbing into the car and driving away.

Only another real car fanatic will understand when I say I felt that the moment had been spoiled for me. I was looking forward to that special moment of climbing behind the wheel for the first time and feeling that it was all mine (or, at least, mine and the finance company's, because I only put down a deposit and paid the rest in instalments). I wanted to be allowed to be a kid, to play with my toy on my own for a while, before sharing it with a burly photographer and twelve million *Sun* readers.

After the Toyota I had a white BMW 320i. It had black windows and a white interior, it was a real beauty. Thanks to my friends in the press I'd only had it a few minutes when I was involved in a crash which wrote off Shirley's new car, a secondhand black BMW she'd bought for herself. We were driving along the M25 after we'd picked up the cars, and we had a chauffeur-driven Jag in convoy with us: he'd driven us to the garage. I suddenly became aware that there was car with a press photographer in it trying to get alongside me, and I remember feeling pleased that I had tinted windows which meant he couldn't see in. The next moment the press car pulled suddenly in front of the Jag, the Jag braked, the roads were wet and although I was only doing 55 mph I went into the back of the Jag. Shirley piled into the back of me: £6,000 worth of damage, and my car five inches shorter than it was when I bought it, only half an hour earlier. To say I was upset would be an understatement. I even had to pay for the repairs to the Jag, and once again the thrill of owning a new car had been tarnished. But I loved the BMW – I had it sent over to France while we were recording the second album, so I could drive it over there. I hated being parted from it.

For the 'Too Much' video we hired a convertible Porsche for a month, and I was smitten by Porsches. I'd dreamed of having a Porsche ever since I'd passed my driving test, but never thought I'd achieve it. After driving that one in France I knew I had to have one.

So I bought my first, a metallic green Porsche 944 which I saw in the garage window and thought was beautiful. I learned a lesson: you should take a bit more care buying a car. It was sluggish, the seats were not leather, and I hated the green colour. I was a prat for buying it. The garage where we bought our cars on a regular basis agreed to buy it back, at a substantial loss to me.

The next car I bought was a Porsche 911, a blue one. This time I did not even go out to buy it myself, I sent my personal assistant. I was very busy at the time, and I also wanted to avoid more publicity. That car caused me a lot of problems. It turned out that it had been rolled and then repaired, but the repairs had never been authorized by Porsche. We found out when it went in for some minor work; the garage spotted that it had had major repairs and checked with the Porsche computer. Porsche knew nothing about its accident, and they had not inspected and sanctioned the repairs. That meant the car was worth considerably less than I had paid for it. My dad got involved and we took legal action against the man who sold it to me. Eventually I got £7,500 back.

After that I hired a Range Rover and then a BMW until I was able to buy the car of my dreams: a red Porsche Carrera. It cost £35,000, but again I was paying for it on the drip. It was the best car I ever owned and I cried when it was taken away, after everything collapsed around me. It was not actually repossessed: I sold it back to the garage I got it from for £5,000 less than I paid for it.

But at least I have the satisfaction of knowing that I lived my dream. Even if it was only for eighteen months.

CHAPTER THIRTEEN

Money

The most hellish equation of all is to be famous and have no money.

Money smooths away the problems that come with fame: the crowds of fans, the lack of privacy. Money buys a comfortable security that you can retreat into from the outside world, where everybody believes they own a part of you.

Billy Connolly, the comedian who, with his wife Pamela Stephenson, has had his fair share of the press spotlight, once said, 'To be famous and poor would be frightening.' Well, the reality is mine. And I can tell you that it *is* frightening.

People who have no concept of what fame does to your life may say that I could opt for a simple life, living in a two-up two-down terraced house, and surviving quite adequately on the money that I have. What they don't know is that fame does not allow you to do that. The fans don't wave goodbye and leave you in peace because they find out you have money problems. The industry you are working in doesn't respect you more because you gear yourself to poverty: the pop world is about success, about front, about playing the part.

And, most importantly, watching millions change hands in our name, we had been seduced into believing we were seriously rich. We geared our lifestyles to being able to afford the things that make fame manageable, the

bodyguards and personal assistants, electronic security, a
house away from the road.

We've been accused of being extravagant: well, I admit
we did spend – but to nothing like the extent that the
public has been led to believe. We were rock stars but we
did not lead a rock star life, night clubbing and partying
until dawn, and we never had drug habits to support, like
so many people in the music business.

And remember: we were very young. How many eigh-
teen-year-olds or nineteen-year-olds would see their
singles shooting up the charts and not go out and buy a
car, a watch, some clothes? How many teenagers would
turn themselves into accountants and start checking
through balance sheets to see just how well off they really
were? Even if we had wanted to do that, or been able to
do it, we did not have the time in those early, heady days:
we slept in our own beds for less than eight weeks of that
first crazy year.

We were paying large amounts of money to men in suits
to look after our affairs. Naïvely, we thought that was what
they were doing: that they put our interests first. Whether
you are eighteen or fifty, you have the right to expect that
if you pay people, they make your concerns their top pri-
ority, and we assumed they did. We were wrong.

In the two years from 'When Will I Be Famous' climbing
to the top of the charts, we grossed £6 million. We paid
out more that £1.5 million in commission to our managers.
And we made, ourselves, £541,000. Remember that for
most of that time there were three of us (Craig was in the
band for the first fifteen months of fame). Divide up that
cake and you will see that we earned about £100,000 a
year each. Nice money, you might think – but peanuts
compared to what we were being led to believe we made,
and nowhere near enough to fund the sort of lifestyles we

believed we could afford. And nowhere near as much as
our managers were making.

There was something seriously wrong.

But we did not know that until we decided to renegotiate
our contract with Tom Watkins and Mick Newton. That
was when, for the first time since the day we signed it, I
looked at the contract. It was also the first time that I
looked at it and understood some of the words used, and
took in what it meant. I'd done a lot of growing up in the
three years since I had signed it.

It was in January 1990 that we decided to renegotiate:
it was a decision that would turn 1990 into the most trau-
matic of my life.

Tom Watkins was a good manager for the first twelve
months of our career. He worked hard to launch us and
he was a very strong presence who made himself felt at
the record company. His methods were not subtle, and I
believe this may have done us a lot of harm in America, where
he was not very popular in the New York office of our
record company. But in terms of getting us noticed at the
beginning, he was able to do the trick. Tom never saw us
as long-life milk: we were gold top, to be drunk quickly
and the bottle handed back to the milkman.

He had good promotional ideas. He made sure that we
had an independent promoter: in other words, we didn't
rely on the record company to get us airtime on radio and
TV. What he could not cope with was long-term strategy.
Having become as big as we did as fast as we did, he had
no idea about how to sustain it, or even ensure that if we
went into decline it was a gradual process that allowed us
to earn big money for a few more years.

We were never close to Tom or comfortable with him.
His partner Mick Newton was the one we related to. Mick

was the one who seemed to care about us, seemed to care about our music. He actually enjoyed being on the road with us, whereas Tom would only turn up at our concerts now and again, and only if for some reason it suited him. He'd sometimes hire a fleet of chauffeur-driven limos to bring his guests to our concerts: backstage at a Bros gig was always a lavish, no-expense-spared event, very impressive. You could tell that this was a serious top band, oozing with money, and that was the way Tom liked it. I was too naïve to know that we were paying for it all and that we didn't have that kind of money.

But it was Mick who was with us whenever he could be, it was Mick who told us he loved us and would look after us. Mick, too, was the one with the real interest in music. When you wanted to get hold of Tom he would be out shopping, or sitting in his office being extremely civilized. Like boxers who become successful sometimes lose their hunger, Tom had achieved with us what he aimed for and his appetite was sated. Mick, we always thought, was a closet musician, one of us. Ultimately, when we discovered how bad our financial state was, it was by Mick that we felt most let down. Even now, I hope that all the things that Mick said to us and all the good times we had together meant something: I'd still like to believe that he wanted to carry on working with us, and that his friendship was not one big act. He used to feel as frustrated as we did when Tom encouraged the idea that he was our Svengali who had created us from nothing. But the bottom line is that if Mick knew about our real problems, the financial ones, he did not care about us enough to alert us.

It was when we came back from the disastrous American tour that we felt serious mistakes were being made with our career. At this stage we had no idea that our earnings were not being handled fairly. Yes, we had been told from time to time by our accountant that we should cut back on our spending, but she had never been heavy with us and explained just how little we had. Yes, our parents (who the management had not previously involved much) were now told to get us to cut back. But we had no idea that, in real terms, we were in what it has now become fashionable to call a situation of 'negative equity': in other words, it was costing more to keep the Bros show on the road than we were making.

We were concerned because the second album had been released while we were away, because the cover was not right, because the single had not been released in America while we were there, because the choice of the Debbie Gibson tour was completely wrong for us. In other words, we could see that the care and attention Tom had lavished on launching us was not being sustained. If we could see such obvious mistakes then our management company, the guys paid to look after our interests, should have been doing something about it. We saw no sign of them doing it.

We also knew, just through three years of kicking around in the professional music business, that we were paying a very high rate of commission to Watkins and Newton: new artists often sign at 20 per cent, but when their earnings soar as high as ours they renegotiate down to 15 per cent, perhaps even less.

So we took our contract to a lawyer. We had no thought of splitting from Tom Watkins at this stage, we simply wanted to renegotiate. It was only when we went through it in detail that we realized that it was an invidious contract, that the clause that stipulated we paid commission on gross and not net profits was intolerable and that the whole thing would have to be torn up and thrown away. The only way to do that was to split with 3 Style Ltd, our management company. We repudiated the contract on 9 February 1990.

We then found ourselves launched on a bitter five-month struggle, during which time our career, without anyone handling it properly, would founder even more than it had done thanks to the disastrous American tour and the badly timed release of the second album. We wanted to be free of 3 Style Ltd: in retaliation they sued us for £1.2 million in damages for breach of contract.

The firm of solicitors we used has an excellent reputation and the woman who handled our case was very professional. Unfortunately both we – and she – believed the case would be settled much more quickly than it was, and in the end we changed to a different firm of solicitors. This was not because the first firm did anything wrong, it was simply because the second firm, Russells, was experienced in handling entertainment industry cases and were rather more aggressive in their prosecution of the case.

Our original solicitor did me one of the biggest favours that has ever been done for me in my career: she introduced me to David Ravden. David turned out to be one of the few pillars that supported the crumbling edifice of my life over the next couple of years. He ranks just behind Shirley and my family in terms of his importance to me, and he came into my life at a time when I was cynical, dejected and lacking any faith in my fellow human beings. David gave me back my self-respect.

David Ravden is an accountant who specializes in working with people in the entertainment industry, and particularly with people in the pop business. He is a partner in Martin Greene Ravden, a well-established accountancy company with several hundred clients, most of whom are in the music business. When our solicitor took our case to a barrister, Andrew Sutcliffe QC, he recommended to her that she needed an expert witness, someone who

understood the business and also understood the figures
on a balance sheet. He suggested David, whom he had
first met when they were both involved in a case involving
Holly Johnson of Frankie Goes to Hollywood.

David is in his forties, but he doesn't come on like a
man in a grey suit. He talks straight and he talks sense.
He left school at eighteen, but didn't go into his family's
fashion business because, like all good Jewish parents, his
mother and father wanted him to become a professional:
a doctor, a lawyer or an accountant. He qualified at the
end of the sixties, a time when there were lots of business
opportunities, a property boom, lots of money to be made.
He worked for companies involved in the entertainment
industry: for a couple of years he was personal assistant to
John Daly, who founded the Hemdale company with actor
David Hemmings. The company produced films and dis-
tributed them, and because it was part of a wider group,
there were subsidiaries including a record company and
a management company. David had been given a great
grounding in many aspects of the entertainment business
and wanted to be his own boss.

With another accountant he then set up his own company, which has now grown to include eight partners. But
despite being a businessman, David is also a human being.
He was introduced into our case as an expert witness: our
solicitor asked him, as someone who is used to handling
music industry contracts and who is respected in the business, to have a look at our contract, to have a look at our
accounts, and give her an expert's verdict on them. He
was shocked, and said so.

He later stated in an affidavit (which means he was
prepared then and is prepared now to say it in court) that
there were clauses in our contract which 'quite apart from
being ludicrously unfair to the artists are actually contrary

to accepted music business practice when the agreement
was signed'.

'It was quite an abominable contract,' says David. 'The
commission rate was high, and should have been renegoti-
ated downwards as soon as Bros began to make real money.
Management means just that: the company should have
been managing the boys' affairs for Luke's and Matt's best
advantage, as they were young and inexperienced.

'Music industry contracts have improved over the years:
in the sixties and seventies, when I first started looking at
them, they were appallingly unfair to the artists, but over
the years, and after a succession of court cases, managements have been forced to clean up their game. The Bros
contract was one of the worst I had ever seen, and I hadn't
seen anything comparable to it for probably fifteen years.
It was right back to the bad old days.'

The accountant we had used since the beginning of Bros
was the same one who had worked for 3 Style Ltd until
July 1989. We were introduced to her by Tom.

It was never kept secret from us that she worked for 3
Style, but it was not until six months before we repudiated
our contracts that she ceased to handle 3 Style's affairs.
She gave them up apparently because of the conflict of
interest.

'There is nothing in law to stop a firm of accountants
acting for both sides, and in fact my own firm occasionally
does it,' says David. 'But we are very aware of the need to
be careful and scrupulously fair.

'If an accountant works for both sides, it is obvious that
if there is a mistake in favour of one of his clients, the
money is coming out of the other client's pocket.'

David found that 3 Style Ltd was being overpaid, even
within the terms of a contract which meant they could
legitimately make a massive amount of money out of us.

As he went through our accounts he discovered that we had paid £188,055 too much in commission to our management company. He also found that we had been paying commission on sums of money paid in advance by our record company to cover the cost of producing records: although this could have been interpreted as 'gross earnings', and therefore due to be commissioned, it was not custom and practice within the music business for that to happen. David described this in his affidavit as 'blatantly unacceptable'. We had also been charged commission on money paid to us to help finance the American tour.

'These sums do not really constitute "earnings" as Bros simply use them to pay towards the cost of performing concerts and recordings songs, both of which are very complex and costly activities,' says David's affidavit.

'Even with the more common and fairer rate of 15 per cent commission, it is most unusual in my experience for such sums to be levied on gross tour receipts rather than on net receipts after payment of expenses.'

Our contract with 3 Style Ltd spelled out that we would not be charged commission for any expenses of sound and lighting when we were on tour, or on fees we had to pay to the tour booking agency. But David found that we had in some instances been commissioned on this money.

In total, we believe that 3 Style Ltd took £614,000 in commission from us which would not have been theirs had we had a contract that was fair.

When we agreed to the contract we had no idea that it was not normal for a management company to collect in money on behalf of their clients, in this case, us. It is the artist that employs the manager, not the other way round, and normal practice therefore is that an accountant working for the client collects in the money, then presents the management with a statement of earnings and the management send in an invoice for their commission. Our contract empowered 3 Style Ltd to collect our money themselves, which they did, and they then deducted their own commission and sent the balance, if any, to our accountant. We paid more than £100,000 in accountancy fees over the time that we were with 3 Style, and David tells us that this covers an enormous amount of work which we thought would normally have been done, and paid for, by the management company.

The contract also included a clause which meant we would be permanently in hock to 3 Style Ltd, because they could claim 20 per cent of all earnings that came from work we did during the time we were under their management, even after we had left them. In other words, any money we ever received from records or publishing from songs recorded or written during the time we were with them could be commissioned by them. According to David, this kind of clause is no longer acceptable or practical and managements have generally cleaned up their acts and started producing contracts that are fairer to the artists. But ours was even worse than most of those old ones: it allowed 3 Style Ltd to take their cut of everything we did, even if it was a song that we wrote but did not record until years later. As David said, this clause would seriously deter any new manager from taking us on, knowing that we would always have to pay off our previous management company for anything done during our time with them.

One aspect of the handling of our affairs which greatly worried David was the manager's 'fiduciary duty' to us. A fiduciary duty means that Tom Watkins, our manager, had a duty to look after our affairs in a trustworthy and honourable way, which includes handling our money properly and producing accounting records which would show us not only how much money we were generating but how much we were actually earning.

Although we had occasional reprimands for spending too much, we were never aware of what was coming in and what was going out. We should also have been given written budgets and estimates for any major project we became involved in which was going to cost a lot: for instance, a tour. Budget figures were drawn up for tours, but I cannot remember if these were shown to us and we were not given copies.

'I cannot see how Mr Watkins and 3 Style could have possibly discharged their duties to Bros when they advised that tours should be undertaken and charged 20 per cent commission amounting to hundreds of thousand of pounds on the income and expenses of the tour without regard to the profit (if any) that would be likely to be generated for the members of Bros,' says David's affidavit.

'In the event, the tours were financially very disappointing to Bros. In contrast, the tours were extremely lucrative to 3 Style.'

You bet. Take a look at these figures:

Our UK tour grossed £1,623,600. It cost £1,332,596. We paid commission to 3 Style of £286,143. And that left us with a grand profit of £4,860 for all those days on the road, nights in hotel beds and bloody hard work. And that profit was split between three of us.

The Global Push tour (excluding Britain and Japan) grossed £1,331,577. It cost £968,090. We paid commission of £254,383, and had a profit of £109,104. The Japanese tour grossed £250,304. It cost £193,038, we paid commission of £50,282 and ended up with £6,984 profit.

In other words, we made £120,948, or just over £40,000 each, from all three tours. By contrast our management company made well over half a million: £590,808.

What's more, when David looked at the figures he knew we had been over-commissioned on these tours alone to the tune of £107,325, which when added to the £80,730 over-commission that he calculated we paid on the rest of our earnings, came to the grand total of £188,055.

At this stage we decided to change our accountants and, not surprisingly, we asked David Ravden if he would take over our business affairs. He agreed, and has been handling them ever since.

When he switched from being an expert witness to being our accountant, he faced a delicate situation. He felt we were not making sufficiently fast progress in the case with Tom Watkins, and he could also see that until the case was settled it was difficult for us to resume our careers. He recommended that we found different lawyers in order to speed things up. He introduced us to Tony Russell, who had also been involved in the Frankie Goes to Hollywood case.

Within eight weeks, on 8 June 1990, the case was settled out of court. It was agreed that we would pay Tom Watkins £42,000 for loss of future earnings, but as he had accepted that he owed us sums that had been taken from us in over-commission we ended up in pocket. It was a great result for us: we walked away free from the contract, which was the main thing, and we had avoided a costly and long-drawn-out court case.

When David took over our affairs in March 1990 he could see they were in a terrible mess. We were insolvent: we owed just under £300,000, and that was without including our tax liabilities. There were creditors pressing angrily at the door and there was no money to pay them. It looked as though we were going to be made bankrupt. Even though I had realized things weren't right, the words 'bankrupt' and 'insolvent' hit me like a sledgehammer. I kept thinking I was going to wake up from the nightmare and find it had gone away. At the back of my mind I was half expecting a phone call to say there had been a big mistake, and we were actually doing very nicely thank you. I could not believe all those hours, days, weeks and months of hard slog had been for nothing.

In the privacy of my own home, I sobbed my heart out. I felt unclean, a failure. I felt I had done something wrong, yet all I had ever done was make pop records that had sold well. I felt I had let people down, yet I was the one who had been let down. It was very difficult to get to grips with the enormity of the problem, and it was weeks before I took in the full implications of it.

For the first time ever, when David became involved, we were put in the picture about our position. He sat us down and went through it all with us. We knew that we were in serious, serious trouble.

It became much worse trouble a couple of weeks later when the *Sun* splashed a story across their front page saying that we owed American Express £58,000. We did: they were our biggest single creditor at that time, but it was a bit precipitate of them to make it so public. The debt was mainly for furnishing the house at Frimley, and we paid it off in full two months later when we were refunded some of the money we had paid in excessive commission. I still have my gold Amex card – I'm going to frame it one day.

However, the damage was done, and our financial problems were public. Anybody running a business will tell you that the worst thing that can happen is that the public lose confidence in you. From the 28 March 1990 onwards, the date of the American Express debt story, it became open season to have a go at us over our finances. The press took every opportunity to cast us in the role of extravagant, arrogant kids who had gone on irresponsible spending sprees. Instead of spitting at us, guys in the street would wave ten-pound notes at us: my one regret is that I didn't take them! Even a little ten-year-old jeered that I was broke at me.

Two days after the American Express story, Tom Watkins was pressing in the High Court for a payment of £63,000 down, and another £6,000 a month as initial payments towards the vast sum he was suing us for. To avoid paying him it was necessary to reveal to the court just how broke we were, and the next day that made a big news story. The figures looked horrendous in cold print: we had spent £117,000 on security, £83,000 on limousines, £83,000 on travel. From that, anyone would think that we were holidaying all over the world, using chauffeur-driven limos wherever we went and surrounding ourselves with bodyguards. There was no explanation given: the travel was the cost of touring for work (apart from three days in Hawaii, the last holiday I had was before I was famous); the limousines were used to get us to and from venues, through hordes of screaming girls, and are part and parcel of normal band expenditure (and were also used by our management people at our expense); the bodyguards: well, I've already explained just how impossible life is when you live besieged by fans.

As for clothes, in eighteen months we had paid out £164,000. But we were appearing on stage, there were three of us for much of that eighteen months, we had to buy outfits for the rest of the band and the backing vocalists: I think if you looked at the clothes expenditure of people who have been in similar positions in terms of their public profile and image, you would find that ours was not excessive.

None of this was made clear. Just printing the figures made us look like we had the good sense of a cabbage: the net result of the publicity was that we were crazy spend-thrifts with no control over our money. The bit about having no control was true: we had never been aware of the true facts of our income, we had never controlled it ourselves, and we had never expected to control it because we believed that our very expensive management were doing that for us. Seeing the figures paraded in public made me feel physically sick: I knew that if I had read them about anybody else I would have been tempted to condemn them, just as people were condemning me.

David saved my sanity. He explained what could be done and what should be done. Since those dark days he has only charged us a very small percentage of any money he has generated for us, and when we weren't working he did hours of work for us for nothing. He insists his motives are not altruistic: he has faith in us, and believes one day, when our careers are off the ground again, he'll get his rewards.

But despite David's support, it was an awful time for me. Instead of making music, which was all I ever wanted to do, I was spending days in meeting after meeting after meeting. The press were desperate to try to get hold of any crumb of a story about us, and we did do some television appearances during this time. It was hell: trying to hold our heads up high and sound positive.

The first step David took was to persuade our record company CBS to provide some immediate financial support. He went to see them to explain that he was in control; that we had torn up our credit cards; that our expensive cars had gone back and the outstanding HP agreements on them had been cleared; that all bills were going direct to him and he was sorting them out. With difficulty, he managed to convince the record company to send us a cheque for £70,000.

'The attitude was that they were a record company, not a bank,' said David. 'Despite the fact that Bros had delivered the goods for them, with two big-selling albums and a string of top ten hits, they refused to feel sorry for them. But I managed to convince them that it was not in their interests to see the boys go bankrupt and that they should reinvest some of the huge profits they had already made from the boys.'

For me, watching my beloved Porsche go back was a very low moment. It summed up everything I thought I had achieved. I could not bear to see it go: I got my assistant to drive it round the corner from my home to hand it over to the man from the garage. But just hearing the engine start up brought tears to my eyes. Even worse was when Shirley's Golf, which I was also paying for on HP, had to be taken. Shirley did not mind: her attitude is that a car is nothing more than a lump of metal on four wheels that takes her from one place to another. She refused to be sentimental or upset about it, but it hurt me deeply because I felt I had failed her.

Our debts were continuing to mount. Our original accountants were owed £18,000, our original solicitors sent in a bill for £104,000 (which was later reduced). We were still in the throes of our legal action with 3 Style, and the High Court had frozen £85,000 which was in our bank account pending the result of the case, and which could have been used to pay off some of our debts.

June 8 was a good day for us, because not only did we settle with Tom Watkins, but David and Tony Russell also clinched a publishing deal with Robin Godfrey Cass, managing director of Warner Chappell. They paid us £175,000 for the rights to the songs on our next album:

the money was used to make a payment of 50p in the pound to our creditors, with a promise to pay the rest as soon as possible. When the press found out about the deal the figure we were receiving was exaggerated to £1 million, which must have raised the hopes of some of our creditors!

David had taken an early decision that he should be as open as possible with our creditors, as any one of them could have bankrupted us at any moment, and he wanted to avoid that if at all possible. He'd spoken to some of them and now he wrote to them all, explaining the position and offering the payment. His policy of *glasnost* worked in that most of them were understanding. Many of them were firms which had made good money out of us in the previous three years: car hire companies, sound and lighting companies, etc.

They accepted that we were not running away from our obligations: it would have been easier for us to go bankrupt and then none of them would have received anything.

However, one of them – and we do not know which one – thought it was clever to send a copy of David's letter to the *Sun*, who, of course, published extracts from it. It was very disappointing, but less of a surprise to Matt and me than it was to David. We knew from past experience that everything we did was newsworthy. But David was angry: he felt we were struggling to do the honourable thing, and we were being undermined. He wrote another letter to all the creditors, telling them that it was a stupid thing to have done, as the more difficult life was for us the less chance we had of ever paying off our debts. Several of the creditors got in touch with him saying that they agreed. They, too, were upset, and they let him know that they were not responsible.

After a great deal more negotiation, David managed to

persuade CBS to underwrite our living expenses for a time.
He produced figures showing how much we needed for
our mortgages, food, HP for one car each, phone, electricity: the basics. We were also still desperately trying to
hold our career together, and there was no respite from
the attention of the fans, so it was decided we needed to
keep a personal assistant to handle the day-to-day running
of our affairs. All in all, CBS agreed to pay £13,500 a
month to cover these costs.

We were totally dependent on them. There was no
opportunity for us to tour, as there was no album to promote, and because we were tied up in London with the
legal negotiations. Things were so bad for me personally
that there was one day when David wanted me to attend
a business meeting and I literally could not afford to put
petrol in the car to get into London.

Against this background, Matt and I were trying to
write new material for an album, and to find ourselves
new management. That we survived the year at all is in
no small way thanks to David Ravden. This is David's
own version of why he got – and stayed – so closely
involved with us:

'It started out as a piece of work for me, what I do for
a living. I didn't expect to like them: I was as much a victim
of the kind of publicity they had had as anyone, and I
probably thought they were architects of their own mis-
fortunes.

'But when I met the guys, I liked them. They were
straight, not at all arrogant. I also saw as soon as I looked
at their affairs that they had had a raw deal, one of the
worst I had ever seen. We are known in this firm as cam-
paigners for artists, we believe the guy with the talent
should be protected at all times. So I was more than willing
to stand in their corner.

'As I got to know them better, I also realized how talented they are. The myth that they weren't really responsible for their own music had gone before them, and it wasn't until I talked to them and listened to their work that I realized they are a great deal more talented than I had given them credit for.

'When I heard the new material they were writing for their third album, I knew they had a real future, and I was happy to be part of it.'

I don't feel bitter about Tom Watkins and Mick Newton any more. At first I did, but I soon decided that if I allowed my life to be polluted by bitterness then I was allowing them to be more important than they deserved. Hindsight would be great if you could have a flash of it before the event: as you can only have it afterwards, it's a useless commodity, and it's not worth spending any time on.

I believe now that Tom, my manager, must have had complete contempt for me and my feelings. He was happy enough to take the title 'mentor' when applied to him by journalists, but he never took on the mantle of a mentor. The only things he taught me were bad habits, like how to spend money.

What I didn't know was that while I was making him plenty of money I had nothing like as much to spend myself. I looked up to him, I was impressed by him, I trusted him. A coach tells you how to do it, when to do it, and if he tells you to jump on the bar and squash your nuts, you do it: Tom was my coach.

Now all I want is for the day to come when he is only a distant memory. I want to feel so secure that I can look back on 1990 and smile about it.

I have seen Tom once since the split, when I bumped into him in Covent Garden. Funnily enough, quite separately, Matt had also seen him earlier the same day. He smiled at me and was civilized. He said, 'I saw your brother earlier.' We did not waste any more words on each other. I had nothing to say to him.

CHAPTER FOURTEEN

Shocked

The special glass my mother has at her house is designed to stop fans peering in: she can see out but they can't see her. I feel as though I spent the first few years of my career encircled by a shield of this glass, only it was facing the wrong way. Everyone could see into me, but I could not see out.

I put a lot of trust in and a lot of dependence on people who did not care about me, which is a bit like standing there and letting someone stick a knife into you. You will inevitably be wounded, hurt, damaged, if you are open and giving with people who couldn't care less about you.

I wish I could recapture those old feelings of trust and friendship and know that they would survive and everything would work out well. Only they didn't survive, because the minute success deserted us so did a great many of the people in whom we had trusted. The 'mates' who had hung out with us on the road were nowhere to be seen. Today I do not have one friend I made during the fame days.

The people around us in those days had as much disregard for money as we did – more so, because it was our money they disregarded! The amount of expensive clothes and jewellery we 'lost' is incalculable, but the total comes to thousands, not hundreds, of pounds. Things disappeared all the time, and we had no more grip on what was happening than anybody else. We did not expect it to be our job to take an inventory of all our own clothes at the beginning of a tour and check it all back in again at the end.

The twenty-first birthday presents that Matt and I gave each other were both casualties of our own – and other people's – carelessness. I took my Cartier chain off for a video shoot, and left it to one side in the studio. After the shoot I forgot to pick it up: but I remembered as soon as I got home, phoned the studio, and it had vanished. Matt's watch went in similar circumstances.

Jackets would often go missing, and they would never be worth less than five or six hundred pounds. I had a special jacket made, covered in watches and clock faces, which I wore when we were photographed for the *Time* album. It had 'The Time' written in studs on the back, and a watch face depicted in studs. It disappeared.

Whenever we missed something we would ask where it was and efforts would be made to find it, but usually it would fail to turn up. This would happen against the background of us being very busy, working day and night on tour, travelling from place to place. Nobody ever had time to stop and hold an inquest. Besides, I'd have felt like the mad captain in *Mutiny on the Bounty* if I'd started a big search for one jacket that might easily have been just mislaid. There were always more important things to get on with.

We paid out a fortune on hotel bills while we were on tour, but I don't regret that. There are some stars around who are booked into top hotels while their musicians and backing vocalists are lodged round the corner in much cheaper joints. I won't name any names, but some really big stars do it. I always felt that was rather mean behaviour, and we would pay for musicians and singers to stay in the same place as us. I think people should be looked after while they are working hard. Even now when I realize how little we made from touring, I still feel it would have been wrong to treat them as second-class citizens.

My loneliness on tour, away from Shirley, was my biggest enemy. I liked having people around me, it was fun, it made life more bearable. So after a show we would all go to dinner together, often as many as twelve people. Anyone who was around from the tour was free to come, and they did.

Whenever the bill was presented, everyone would avert their eyes and suddenly be very busy talking to their neighbour. Nobody would look at me: it was as though I was the camera and they all wanted to avoid looking into the lens. Nobody ever offered to split the bill with me, apart from Scott Davidson, the keyboard player, who I really did feel was a true friend in those days. Somebody once offered me £20 for a meal of which their share was about £100, but that was an insult really. I always ended up paying: once, in New York, the bill for twelve people was $3,000. The champagne they had been drinking was $180 per bottle.

I admit I developed a taste for good wine and good food in those days, and so did everybody else – but at least I was doing it at my own expense! Looking back, I don't know whether all those people really were playing me for a sucker or if they, like me, genuinely felt there was so much money washing about that one more expensive meal didn't matter.

All I do know is that since the bubble burst not one of them has been in touch. One minute you smell of roses and people can't get enough of you, the next you smell of dead fish and nobody wants to be around. I never thought I was buying friendship when I picked up the tab for everybody's meals: I genuinely thought we were all mates, and

I just happened to be the one with some money so I would pay. I assumed that if it had been the other way round, somebody else would have paid. I didn't rate money highly enough to imagine that was the motivation for people hanging out with me. Now I'm afraid I believe it was. I'm now very cynical about people, I've learned the hard way. I *was* buying friendship, and it wasn't worth the price I was paying for it: not the financial price, but the emotional one. The pain of finding that was all people wanted me for went very, very deep.

I have heard people say how, when some big tragedy like a death comes into their lives, people avoid them because they do not know how to talk to them. Perhaps that is what it was like with us: people didn't know what to say to us when they heard we were in a deep financial mess. But I don't believe I would have reacted like that towards friends of mine. After all, people in the same industry can always find plenty to talk about. But the phone stopped ringing.

You never really know who your friends are until you can give them nothing, there is nothing they can get out of being around you. There are people who enjoy hanging around with someone who is famous, and there are plenty of others in this industry who only want to know you if you are of benefit to them. There were a lot of people on our payroll: when we stopped paying the wages the friendship stopped, too.

I was very sad when Scott Davidson chose to work with Craig. I thought Scott and I would have been friends for many, many years to come. We got on very well and he played on the first two albums. He did the American tour with us: he bought me a small silver flask, which I used to fill with Hennessy Cognac, which is what I reckon kept me going in America. It was the only time anyone from the band ever gave me anything. But when we got back to England he phoned to say he had been offered a lot of money to work with Craig, and he was going to accept it.

I took it personally: I felt betrayed. He was the one artist on the whole planet I felt was there because he liked me, not for the money, yet he was leaving for money. He had seen how deeply unhappy I had been when we split with Craig, and he knew how much we had suffered from being cast as the baddies while Craig was seen as an innocent victim. He'd told me how unjust it all was. I was as upset when Scott left as I was when Craig did.

My dad discovered one way in which we were being ripped off when he got a lift home one night with a driver from one of the car hire firms we used. Dad's a very experienced detective and he's also a nice friendly guy who people find it easy to talk to. He sat in the front seat next to the driver and before long he'd heard how we were being ripped off for the cost of phone calls from some of the limos we hired. Cars like that all have their own phones, which are costly to use. We were being billed for calls which lasted sometimes for almost the entire length of time that we had hired the car for – even though for much of that time it would be sitting outside waiting for us, and we wouldn't be anywhere near the phone!

The driver who talked to my dad put his neck on the line tipping us off, and I really appreciate that: he did it, he said, because he had always found us to be two decent young men, and he didn't like to see it happening to us.

We suggested at an early stage that we should buy our own limo and employ a driver, but we were told that it was too expensive. In fact it would have saved us a fortune, we'd have recouped at least three-quarters of what we paid out in car hire. About a year after we first suggested it,

Tom Watkins did it for himself – he bought a Jaguar and hired a driver.

While the car hire bills were being checked we discovered that we had even paid inadvertently for a van hired by Craig, after he had split from us, to move some of his equipment. He had asked my bodyguard, Kelly, to book it for him, so it had been put down on the Bros account by mistake.

Shirley had put her own career on the back burner while Bros were big: she promoted her own record, but had given up singing backing vocals, which is where she could have been making good money. I didn't see any need for her to work if she didn't want to, and she had already spent so many years in the business that she was happy to give it a rest. When she sold her house she gave a large chunk of the money to Jim, and the rest went on her tax bills and on paying for things for the bungalow.

It was difficult for her to work: I was very bad news for her, career-wise. People in the business knew that she was with me, and they were reluctant to employ her because of our lack of credibility. Or they assumed she wasn't available and didn't bother asking. She was always furious when she saw newspaper articles that suggested we were hyped: she'd been in the studio when we were unknowns, making our first album, and she knew we could do it. Shirley was always ready to leap to my defence if anyone said anything about me in her hearing: on more than one occasion she's had to be restrained from clocking someone.

Although she's been in the business longer than me and was far more cynical than I was about the sycophants and the hangers-on, Shirley was as shocked as we were when we found out about the money problems. Although she did not like Tom Watkins – he did not make any attempt to make himself likeable to her – she had assumed that we were being managed well financially.

'I could not believe it when Luke told me there was no money,' she says. 'All I had seen for two years was Luke working himself into the ground. He was never not working, and the hours were horrendous. I assumed, as everyone did, that he was rich. He had managers and accountants, after all, and I assumed they would be looking after him. I never asked about money.

'To my knowledge, he had never been given a spending limit. He had never been made to sit down and look at any figures. Sure, I knew that occasionally the accountant had told both him and Matt not to spend so much, but it was never heavy. They were never given budgets to look at, never forced to look at the reality of where their hard-earned money was going.

'David Ravden was the first person to do that.'

David put us on a budget of £800 a week at first, which sounds a lot of money but we were still paying for a personal assistant each, and we had to try, for the sake of our careers, to keep up appearances. But after a few weeks he reduced the budget to £500, and then to £300, by which time we had got rid of our assistants.

That's how it still stands today. It sounds a reasonable amount of money to many people, I know, and we manage well enough on it. But it was an enormous adjustment to make, from having to never even think about money to having to watch every penny. I'm not complaining. But I do know that it is harder to set your sights down, financially, than it is to set them up. If you creep up to £300 a week, it seems like a lot of money. If you come down to it, from literally thinking that you are a millionaire, it seems a very small amount to manage on.

Luckily, Shirley is not the sort of woman who thinks

love is something that goes with diamond rings, expensive dinners and £50 bottles of perfume. She's had all those things, and I know she's enjoyed them. But when the good times stopped rolling she never for one moment reproached me, never complained, never made me feel in any way that I'd failed her.

David was astonished that we had not been given a spending allowance before, not since the early days of our first recording contract.

'If my company had been handling their affairs from the beginning they would never have got into the mess they were in,' he says. ' Not only would they have received a far greater chunk of their own earnings, but it would have been handled better.

'It was no good their accountant complaining that they spent too much. Something should have been done to make sure that they didn't. They were only really extravagant in one way: the cars. The amount they spent on clothes was very reasonable considering the profession they are in: it might sound a lot to the man in the street, but when you are appearing on stage, and on television, and your career depends to some extent on how you look, clothes are a necessary expenditure.

'The travelling bills were all associated with their work. They were picking up the tab for everybody, and at the same time their management, who were helping incur the expenses, were taking commission on gross income without deduction of any of those expenses. It was a recipe for disaster.

'They lost money on cars, because everyone knows that new cars depreciate very rapidly, and they changed their cars too often. But even so, the losses should have been sustainable within the kind of massive amounts of money they were generating, if only a reasonable share of that money had been going to them.

'And who can blame two teenage boys, who thought they were earning millions, for wanting Porsches? I would have been the same at their age if I could have afforded it.

'Our company handles young artists who are just breaking big into the business, and we keep them on a tight rein. If they are determined to spend too much we tell them, forcibly, that they can't: we don't just let them do it and then whinge about it afterwards. That would be failing in our duty as I see it. An accountant does not have to be popular, he has to wield a big stick at times. Later he gets thanked, but not always at the time.

'Nobody cared enough about Bros to wield the big stick. They are intelligent boys who would have understood the score if they had been forced to look at it.'

Mum and Tony and Dad were terrific throughout the bad times. There was never any element of 'I told you so' or 'Why didn't you listen to us?' They understood that we had been paying for top management, and that we had therefore assumed that we were being looked after. Dad himself admits that he was very impressed when he sat across the desk from Tom Watkins in his swanky office.

'I was concerned, because of the vast amounts of money that were flying around, that nobody would notice if a million or so went missing,' said Dad. 'I'd heard about other stars who had ended up broke. I told Watkins of my fears. He pointed out that Bros were not his first band, nor would they be his last. He said with great aplomb that it would not do his reputation any good if, after a couple of years at the top, Matt and Luke "did not have a pot to piss in", to use his exact words. He told me that the boys had good accountants who were looking after the investment side of their affairs.

'I was not a naïve eighteen-year-old. I was in my forties, I'd been a detective for years, I knew my way around. Yet

I was taken in by him. How could I ever think any of it was Luke's and Matt's fault?

'It came as a shock to realize how little they had for all the work they put in, and I felt furious towards Watkins, after he had deliberately reassured me. If I had met him at that stage I think I would have chinned him – which would not have been a good idea from my career point of view.'

Mum felt very upset for us.

'It is like watching your sons being dropped into a tank of sharks and picked to the bone. I felt so helpless,' she says. 'When they are little you can kiss them and make the bogeyman go away. But this was real. I felt shocked, even though I am much older than they are and have had plenty of problems in my own life.

'In the end, after my initial anger, I have come round to feeling sorry for Tom Watkins. One day his conscience will catch up with him. One day he will look in the mirror and see a person he does not like very much.

'Luke and Matt had to take so much bad publicity, so many abusive remarks in the street. They took it all with dignity and pride, and they did their crying in private. On the surface, Tom Watkins appears to have come out better off. But money is only a very small part of life: I don't think he could claim to have any dignity or pride.'

Tony, ever the businessman, was incensed that we had paid 'top prices for unsatisfactory service'.

'It is a lesson to everyone: never assume that because you are paying through the nose you are getting something better. Luke and Matt paid a phenomenal amount to have their affairs looked after, and so they naturally believed they were being taken care of.

'They made the mistake of thinking that people are basically decent and fair. They were willing to pay for everything, and there were plenty of people who were willing to let them do that. Those people have now moved on to the next money pot.

'The management team didn't have to see Bros as a long-term proposition. Their attitude was: come for a ride, let's make money while we can.

'The saddest part of it all to me is that they have come out of this without any friends. It seems that everyone they knew in those days was only out for what they could get from them. When the money stopped, so did the friendship. Isn't that a terrible comment on humanity? Luke and Matt are likeable young men, good company, generous, considerate. It isn't difficult to be friends with them. But it became fashionable to knock them: the press had a field day when their financial troubles became public, and none of their so-called friends was willing to stand up and be counted for them. It's enough to make anyone cynical.'

When we split from Tom Watkins we had David in charge of our business affairs, but we needed someone to look after our career for us. While we were in the throes of a court case with Watkins no other management would be likely to take us on, so we made our own arrangements. Mark Evans was one of Watkins's staff, and he had looked after our affairs on a day-to-day basis for some time. He knew what we were doing, he was used to working with us, and he was efficient. We asked him to leave Tom and come with us.

He was happy, but he too faced legal action from Tom to whom he was under contract. We agreed to pay his legal costs which, in the end, came to £21,000, more than he or we expected. He was very embarrassed about it, but we honoured it, even though in the end we had to pay it off in instalments.

Mark was the greatest second-in-command in the business, a really good person to have on your team. He had great faith in us and our talents. But the responsibility of taking us over completely was huge, and I think he felt out of his depth. We were also going through such traumas in our personal lives, and such bad publicity, that it was difficult for him to generate the level of work we needed to get ourselves back into good financial shape. He didn't have the clout in the industry: other people were so used to dealing with him as a number two that they found it hard to relate to him as the main man.

Mark took a big risk on our part, and I will always be grateful to him. He was with us throughout 1990, which was a time when we needed someone solid like him around. But in the end it fell to me to see him and tell him that it wasn't working out – because we weren't working. In a strange sort of way, I think he felt relieved, and we parted on good terms.

The year ended on a good note for us. Our financial situation was still bleak, but David Ravden was in control and we knew that we could rely on him. And our career was looking up.

We had found a new management team. John Reid, Elton John's manager, had agreed to take us on.

CHAPTER FIFTEEN

I Quit

Our new manager, John Reid, lived in great style in a mansion near Rickmansworth, Herts. We were invited to spend a weekend with him soon after he had signed us, and when we arrived in my second-hand, filthy dirty Jaguar Sovereign we knew before we had crossed the threshold that we were out of our league. The other cars parked outside made my old Jag look like it had gate-crashed a party.

There was no party though, as we four – me, Matt, Shirley and Matt's girlfriend Mel – were the only guests. John personally cooked a meal for us, and it was a relaxed, happy evening.

In contrast, on our second night there, John held a dinner party and we felt rather like gate-crashers ourselves. The conversation round the table revolved around how many millions the guys there had each made in the previous year. One of them asked John, almost like it was a party game, what his worst recent year was, and he said something about being down to two million. When I was asked the same question I said, 'I think you all know what my situation is.' It was like being an alien from another planet, sitting amongst that lot and their wives and girlfriends, who were dripping with jewels – especially as I knew that most of them were nothing like as big in the business as John, either. They were what I call 'hoitys', music industry snobs trying to convince each other they were wealthy.

In the middle of the table as a centrepiece was a diamond-studded tortoise, and when you pressed its tail a bell rang, summoning the staff. John's wealthy guests loved it and kept pressing the tail for the hell of it – without a thought for the waiter who had to keep running in and out to see why he had been called.

John himself was always very charming. The following day he lent his own cars to us so that we could go out shopping: Matt, his favourite, and Matt's girlfriend Mel were given a Bentley convertible, and Shirley and I were given a Mercedes 500SL two-seater: he didn't know it, but I much preferred the car I got, and Matt would have, too, even though the one he was driving was worth about £130,000.

On our return, when we went to our bedrooms, we found presents laid out on the beds for us. Shirley got a pair of silk pyjamas and a pair of silk boxer shorts with 'John Reid' embroidered on them. I also got a pair of the boxer shorts. Matt was with us, so I went with him to his room to see what they had got: Mel got a cushion, a beautiful scarf and a pair of the shorts, and on Matt's side of the bed was a John Paul Gaultier jacket, plus his pair of shorts. The jacket could not have cost less than £600.

If there was a message there, it was pretty blatant. It was so blunt and obvious that I really do wonder to this day whether it was not a mistake: although there was no doubt that John preferred Matt to me, at the same time I find it hard to believe that he would be crude enough to show it like that. Matt was embarrassed and upset because he thought that I minded: in fact, it struck me as funny. I've heard about people dropping hints, but this was hurling them . . .

At some point while we were staying there, John took us to look in his safe. I think one of us must have asked him about his jewellery. Out came the most amazing collection of gold Rolexes, diamonds and brooches, it was like being in Cartier's in Bond Street. I walked out of the room halfway through the exhibition: partly because there are only so many gold Rolexes you can enthuse over, only so many canary diamonds you can admire, but also because I was horrified by the ostentation. It was a world we had become a part of, and I had learned to love jewellery myself, but I could still keep a sense of proportion about it. It seemed obscene for one man to have so much, and to have to keep it locked away in a safe. I admit I also felt hurt: I was in the process of selling off all my jewellery in order to pay bills and survive, and it seemed tactless, especially as John knew the details of our situation, to have to stand there and see so much paraded before us.

It was through Elton John that we became involved with John Reid. Elton, who has always been managed by John, has been very good to us and has said a lot of nice things about us. On more than one occasion he has said publicly that we were underrated, and more talented than we were ever given credit for. He knew when we split with Tom that we were looking for management. Muff Winwood, head of A&R at our record company (CBS had by now been taken over by Sony, the Japanese giant, and was known as Sony Music) also knew John Reid, and mentioned us to him.

John Reid's company is no doubt brilliant for the artists they handle: they have big stars like Elton, Billy Connolly, Barry Humphries, Viscount Linley. These guys don't need anyone to go out there and find work for them, or hustle for them. They need management which is good at organization, and that's what John Reid's company is.

We needed something else. John himself is very much

a figurehead, or at least he was in our dealings. He has had tremendous success for twenty years or more, and he did not need to be in at the cutthroat end of the industry.

It was Steve Brown who took over the main responsibility for our affairs, with a girl called Dee Whelan running them on a day-to-day basis as our personal manager. Steve is terrific, one of the very best, and I believe that if we could have had 100 per cent of his attention we would have done very well. But he spent much of his time in America with other clients, who all needed their share of him.

John Reid's company never ripped us off, but they didn't contribute much to our career. On a personal level they were all very polite, but I don't need to feel grateful for that because I, too, am always polite. After we had left, one of John Reid's staff publicly branded us as 'prats', which was wounding and unprofessional, as we did not part from them on bad terms. I was astonished by his comments: a company like theirs should have too much class for that.

Our careers were a headache, I know, but given the right tablets a headache goes away. Unfortunately, they didn't know which tablets to prescribe.

Dee worked very hard on our behalf, and she shared our frustrations. She did not have the authority to make decisions, and she did not have the clout to make her presence felt at the record company. We were already immersed in writing our third album when we signed to John Reid, and we were pleased with the songs we were writing.

Changing Faces should have been the answer to all our financial problems. Launched properly and quickly, with good promotion, it would have made money for our record company, it would have cleared our debts, it would have given us a future career. And, most important of all, it would have taken us across the very difficult bridge from pre-pubescent pop to the grown-up world of real music – because it was a great album, much the best thing Bros ever did. The third album is always the crucial one, it needs as much care and attention as a debut album.

We were older, more experienced, and it was reflected in our songs and our music. We were writing about things we'd had no experience of at eighteen: we were growing up, and it was there on the album for everyone to hear it. Our musical competence had grown and so had our musical confidence, despite all the knocks we had suffered. We were ready to move on. It was as if we had been driving down an A road and needed to get on to a motorway: the third album was going to be the slip road. We did not want to stay locked in the fantasies of little girls for ever. We'd always been criticized for being pop: this album was the answer to our critics.

But nobody buys a record they don't know about, and nobody knew about *Changing Faces*. It took so long to release that all the impetus of our previous success had been dissipated by the anti-Bros feeling whipped up by the press. The main problem was that Sony was paranoid about the album being 'right'. We ended up writing over forty songs for it. You obviously have to write more than the ten which are going to be recorded, but usually fifteen or so would give a good enough choice (and, in fact, the ones eventually recorded on the album were mostly the earlier ones we wrote). It seemed to us that they wanted all ten to be hit songs, whereas what you need is three hits and seven good songs on an album. We ended up putting our heads up our backsides till we ended up inside ourselves, trying to produce the songs that they wanted.

Matt and I did not let our business problems get in the way of our music work any more than was absolutely necessary, and we could have recorded and released that album in four months: in the end it took eighteen months and cost the record company a third of a million. During that time we had nothing to promote, so touring was out of the question. Apart from money we were earning in rights from the songs we had already published, we had no income other than the money from the record company. We were pinning a lot of hopes on the album.

The songs were good: we knew that, and so, eventually, did the record company. Muff Winwood said that if he could have been given his perfect Bros album, this was it. He could not, he said, have asked for more. When we played 'Are You Mine?' to Piers Morgan, editor of the *Sun*'s 'Bizarre' page (featuring pop and show business stories) he wrote:

> It's a superb ballad – easily the best thing they have ever done. And, like George Michael's 'Careless Whisper', this could be the song that catapults Bros into a new, more mature league of stardom. They've earned the chance.

Unfortunately, the album release could not have been more disastrously handled. The executives at CBS were like a team of synchronized swimmers who had decided to swim off in different directions. They may all have been technically very good, but there was no sense of teamwork. There was no planning, no coordination, no effort to make sure we got played on radio. We had a few press interviews arranged by Dee Whelan, and she also set up a radio promotional tour, but that was all. Considering they'd had eighteen months to get ready, it was abysmal: our management should have had someone hassling the record company three or four times a week to make sure everything possible was being done.

Radio plays were always difficult for us. Some of the independent local radio stations liked us, but at a national level and a London level we always had a hard fight. Radio One played records according to the dictates of a 'Playlist Committee'. The committee, made up of producers, met once a week to decide which new releases would go on one of three playlists. The A list meant the record would get played a lot and would be used on all shows; the B list meant it would get occasional plays; and the C list meant it would only be played in the slots where the DJ and his producer could insert records of their own choice. We never, not even when we were churning out top ten hits, went straight on to the A list. It was only when our songs were right up in the charts and the fans were demanding them that they got a decent amount of airtime on Radio One. We were rarely played on Capital Radio, the independent London station. There the playlist choice was dominated by the opinions of the programme controller, and he never rated us.

So coming out with an album after eighteen months away, a lot of care and consideration was needed to make sure we got the exposure we needed for the fans – and people who had not liked our previous stuff – to get to hear our new sound. The record company and our management team should have been talking to radio people, persuading them to listen, selling us again as if we were a new group – or, at least, a very famous, well-established band but with a totally different sound. The curiosity value alone of Bros doing something so different should have merited some plays.

Our career was like a ball that had been rolling along

fast. Then it had changed shape, to a square or a triangle, and it didn't roll so easily. But with a bit of pushing it would roll, and as it went further and further the corners would wear away until it was rolling fast again. We needed the push.

It didn't happen. A senior executive at CBS admitted to David Ravden that if it wasn't for the fact that he worked for the company, he would have had no idea we had a new album out. Another executive asked us when we were going to cut a single from the album: it had already been done.

They did not know, and we got the impression they did not care, what happened to our album. The only really good radio publicity we got was when, on our way to sign copies at the Tower Records shop in Kensington, Matt called up Phillip Schofield, who was on the air with his Radio One show at the time, and Phil talked to us live while we were doing the signing. So his listeners at least knew about the album.

There was an amusing – in retrospect – incident in Vienna, where we went to do a press conference to promote the album.

A couple of years earlier we had cancelled a concert in Austria when we found the basketball court where we were booked to appear was totally inadequate. The stage ran the wrong way along the hall, and it wasn't strong enough to take our rig: the average band travels with about ten tons of lighting alone.

We arrived at the press conference to find two detectives there, with a summons for our arrest. The promoter of the cancelled show was claiming £10,000 in damages, and the policemen wanted to seize our passports to prevent us leaving the country. Although we had our passports on us, we had the forethought to say that they were back at the hotel. The detectives agreed to follow us back there.

We legged it to the van we were using for the European promotion, and as we began driving I frantically telephoned the British Embassy. The Embassy staff advised us how to get to their address – we were skidding around the narrow streets pursued by the police car – and when we arrived at the Embassy the gates were open and we drove straight in. It was a bit like something out of a James Bond film but I was determined I wasn't handing my British passport over to anybody!

We spent hours in the Embassy, being amusingly entertained by the consul, who was unflustered and very helpful. I expect he is used to dealing with far more delicate situations than ours, although he wasn't used to being besieged by the police, the press and fans. He finally arrived at a solution: we would be allowed to carry on with our press engagements that day, and the following day we would appear in court to sort the matter out.

In fact, it was less of a formal court appearance than we expected, more of an investigation. Matt and I were taken into separate rooms and gave long detailed statements, for about forty-five minutes, about why we had refused to play the concert. We were each provided with a translator. Our statements matched perfectly and, after a few more questions, the examining magistrate concluded that we did not owe anything; that our decision not to play the concert had been sensible and fair.

In the circumstances, the *Changing Faces* album did very well: even without properly organized publicity it went into the album charts at number sixteen and sold a reasonable amount. We had two hit singles off it, 'Are You Mine?' and 'Try'. We made no money because so much had already been advanced by CBS, which they needed to recoup from sales. We were simply hoping to have picked up merchandising and other spin-offs, and get our career back on the rails.

But then somebody at CBS seemed to realize that they had handled it badly, and it was decided that they would withdraw the album (by simply not sending out any more copies to shops), design a new cover with a new name, and relaunch it with lots of promotion and publicity. We went along with that: we thought it still had a chance. Looking back, it would have been much better if they had gone mad and pulled out all the publicity stops when it hit number sixteen.

I don't know whether CBS were ever sincere in their intention of re-releasing it, but it soon became apparent to us that they were not going to do so. They started talking about a 'Bros: Greatest Hits' album, which would have been a disaster for our career. Record companies are funny creatures: you would imagine that having put a lot of money into it, they would have been prepared to spend just a little bit more promoting it. But because it didn't go off like an atom bomb they pulled back and counted their losses.

It did not sink in straightaway. We had worked on the album for so long, we were very proud of it and we knew everything hinged on it. It took me a few days to take on board what was happening: there was no album any more. I woke up one day and realized I had nothing to look forward to. I was in debt to the tune of quarter of a million pounds. There was very little work lined up, no means of ever getting the money to pay off the debts.

I also knew that, as far as anyone in the music business was concerned, whatever credibility Bros had belonged to Matt. Nobody had ever given me any credit. I had heard, second-hand, that an executive at my record company had described me as 'the one who does fuck all'.

I'm a performer. From the age of twelve onwards it is

all I have ever wanted to do. I didn't come into the business to make big money, I didn't come in for the fun of it, although I've enjoyed both the money and the fun. I came in for the music. Now, here I was, enduring the ongoing nightmare of debt, being jeered at and sneered at in the street, and not even being given credit for my involvement in the music.

I had never thought about Bros breaking up, even when I hated the situation we were in, even when the band was nothing but a pain in the bum, even when Matt and I talked about the different things we wanted to do musically. I always thought Bros would be there in the background: that we would go out and do different things, but that ultimately we would always be together in the band.

But now I could see the impossibility of it all. Despite all the subtle ways it had been suggested to him, I knew that Matt would find it almost impossible to make the decision. He would have been worried about leaving me – and it riled me that anyone would worry about me, because I'm proud and capable. But I could see that Matt, who has a great voice, would never get the recognition he deserved while we were Bros and identified only with our teen fans. I didn't want him to grow to feel resentful about me, nor did I want him to feel guilty if he ultimately made the decision to split. I knew it had to come from me.

It was a sudden decision, made when I woke up one morning. I'm glad I did not agonize over it for long. It's hard to give up something secure, something that works: it's a bit like giving your house away. But the Bros house was leaking and draughty, and although it was a roof over my head I didn't feel I had the energy left to repair it.

We could have issued a 'Greatest Hits' album and spent the next ten years cashing in on what little bit of left-over fame there was, like the sixties groups who are still playing the local night spots up and down the country. But I was only just twenty-three, I didn't want that. I wanted to put my talents, my enthusiasm, my effort into something new and fresh.

I finally knew that Bros had reached the end of the road. I picked up the telephone and called Matt.

Chapter Sixteen

Tears On My Pillow

He would probably not admit it even to himself, but I think Matt's main emotion when I told him I was leaving Bros was one of relief. He had been told for so long, and by so many people, that he was the talent in the band, and it had been insinuated that I was holding him back from a brilliant solo career: ultimately he would have found it hard to resist believing at least some of it.

I realized after we split that I had spent five years playing second fiddle to him, never promoting myself and my involvement strongly enough. It was a reversal of the roles we had had for the first eighteen years, when I was the dominant one, the one with the will and determination to get a band together, and he was my little brother Maffy. But I was still that same strong personality: it simply took me a few painful months to get back to knowing it.

When I told Shirley about my decision, she agreed, although she would never have suggested it. I don't think Matt could take it in at first, and then he cried, which made me cry too. After speaking to him I called John Reid's company, and they told me to take a day to think about it. But my mind was made up, and the more I thought about it the more resolute I became.

When I contacted our record company they were happy to let me go, and clear all our debts to them. It was the first time in my life I was glad to be regarded as a complete waste of space. It meant they put no obstacles at all in the way of me leaving.

I rang the company that handled our press affairs and asked if they would put out a statement saying we had split.

The immediate reaction shook me, but was only a sign of things to come: who, they wanted to know, was going to pay for them to put out the statement?

I hoped that Steve Brown, at John Reid's company, would be interested in managing my solo career. I asked him, and he said he'd get back to me. When he didn't call I rang him and said, 'You don't want to do it, do you?' He said, 'Probably not.' It was a severe blow to me, but I handled it coolly and thanked him for being straight with me. Within less than a week I had become organization-free: I had gone from having managers, a record company, a publishing company and a partnership with my brother, to having nothing. For a day or two there was a phoney feeling of elation, of being demob happy.

Then it hit me.

When it looked as if my creditors would make me bankrupt, I knew the first thing to go would be my house. I'd already watched my car being driven away, I could not face being in the house when the bailiffs arrived. I put it up for sale, and we thought we had been lucky and found a buyer straightaway: but like so many people, our luck didn't hold and the sale fell through.

I decided to move out into a rented house. It was difficult living in the bungalow while it was on the market: when anyone sells a house they get a certain number of 'trippers' looking round, people who seem to spend their free time gawping at other people's homes without any intention of buying. When you are famous the problem is much greater.

Two weeks before Christmas 1991 Shirley, Carli and I

moved into a house just outside the village of Elstead in Surrey, where we lived for the next year. Finding the house was, in itself, a nightmare. If you want an example of the way my luck was running during this period of my life, listen to this.

The car I had at the time was a second-hand Jaguar Sovereign, bought with David Ravden's approval because I had, until the split with Matt, ostensibly had a career to keep on the road.

Shirley and I set out to see a house that was available for rent at a price David said we could afford. The owner of the house gave us directions on how to get there. She told us we would have to drive through a ford, which might look deep but was easily crossed. Except that when we got there it had been raining steadily for a few days, and the water really was deep – about three and a half to four feet deep to be precise. We discovered this when the engine cut out because the exhaust was submerged, and moments later water washed over the bonnet. When I climbed out it was above my waist.

Shirley was terrified, but I managed to pull her out through the sunroof, and carry her twenty feet to dry land. It was winter, but my jacket was in the boot of the car, and all I had on was a silk shirt and trousers, which were by now soaking. As we stood on the higher ground we watched the Jag float away down the river and lodge itself against a bank. We were in the middle of the countryside, on the edge of a golf course and only a few hundred yards away from the house we had intended viewing. Luckily I had a mobile phone, and I was able to get through to a twenty-four-hour recovery service, but I almost froze to death waiting for them. A gaggle of schoolgirls appeared from nowhere to gawp at me. It cost £100 to get the car rescued and towed away, and it was a write-off. The insurance money did not cover the repayments I had to make on it, so I was even deeper in debt and without a car.

I don't think we even bothered to view the house, certainly not that day, but soon afterwards we found the one in Elstead.

That Christmas was a very strange time, very special and precious, as though we were trapped in a tiny capsule of happiness, before being thrust out into the pain and reality of what was happening to us. For a week or two the whole nation is on holiday and so I was insulated from my own forced idleness: it did not matter that I wasn't working.

My family came to stay over Christmas: Mum, Tony, Granddad and Matt, Shirley's mum Lil, who is one of my dearest friends (I know you aren't supposed to like your mother-in-law, but Lil and me get on great), Shirley's sister Patsy, Patsy's husband Taffy, and my aunt Sally.

It was painful for me only being able to buy token presents for everyone: it may not sound a serious problem to most people, but when you are used to being able to spoil those around you, it takes a lot of psychological bending to accept that you can't. But that did not stop us having a good time. Everyone got on brilliantly. Mum and Shirley are now very close, and Mum and Tony adore Carli: they sometimes babysit for us at weekends, and Carli always looks forward to it.

The only tension over the whole holiday was between Matt and me, and that spilled over into a fight on Christmas Eve.

We knew that just after Christmas Matt was leaving the country to work in America. John Reid's company was still managing Matt, and they were paying for him to fly out there to make some demo discs as a solo artist, whereas they had turned me down flat when I asked for £1,500 to make some solo demos.

It would be the first time we had ever been apart for a long stretch (as it turned out, we did not see each other for a year). We knew the parting was necessary, but neither of us were very good at handling the pain we were in because of it.

There were times in our career as Bros when I wished that Matt would speak up for me more, push my talent more: but I can't blame him, because I know I was being subtly undermined all the time by people who were dripping their opinions into his ear. Matt and I always loved each other, but it was as though other people put a panel of misty glass between us and we could not always see each other properly, or reach out and touch each other. It was not my place to smash that glass: it was his. I told him at times that I did not believe I was getting the credit I deserved, and by doing nothing about it he was validating the opinions of those who treated me as nothing more than a nuisance, but he could not see it through the misty glass.

We've always fought. Brothers do. And we can both pack a punch. But for years now we've cooled the physical side of our rows, because neither of us wants to get into a real brawl. We push each other and shout at each other, but we pull back from smacking each other in the head. That's what it was like on Christmas Eve: a really nasty row in the kitchen, with us each shoving the other and saying things we afterwards regretted.

I expect other twins are the only people who will understand how close you are to someone who has shared your life from birth. I would die for Matt: if an angel gave me the choice of one of us dying, I would not be strong enough to stand by and witness his death, I would much prefer to die for him. It is a bond that sometimes, like that Christmas

Eve, is too strong for either of us to handle.

When the moment came for him to leave we both broke down completely. We were crying and holding each other, tears running down both our faces: it seemed so big, so final. My mother was in tears too, and so was Shirley. Everyone close to us, especially Mum, knew how difficult it was for us to split after a lifetime together. The only words we said to each other, over and over, were 'Love you, love you.' I was grateful then that, as a family, we have never been frightened of showing our emotions and expressing our love: it would have been dreadful if our parting had been a macho slapping on the back and a fighting back of tears. At least we were able to let it all out. We clung together, reluctant to accept it was happening and yet both realizing it was inevitable.

When Matt eventually climbed into his car he wound the window down, and I walked alongside him down the drive to open the gate for him. His last words were, 'Luke, I'll always love you.' As his car pulled away I could not watch, I was blinded by my own tears and I stood for a moment at the gate, looking down, struggling to control myself.

Then, as I lifted my head, I saw a bright light streak across the night sky: it was a shooting star. I made a wish, for health and happiness for both of us. It sounds so corny, but I'm sure that star was an omen. It made me feel better and I was able to walk back to the house with a lighter heart.

I was incredibly lonely and scared when Matt went away. We had been together all our lives and we had worked together from the day we left school. I felt almost as though a part of my own body had been amputated: something that had always been there was no longer there. Sure, we talked by telephone all the time, but not being involved in the day-to-day running of each other's lives inevitably put as much distance between us as the jet that flew Matt to Los Angeles.

In the months after he left I went through what was probably almost a nervous breakdown, but I did it on my own and I came through without any professional help. I am a very proud person, and it is hard for me to describe – and even accept – what happened to me in those months. But if it helps even one person realize that there is a way out of deep depression, that it is possible to go as low as you can psychologically and still come back up, then it is worth sacrificing my pride.

My life had become a negative of itself in half a decade. The first three years of my career was a positive image, the next two were a negative of the same picture. Instead of being lauded and having people hang on every word, I felt I was a complete nothing, worthless. Instead of having money, I was poor and in debt. Instead of having friends, I was alone.

Acclimatizing to loneliness is very hard. I became very, very afraid. I was afraid to go outside, afraid to see anybody. I thought people would say things, would think I looked poor, or ugly. I was afraid that if I spoke, they'd tell me off or say hurtful things. I was one big walking insecurity.

I looked terrible. The hair on top of my head came out in clumps (though thankfully it has re-grown). My skin was blotchy. I lost weight, dropping from over eleven stone to nine and a half stone. Worse, I lost interest: I can remember looking in the mirror one morning and I had not shaved for about four days, I was bleary-eyed from drinking too much the day before, and I was wearing a tracksuit, trainers and no socks. I thought, 'What have you become?'

When I was really depressed I felt as though my insides were dirty, as though my liver, lungs, stomach and all my internal organs were coated with dirt and mud, and I wanted to put a hosepipe down my mouth to wash everything, my blood as well, away. It was a weird feeling.

The worst moment of every day was the morning, when I first woke up. It would take a few seconds for me to remember: I've lost my home, I've lost my car, I owe a quarter of a million pounds, I can't go out, I can't support myself or my family, I'm a failure. The debt felt like a great heavy bag tied to my ankles, stopping me from walking.

For eight months I hardly went out. The rented house had leaded lights at the windows, and I remember standing at a window watching the rain driving across the garden and feeling that I was behind bars, a prisoner. At times like that I sometimes had such severe anxiety attacks that I would hyperventilate and start to shake. At other times I would cry: I would collapse on the floor wherever I was, in the hall, in the lounge, in the bedroom, and it would all come out, huge uncontrollable sobs. Sometimes I would be full of resentment, pacing about like Mr Angry, and on other days I would have no energy and would talk in a flat monotone.

There was nobody I could call, nobody I could share it with. To the rest of the world I put up a continual camouflage. I did not want Mum or anyone else, except Shirley, to know what I was going through, how low I had sunk.

If Shirley was working she would be up and out of the house by nine in the morning, and I would be on my own until Carli came home from school. I'd be cooking dinner for Carli and I'd think, 'I'm nothing but a bloody housewife. I'm a young man of twenty-three, I ought to be out in the world, working, enjoying myself, and I'm trapped in this house cooking dinner.'

There would be fans outside the gate: the number has dwindled to a small knot now, but in the early days of the split there were never less than thirty or forty girls there. I would wander around in a bathrobe or sling on a tracksuit: there seemed no point in dressing up to stay home, but with the girls at the gate I could not, on a point of pride, walk out looking terrible. I was trapped, living like a hermit . . .

One day I realized that it was three weeks since I had even been outside the door of the house. I had to force myself to go into the garden. I got out of my chair and I was aching everywhere, I felt so low and lacking in energy. But I did it: and then I started crying again because I realized how pathetic I was becoming.

I stopped buying clothes completely: I was used to being able to afford the best, but now I could afford nothing, not even small things like replacing underwear. New clothes make you feel good, they are a psychological boost, they make you feel like going out and meeting people. If you are constantly wearing old things you don't feel great, you don't ever have a day when you feel really good. And there are an awful lot of days in the year to not feel good about yourself. I started drinking. I've always been able to drink and I've always enjoyed it. But on the American tour I was drinking Cognac, and when I got home I realized that I missed it: I knew then that I would have to be careful as I could easily become dependent on it. At home on my own I started having a beer at ten in the morning, just to quench my thirst – even though a soft drink or a cup of tea would have done that. Then I had a few more beers at lunchtime, and in the evening I'd have a bottle of wine, sometimes two. I'd wake up every morning feeling slightly hungover, slightly off colour.

I was frightened of answering the phone: every call

seemed to bring more bad news. My so-called 'friends' all seemed to have lost my number: nobody rang just to see if I was OK. Thank God for David Ravden, who spoke to me most days and always put the financial problems into perspective: he'd tell me there was nothing we couldn't deal with, and even if I was forced to go bankrupt it was amazing how soon people would forget that. He also worked non-stop preventing us from going bankrupt, pacifying creditors and persuading everyone to give us time. I knew, in my heart, that going bankrupt would be a terrible psychological blow, and that it might be more than I could take. I would feel I had completely failed if that happened, and I would also feel personally responsible for letting my creditors down.

For the first couple of months after moving I struggled to pay both the mortgage on the bungalow and the rent on the house, but that soon became impossible and I let the mortgage lapse into arrears. Because of the property slump, the house was worth a lot less than I bought it for: it was on the market for £160,000, when I had paid £250,000 and had a £200,000 mortgage on it. I was in no worse a situation than thousands of families all over Britain, but again the press reacted with glee when the bungalow was repossessed. 'Pop glory years fade away as Luke's £1/4 million home is repossessed' said the *Sun* headline, making out in the story again that I had let a fortune slip through my fingers and was the cause of all my own problems. If I'd been going out every night and pissing it all up against a wall I'd have understood, but in all my time at the top I reckon I can count on two hands the number of parties I went to, and there were even fewer evenings in nightclubs. We were rock stars but we did not live like rock stars, and the minute we found out the scale of our financial problems we did everything we could to sort it out – yet we were pilloried over it.

Luckily Matt and I have not been made bankrupt. By the end of 1992 David had persuaded all our creditors to accept a voluntary arrangement with us: over three years we have agreed to pay off 30p in the pound of all our debts. Had they pushed us into bankruptcy they would probably have received nothing, because we have no assets left.

Selling my jewellery was painful. I went from having £35,000 worth, including two Rolex watches and two Cartier watches, to £30,000, then down to £20,000, £10,000, £5,000 and finally nothing. My stuff went first: my car and my jewellery. Then Shirley's car, and even the two and a half carat diamond ring that I had given her, telling her how much I loved her as I slipped it on her finger, had to be sold. That was the worst moment by far. All in all, I got less than £10,000 for everything I sold: it had proved to be a terrible investment. It was embarrassing and humiliating selling things off to people I knew, but the money was needed to pay the rent. In the end I was left with one watch, but eventually that had to go too: it raised enough money to buy the very basic recording equipment I needed. The Ford Granada that Matt and I had jointly bought for Mum and Tony was the only thing we did not sell. I think I would rather have died than be forced to take their car back.

I know that our poverty was not as great as that experienced by thousands of people all over Britain. But having been able to afford nice things, it was much harder to get used to watching the pennies. I had never had to think about things like the cost of heating, petrol or food.

Lots of people lose their jobs, their homes. But at least they can keep their dignity intact. Nobody need know their pain. Everybody knew mine.

Shirley would sometimes persuade me to go out, because she knew it was good for me. I was not insured to drive the little car she has, but she would take me to a pub for a drink where I would have to endure the smirks and sneers, the comments and the laughter. I could not fall back on a display of front.

I never understood the glee people got from my misfortune: I hope I would not be capable of feeling like that about anybody else and certainly not about somebody I had never met. I had idolized Duran Duran, seen film of them stepping out of limos and Lear jets, but I didn't resent their wealth and I didn't start hating them and mocking them when they ceased to be in the charts. I wished often that I could go up to these people and sit down and start talking to them: would they still hate me then? Our image as Bros had been so two-dimensional: if they knew the real three-dimensional me, would they laugh and sneer?

There's a peculiarly British thing about not liking success. There's a feeling that we should never let people get 'too big for their boots' – and if they do, we ram a hobnailed British boot down their throats and choke them to death. Then we take great delight in listening to their death rattle.

When I did venture out, the level of verbal abuse shocked me. Guys I had never seen before in my life would swear at me – and I really mean swear – in front of Shirley and Carli.

I've said it before in this book, but it was a thought that played through my head endlessly: what had I done wrong? I'd made some pop records and lost some money, was that a reason to treat me so badly? I didn't know why I couldn't hold my head up high, I didn't know what I had done to be ashamed of, and yet I felt embarrassed about who I was and I wanted to hide. If ever I went out, I literally used to walk with my head bowed down. I asked myself: is this what it all adds up to? We had twelve hit singles and even our last one reached the top fifteen, yet everywhere we were branded as failures.

For over a year I did not have a car at all. The insurance company wanted £2,000 to include me on Shirley's insurance: they argue that famous people know other famous people, and if you have a crash and a famous person gets hurt the damages claim could be off the scale, company-threatening. In any case, Shirley's second-hand Renault 5 is not big enough to accommodate my legs in the driver's seat. But I hated not having the freedom to get into a car and drive away: I have always found that driving clears my head and helps me to think straight. Not having a car was another reason why I felt I was in prison.

On Shirley's birthday I could not afford to spend much on her, and I could not get out of the house to get anything. It was humiliating: I gave her some money to buy something for herself. Because she's strong and doesn't care about material possessions, she did not mind. But I minded.

We were never the sort of show business couple who went to parties or clubbing, so we never missed that side of success. But we always enjoyed eating out, which we can now only do very occasionally.

My twenty-fourth birthday was very strange because it was the first Matt and I had ever spent apart. Because he was starting to get his life together again, he sent me a good present: a watch. I sent him an electronic organizer, which cost a lot less than the watch but was all I could afford. It made me feel bad.

Matt was very homesick in LA, even though Mum and Granddad had both been out to visit him, and he wanted

to be back with me for our birthday. But I persuaded him
to wait until Christmas: I wanted to be able to relax and
enjoy his company, not still be struggling to get my life
together.

It was always going to be easier for Matt than it was for
me, he had a lot more respect within the industry. At first
we both thought that John Reid was going to continue to
manage him, but after a few weeks he realized that it was
not working out. He found a new manager straightaway;
Michael Lipman, who used to be in a partnership that
managed George Michael and has only recently set up on
his own, took Matt on straightaway. Michael has something
to prove to the industry, which means that he will put
everything into launching Matt's solo career well, and he's
already fixed him up with a deal for his first solo album.

   It was easier for Matt, too, working in Los Angeles, away
from all the pressures of fans and press. He's unknown
out there, he can live a normal life. Even the burden of
our financial problems is something that he hears about
by telephone every so often: he does not have to live with
it day by day.

   Matt's private life is now happy, too. He started going
out with Melanie Sykes after he was introduced to her by
a friend. It was difficult for Matt to find the right person.
When he didn't have a girlfriend the press branded him
as gay, which was very unfair. Because he didn't issue
tickets for photographers to bring their cameras into his
bedroom, he had to be gay – that's the way they see it. I
often wonder if the journalists who write stories like that
ever think about the people whose lives they are turning
over. Poor old Matt went through agony over it. At one
time we talked about whether he should go out with someone just to scotch the rumours, but he decided he would

not be pressured into a relationship by the press: he wanted to meet the right girl. In one interview he said that the girl for him was probably working in the local greengrocer's. He didn't mean it literally: he simply meant that he was looking for a normal girl, but that because of our fame it was impossible to meet normal people on equal terms. When he started going out with Mel, who is a successful model, there were snide cracks about that. What happened to the greengrocer's assistant? they said. You can't win.

When he started living with Mel I was very suspicious of her: I understood properly for the first time how he felt about Shirley in our early days. Matt and I love each other and are very protective towards each other, and neither of us wants to see the other get hurt. I didn't want anyone taking the piss out of him: I wanted to know that she loved him. But I had to curb my anxieties, because I realized it was something that was between the two of them. Now I know that it is a real relationship, and Matt is happy, so I am happy for him.

Originally, I was going to go to LA, too, although not to work with Matt. I knew it would be much easier to be out of this country. But there is a strong streak of stubbornness and determination in me: I wanted to beat whatever was working against me in Britain, I did not want to roll over and die because I was the victim of my distorted reputation. I wanted the chance to show what I was really capable of, to the people who had mocked and derided me.

A friend of ours, Gardner Cole, came over from LA and spent a week with me, and we talked about working together to write songs. Then the next thing I heard was that Matt was going out to America to stay with Gardner and they were going to work together. At first I felt I had been kicked in the teeth again, but now I realize that it was a good thing: for a few months I was forced to work on my own, find my own depths of talent, rely on myself – and work through my own depression.

It was not a happy time, but in the end I have come out much stronger and with a great deal more confidence in myself. I now do some work with a partner, Simon Burton, but I know that I can do it on my own: I had written about twenty-five songs before I teamed up with Simon.

It was work that saved me from my breakdown.

CHAPTER SEVENTEEN

I Owe You Nothing

I knew I could write songs, I could sing, I could play. If I had been all the things people thought I was – talentless, hyped, dependent on my brother for success – I probably would have gone under, ended up in therapy, a headcase. But the bottom line was that I never lost faith in myself: my faith was shaken, it came close to being obliterated, but it was always there. In the end I knew I had a responsibility to myself, to those around me, and to those whom I owed money: I got on with the job of rebuilding myself and rebuilding my career.

I was moping in bed one day and Shirley literally kicked me out, took hold of my last watch and ordered me to sell it and buy some equipment. She said, 'Luke, I'm not standing by and watching all your talent go to waste. Get off your backside and work!' It was what I needed, and I bought a keyboard and a four-track studio with the money I raised from selling the watch. The transaction gave me more than just the equipment I needed to start working: it introduced me to Rob Ferguson, who worked for an audio supplier. Rob has become a true friend, somebody I met when I had nothing and who has been prepared to help in every way that he can, supplying me with equipment and allowing me to pay later. For my birthday he sent me ten DAT cassettes, the type you need for recording music: a real boost and a terrific gesture.

Working was hard at first because I had always worked

with Matt before, right back to when we composed songs together in the summerhouse. But I taught myself how to use the computer, I got to work and I soon discovered I enjoyed it. The songs were written by me, to my taste and specification, the way I wanted it. With Bros, I overdosed on compromise; every decision was made with an eye on what other people would think, how the fans would react, what the opinion of the record company would be. This time, I was determined there would be no compromise. The Bros career was built on a musical lie, it was not my music, it was the music everybody around us thought was right for our fans. But a building without strong foundations won't stand up for very long: as soon as we tried to progress musically (with our third album), the whole structure came tumbling down.

This time round, I'm going to be happy with my career from its footings upwards. I could have employed some hotshot to write songs for me, but I did not want that, I wanted the music to be my own. So I put my head down and got on with it. 'I've got to get it right, I've got to get it right', was like a one-track song, playing in my brain, keeping me at the keyboard long after the rest of the world had gone to bed.

I would start work at about one in the afternoon and I'd still be going at four in the morning. I have always been a hard worker. I don't think anybody, apart from a few teachers at school, would ever say I was lazy. Luckily, as far as writing songs goes, I'm prolific. Put me in a studio and I don't come out until I've created a song. I'm an insomniac at the best of times, and at the worst of times sleep becomes my enemy: I don't want the bad dreams, I don't want the horrible experience of waking up and remembering all over again the mess my life was in.

One of my songs, 'The Shadows On Me', reflected these feelings:

> Some nights I lay in bed
> Closed eyes can still see
> You wouldn't believe
> What's floating around me
> All night is a conscious dream
> I wish these thoughts would let me be.

Shirley helped me with my singing. I lacked confidence at first, I wasn't sure whether it sounded right. I told her not to pull punches but to tell me if I was awful, and she was a tough critic; I know that nobody is going to give me any leeway, nobody is going to make allowances, I have to get it right. The pens will be poised, ready to tear anything I do to pieces. After all I have been through I am resilient enough to ride any gratuitous criticism, but I need to feel confident myself that it is good.

Shirley helped me get the strength and power into my voice that I need; I don't want to sing two verses and a chorus and fly the rest of the choruses because my voice wouldn't take it. I want to sing it live the way it will be on the album.

I went for it so hard that I used to wake up in the morning coughing up blood. I panicked the first time, but Shirley explained it was my throat bleeding because I had been singing for six or eight hours the night before.

Once I had got four good demo tracks together, not professionally produced in an expensive studio but made at home on my own equipment, I set out to find myself a new manager. It was a struggle. As far as people in the business were concerned, my experience counted for noth-ing. When you just play drums on stage people think that's all you can do – and in my case they didn't even believe I did that. In reality I co-wrote and co-produced the songs. I may have done a Wembley Stadium show, I may have toured the world, I may have done over fifty television shows, I may have had twelve hit singles and I may still have had a fan following, but I was like a complete new-comer when it came to finding management.

For some reason, people think that when you lose your money you lose your experience. They patronize you, as though everything – including your brains – disappeared with the cash. Because we started in the business so young, we were still very young by the time the bubble burst: had we started at twenty-four we would have been in our thir-ties by now, and we might have been given more respect. But our experience would not have been any greater and our potential, because of our age, would have been less.

Yet it took me eight months altogether to find new man-agement, and during that time I felt I was a voice crying in the wilderness. I not only had to swallow my pride but digest it and get rid of it, to bring myself to walk around the offices of management companies, trying to sell myself. After the initial surprise that I could write and produce any music, the reaction was depressing: everyone wanted an obvious hit before they would agree to manage me. I had to face the harsh reality that I had absolutely no credi-bility within the industry and that my only fuel was my own enthusiasm.

Eventually, my new management team approached me. Peter Powell, Colin Lester and Ollie Smallman have teamed up together in a unique deal to be my new man-agers. It was Peter who initially got in touch, through David Ravden. When David contacted me I said, 'Do you mean the Radio One DJ?' which is how Peter will doubtless always be known, even though he has found a role in life which he enjoys far more, managing other artists. His company looks after Sarah Brightman, Phillip Schofield and many others. Peter realized what a rough deal I'd had, and he heard how passionate I was about my work. When he came to see me I played him the tracks I had recorded myself, and before I played them Peter tried to politely let me know that he wasn't expecting them to be brilliant. After a minute or two I noticed that his foot was tapping, and a big smile came over his face. He was amazed that I had done it all myself.

I think he was also amazed that my voice is so different from Matt's. It's much deeper, more gravelly, and very powerful, probably more the way Matt's would have been if he hadn't idolized Michael Jackson and Stevie Wonder.

It was Peter Powell who introduced me to Simon Burton, who has collaborated with me on songwriting.

Peter's arrival in my life was like a reassuring hug after you haven't been cuddled for months: he is a professional, he knows what he is talking about, and he wants to be on my team. My confidence soared.

Guitarist Greg Bone, who is a great friend of mine and a terrific musician, played with me on my demo tapes. Greg is lined up for my new band.

I tell Shirley that I had her when I had everything – money, fame, a successful career – and I have her now, so I will never be poor. I don't have to make any payments on her: she's there, and I want her to know how much I love her. Without her I would have been like a cornfield stripped by locusts, there would be nothing left of me worth having. She has been so supportive. At times she has cried with me, at times she has pleaded with me, and at times she has been tough with me, when I have needed it. But at no time has she moaned at me because I was being a miserable bastard, or negative, or flying off the handle for no reason. She understood it all.

She has seen me grow from a boy to a man in the time she has known me, and she tells me that she believes I have been dignified and brave. She doesn't tell me in an ego-stroking way, because I would see through that after all my experience with it: she tells me because she has seen me contain myself when it would have been so easy to thump someone, she has seen me struggle on with my work when it would have been so easy to throw in the towel, and she knows how determined I was not to go bankrupt and leave my creditors with nothing.

Our love has grown very much stronger through the last two years. We have spent so much more time together, which would have been disastrous if there had not been a really deep bond already there. If there were any cracks in our relationship, the trials we have been through would have opened them up wide. When I want to write a love song, I just think about Shirley and it all flows. I've written a song for her called 'For Ever':

> There's no substitute for the way you look
> In the morning sun
> My heart you've won for ever
> Our love's a spider's web
> It wouldn't last they said
> For ever

A spider's web may be very fragile and may break, but it is incredibly strong, the strongest substance known to man in proportion to its dimension, and when it breaks it is always there again when you come back. Her own work is building up again now, and she's hoping to break into television as a presenter: she's recorded some shows for an independent company. I'm pleased for her, she will be able to show people she's intelligent as well as talented and great to look at. I hope she will be a great success. I know that it will be hard for me if she finds success before I do: I'm very proud and independent, and I would not want to tag along on her coat-tails. But I hope I would be mature enough to handle it.

I haven't turned into a house-husband in the last two years, and I don't think I ever could. Although I have not been working outside the house, in the studio I have been putting in full days. I've done some cooking, but I don't enjoy doing it every day. I don't mind doing barbecues and occasionally cooking a special dinner, but I'm not into thinking up ideas for meals all the time. Shirley enjoys cooking, but I don't expect her to do it any more than I do: she only does it because she wants to. She also does the cleaning and other household jobs, and I thank her for it because I certainly don't believe it's her job to look after me.

I have grown much closer to Carli because I have spent so much more time with her. She's comfortable with me now and I love having her about. Relationships that have a few problems in the early days usually turn out to be stronger than those that start on a high: Carli and I have both learned to make concessions to each other and we now enjoy being together.

Shirley and I have been together now for more than twenty per cent of my life, and virtually the whole of my adulthood. I missed a bit of my youth by meeting Shirley so young, but youth contains nothing that I care about. All that happens when you are young is that you make a lot of mistakes, and I've had my share of those in other ways. I just thank God that when I was eighteen something happened to me that was no mistake: Shirley.

We laugh together at the way people suddenly give her a lot of credit for being with me. They say Shirley has 'stuck by me' as though all she ever valued me for was the money and the fame. When we were famous everyone slagged her off and disregarded the fact that she had known me before Bros were big; now they talk about her as though she's St Joan of Arc, a martyr for sticking with me!

Here, in Shirley's own words, is what it was like living with me after the break-up of Bros:

'There were days when Luke was so depressed that he did not want to get out of bed. He slept too much, drank too much, didn't work. I let him do it: I knew there was no point in telling him to stop. I simply had to let him work it out, until he reached the day when he felt disgusted with himself. It broke my heart watching him, but I understood how he felt. He was scared, scared that he couldn't do it professionally on his own after always being part of a team.

'But I knew he could, and as soon as he got started he knew it, too. Then he began to enjoy it, his confidence started to come back, he loved the freedom of making the sort of music he wanted to make. I'd been around him long enough to know that he had a good voice. I'm a professional singer and I would have told him, no bullshit, if I didn't think he could do it. It was just a matter of getting him to believe in himself.

'He should have been singing all the way through with Bros. But it suited everybody to keep Matt up front as the singer and keep Luke on the drums, and he was never sure enough of himself to challenge that. He was too talented to stay in the background, but Matt was insecure too: they fed on each other's insecurities.

'It wasn't easy for me. He needed me there, as a companion. I had to spend hours with him in the studio, just listening to his work. I couldn't work at first because I wasn't sure whether he would survive left entirely on his own, but it soon became financially necessary for me to take any work I could get. The trouble with my business is that if you are not around, people forget about you, and at first there were not too many offers coming in for me. I also had to be very careful about Luke: I think it would have destroyed him in those early days if he had seen me rushing around being busy.

'It never bothered me selling the jewellery. I'd rather pay the bills than have a diamond ring on my finger. Possessions are only possessions, they don't feed you or keep you warm. Whatever strains there were on our relationship, everything we went through strengthened it. We have never, ever, been as close or felt as strong as we do today, I have never felt so loved and so cared for.

'I really resent it when I hear people saying how much they respect me for staying with Luke. What do they think our relationship was all about? Luke is considerate, gentle, funny and very loving, and we have a good life together. The bad times are over because he has got his self-respect back, and that's the most important thing.'

As well as Shirley, the rest of my family have been wonderfully supportive. Both Mum and Dad gave me birthday cards for my twenty-fourth birthday which moved me deeply.

Mum wrote on hers that I am not just her son, but her friend. It meant a lot: you take a mother–son relationship for granted, and children take advantage of their parents without thinking twice about it. But friendship is not something that comes as a right, it has to be earned. You have to like someone to think of them as a friend.

Dad wrote his own verse in his card:

> In and out of paper shops,
> Lots of cards with fluffy toys,
> But the only decent ones for sons

Are the ones for little boys.
So I thought I'd send a funny card
With a message from the heart,
But I could only find this silly crap,
A sort of glossy paper fart.
But at last I get the chance to say
What a treasure you've become.
I love you very much, Luke,
I'm so proud that you're my son.

I was very touched that he should take so much time and put in so much effort for me. We had our problems with our relationship with Dad when we were little, but these days I could not ask for a better father.

Mum was devastated by Matt and me splitting, although she had seen the writing on the wall for some time. She had been worried about me not getting the credit I deserved from the very beginning.

'I saw what was happening to Luke before he saw it himself,' she says. 'I realized that people around them were making out that Matt was the one with the talent, as though Luke was just hanging on. But I've known them all their lives and I know that Luke is just as gifted as Matt. When the third album did not get the support it should have had, I knew the boys would split up, but it still broke my heart.

'I watched Matt walk to his car after Christmas, his shoulders shaking and sobs racking his body, and Luke just behind him, his hands up to his face. I will see that picture in my mind forever.

'But since then I have watched Luke grow in stature. He has become stronger, more secure. It took courage to get through what he had to face and he did it without complaining. I believe that when people hear the music he has written now, they will have no doubts any more about his talent. He needed to get away from Matt to prove it, to himself as well as to the world.

'Nothing will ever stop Matt and Luke loving each other. They may be thousands of miles apart, but they are still incredibly close. When Bros split, they did not: they are still brothers, still twins, still there for each other. That's their greatest triumph, in the face of what happened to them.'

Dad says that, on a purely selfish level, he enjoys the fact that he gets to see a lot more of me now that I am no longer half of Bros than he did before.

'I've really got to know Luke over the last couple of years and I feel desperately proud of the way he's handled everything. I don't know how he and Matt survived those mad years. I had one very bad experience with the press, when the *Sunday Mirror* distorted the facts of their child-hood and made me out to be the sort of father who only had time for them when they became successful; reading it was like being thumped very hard in the stomach. They put up with that kind of twisting of the truth every day. They had no normal youth, no normal growing up. But they have coped brilliantly. They are a delight: not many men can have had as much pleasure out of their sons as I have had out of mine.

'In the last few months I have been listening to the work that Luke has been doing and, even though I knew he was talented, I have to admit I have been thrilled by how good it all is. It is mature, solid, really excellent. He has a great future ahead of him.

'As a father I couldn't be more pleased with the way his personal life has worked out, too. Shirley is terrific, and they make a great couple. At the end of the day, that's one amazing bonus, to be with someone you love. I could always see that Luke was not getting enough credit for his input into Bros, that Matt was taking the glory. But at the end of the day Luke was the lucky one: he had his private life together.'

Tony is one of my biggest fans, and he has no doubt about my future success.

'Listen to the new music: you would have to be a real idiot not to be able to sell it. I have one hundred per cent faith in Luke's talent. I've known since he started to blast away on that drum kit when he was twelve that he had something extra, something special. Music is what he understands, what he enjoys, and what he is lucky enough to have a great gift for.

'Seeing them split was very sad, but they are only apart professionally: nothing on earth could separate Luke and Matt for good. Luke's had a tough time, but he got on with what he had to do, took one day at a time. I've had plenty of financial problems in my life, so I have some idea what he has been through: but I had the right to privacy, which he has never had.

'He and Matt had to do their growing up in the spotlight, with cameras trained on them. It was very hard. But essentially they are two very nice straightforward young men, and that is what has carried them through. I'm pretty proud of the whole family.'

As for my granddad, well, he admits he is a Perry Como fan, and next in his own personal charts come Mozart and Bach, so turning him on to Bros was always a bit of a struggle. But we got him there in the end; he used to come to our concerts and he admits he enjoyed himself. The first time he came somebody gave him a pair of earplugs, but he never took them out of his pocket. He has heard my new music and he reckons he likes it better than the early Bros songs.

My granddad gave me something very important, something that has helped me through the bad times: my faith. He is a spiritualist, and he sat in a developing circle for some years to increase his healing and psychic powers. He's been successful helping quite a few people with problems such as arthritis, nervous complaints, drug addiction and even cancer, although he is reluctant to claim too much credit.

He never forced his religious beliefs on me, or anyone. But over the years I have come to share his views: I know that life does not end with death and I believe that there is a spirit world that can, sometimes, be contacted. From time to time I, too, seem to have flashes of psychic power, which one day I would like to explore more fully. But the simple act of believing helped to keep me sane during the dark days. However bad I felt, I always tried to remember that there were others stuggling under far worse burdens.

Having come through the last two years, I am now a very strong person. I have learned the power of positive thinking; I refuse to dwell on all the negative aspects of my life. I wake up in the morning and think about what I have got going for me, not what is against me.

The only luxury that I want today is security. The security to wake up in my own home, surrounded by my own family, and the security of doing a job that I love. Once, success to me meant a Porsche Carrera, or a Mercedes, on the drive and a gold Rolex on my wrist. Now I know that peace of mind is worth far, far more.

I would, of course, like to be successful again – I intend to be. But there is a fine line between fame and succes. Last time around I had the fame, but I did not have true professional success. This time I mean to reverse the equation. I want the success, the respect, the career that my music deserves. Whether or not I have fame is incidental, and I know I will never again be excited by fame.

If I have made some mistakes, then at least they were honest ones and I made them at my own expense. I'd much rather lie on my deathbed and say I wish I hadn't done certain things, rather than have a list of things I wished I had done.

When I first became famous I felt I owed a great deal to the fans who bought my records, screamed at my concerts, made me a star. Someone said to me recently, 'You owe everything to them, they gave you everything you had.'

It has taken me a long time to realize that I don't owe them anything. They had a good time, they got pleasure from my records. And it was the records they were buying, not me. The only debts I have are financial. I have paid all my other dues.

I hope that those of you who have read this book have enjoyed it, and I hope that you have come to see me as a human being, not the two-dimensional Bros clone that I was made out to be. But at the end of it, this is all I am giving of myself to anyone. I don't belong to you any more than you belong to me. I owe you nothing.